Back to the Table

Episcopal Church Women

Christ Church
Raleigh, North Carolina

Episcopal Church Women
Christ Church
P.O. Box 25778
Raleigh, North Carolina 27611-5778

Nora Shepard, Front Cover Art
Sara Emrich, Back Cover Art
The Rt. Rev. Robert Estill, Pen and Ink Drawings
Mike Hoyt, Writer

First Printing   July 1998   5,000 copies

ISBN: 0-9663382-0-0
Library of Congress Catalog Number: 98-070302

Printed in the USA by

WIMMER
The Wimmer Companies
Memphis
1-800-548-2537

In the South, eating is a big part of life. And churches play a big part in the tradition. There was always a church picnic. Or a big Sunday dinner at home after the eleven o'clock service. Or the headlong rush to beat the Methodists to the cafeteria. The Baptists always took longer, of course.

Traditional "feasts" — we called them "dinners" — celebrated Christmas and Thanksgiving, and Easter with its traditional ham and yams with marshmallow topping. Dinnertime, holiday feast or not, was always family time. A time for sharing. A time for getting to know each other better. A time of love and care and laughter.

Dinners were the glue that held folks together, whether aunts and uncles or the new people from next door. Even a simple family supper began with a prayer. There was the holding of hands, a bowing of heads. And, with one eye half-open to be sure brother didn't take a swipe at the mashed potatoes, we thanked God for his bounty. Silently, we gave thanks for each other, and for these special moments together.

But times have changed. More moms are going to the office. Small towns have turned into shopping malls. Dinner times as we knew them have gone the way of American Flyer wagons and fat-tire Schwinns. The magic and wonder of a time when families gathered around the table has become a wistful memory of another era.

These days, we "grab a bite" or eat "on the run" or order a pizza. The family table has been replaced by TV trays or the kitchen counter or the back seat of a Suburban on the way home from soccer practice. Or, worse, it's become a drive-through window.

Now, this book can't change all that. But its aim is to remind each of us of that special time we call "dinner" and perhaps even revive this wondrous tradition. A sacred time of togetherness, a communion with each other and with our God. A moment when we are reminded that, in its own way, eating together with people we love is a powerful form of prayer.

So we invite you to come with us, again, to the table, to come home, and to join in the feast.

A short history of Christ Church

North Carolina was still in its infancy when Christ Church was born in 1821. A group of Episcopalians who had been worshiping in a Raleigh museum formed a parish that year, and the Right Reverend John Stark Ravenscroft, the diocese's first bishop, became the new church's first rector.

A wooden sanctuary was erected at the corner of Edenton and Wilmington Streets in the heart of the city. Over time, the church was enlarged and, over the rector's objections that it was "too frivolous," the first organ was acquired. In 1848, the cornerstone of the present sanctuary was laid.

During the War Between the States, Christ Church ministered to soldiers from both sides, and weathered the Yellow Fever plague and the hard times of the 1860's. At the end of the war, it was said Christ Church's gilded weather cock "was the only chicken left in Raleigh" following the city's surrender to Sherman.

In 1914, the present stone Parish House and Chapel were added, replacing a 19th century wooden annex. A new wing and other additions to the church were completed in 1970.

With over 2500 members, Christ Church carries on outreach programs that touch the lives of thousands of less fortunate throughout Wake County, and beyond. And the Episcopal Church Women (ECW) at Christ Church are at the center of all.

This ECW cookbook is but another step in the vibrant and expanding life of the church which spans almost 180 years. It is intended as a true offering of love, not only to members of the church but to the many communities we serve.

Table of Contents

BACK TO THE TABLE
Appetizers & Beverages

Marriott Little

Getting started

You could ask, "Well, if you come to the table hungry, why do you need an appetizer?" One answer is, "You gotta start somewhere." Or, as the old Southern adage suggests, "in order to finish well, you have to start off on the right foot." Now, some folks don't fully understand all this until they put it to the test at suppertime.

When folks head out to a fancy restaurant, they'll usually order an appetizer. Lowbrow places call 'em "starters" as in "What'll you have for starters, honey?" And when neighbors come over for supper, they're served a little something to rev up the taste buds. Usually a small glass of V-8 and some celery stalks filled with pimento cheese spread. Or carrot sticks. Or a little plate of deviled eggs. Or some melt-in-your-mouth homemade cheese straws. Or if you're really lucky, some bread and butter pickles Aunt Martha picked up at the State Fair last fall.

When the neighbors dropped by, Mama would add some little Velveeta cubes with a pickle on top skewered with one of those frilly-top toothpicks. Most men concoct their own "appetizers," mostly made up of whatever's handy that sticks to the top of a Ritz cracker and goes down easy with a cold beer.

Now in this section, we're talking about really fancy stuff — appetizers made with seafood, cheeses that don't come pre-sliced and single-wrapped, fruits and vegetables folks don't grow in this country, and tasty sauces and garnishes they serve in the big name restaurants or over at the country club. So, if your special meals aren't getting off on the right foot, turn the page and read on. You're about to take a big step toward getting folks back to the table around your house.

Oh, and don't forget about the beverage section. It's hard to enjoy a good "starter," or the rest of a special dinner without something to wash it down. So you'll find a generous helping of good things to drink: special coffees, teas, and a juice drink or two. So let's get started.

Christ Church Sugar and Spice Pecans

1 egg white, at room
temperature
1 tablespoon butter, melted
2 cups pecan halves
½ cup sugar
½ teaspoon salt
1½ teaspoons ground
cinnamon
¾ teaspoon ground nutmeg
¾ teaspoon ground allspice

- Preheat oven to 300°.

- Beat egg white at high speed with an electric
mixer until stiff peaks form; fold in butter. Add
pecans, tossing gently to coat.

- Combine sugar and next 4 ingredients in a small
bowl; sprinkle 2 tablespoons on an ungreased
baking sheet.

- Dredge pecans, ¼ cup at a time, in remaining
sugar mixture. Spread pecans on baking sheet,
and sprinkle with remaining sugar mixture.

- Bake at 300° for 20 minutes, stirring once.

- Remove from oven; separate pecans with a fork,
and let cool.

- Store in an airtight container.

2 cups.

Peppered Pecans

¼ cup sugar
1 tablespoon salt
1½ to 2 tablespoons
coarsely ground pepper
1 cup pecan halves

- Combine first 3 ingredients.

- Cook pecans in a large skillet over high heat,
tossing constantly, 1 minute. Sprinkle with half
of seasonings.

- Shake the pan 1 minute or until sugar melts.
Add remaining half of seasonings, shaking until
sugar melts.

- Remove nuts from skillet, and let cool.

- Store in a zip-top plastic bag.

1 cup.

Easy Cheese Straws

1 package pie crust mix

2 cups (8 ounces) shredded or grated *x*-sharp Cheddar cheese

¼–½ *t* Ground red pepper

Powdered sugar

- Process first 3 ingredients in a food processor or mix by hand until well blended. Chill.

- Roll dough out, and cut using cookie cutters.

- Bake on an ungreased baking sheet at 375° for 8 minutes.

- Remove from oven, and sprinkle with powdered sugar.

- Store in an airtight container.

The sharper the cheese, the better! This recipe is foolproof. They freeze well, too. You can also use a cookie press to make straws or chill dough until firm and slice.

Mixmaster Cheese Biscuits

½ pound butter or margarine, softened

2 cups (8 ounces) shredded extra sharp Cheddar cheese, softened

2 cups all-purpose flour

½ teaspoon cayenne pepper

1 teaspoon salt

1 teaspoon lemon juice

- Preheat oven to 300°.

- Beat butter and cheese at medium speed with a mixmaster until smooth.

- Sift together flour, red pepper, and salt; beat into butter mixture. Add lemon juice, and beat 20 minutes.

- Drop dough by teaspoonfuls onto a baking sheet.

- Bake at 300° for 20 to 25 minutes, placing another baking sheet under pan while cooking to keep biscuits from browning.

- Remove from oven, and let cool on paper towels.

- Store in an airtight container.

Serves 25.

Christ Church Cheese Straws

4 cups (16 ounces)
shredded New York
State sharp Cheddar
cheese

3 sticks margarine

1 teaspoon salt

1 teaspoon ground red
pepper

4 cups all-purpose flour

- Preheat oven to 375°.

- Beat cheese and butter at medium speed with an electric mixer until creamy. Beat in salt and pepper.

- Work flour into mixture. Knead until soft and right consistency for using cookie press.

- Use a cookie press fitted with a number 2 star disc to shape dough into straws of desired length, following manufacturer's instructions.

- Bake on a baking sheet at 375° for 5 to 8 minutes. Do not burn.

- Store in an airtight container.

20 dozen.

You can also roll dough out thinly on a lightly floured surface and cut using a 2-inch round cookie cutter. Rounds are good with a piece of crystallized ginger on top. These freeze well.

Cheese Olive Delight

2 cups (8 ounces) shredded
New York State sharp
Cheddar cheese

½ pound butter, softened

2½ cups all-purpose flour

¼ teaspoon ground red
pepper

¼ teaspoon salt

1 (6-ounce) jar pimiento-
stuffed olives, well
drained

- Combine cheese and butter, stirring well and using your hands if necessary, until smooth.

- Sift together flour, red pepper, and salt; add to cheese mixture. Mold dough around each olive.

- Freeze olives on a baking sheet. Place in zip-top plastic bags, and freeze until ready to serve.

- Let stand at room temperature 1 hour before baking.

- Bake, not touching, on baking sheets at 375° for 20 minutes.

- Serve immediately.

Marinated Chèvre

8 (2- to 3-ounce) goat cheese rounds

1½ cups olive oil

4 bay leaves

1 tablespoon mixed peppercorns

1½ tablespoons dried thyme

3 garlic cloves, cut into slivers

3 tablespoons chopped fresh basil

- Place cheese rounds, not touching, on an ovenproof platter.

- Cook oil and next 3 ingredients in a small saucepan over medium-high heat until mixture begins to sizzle and pop. Immediately pour over cheese rounds.

- Sprinkle evenly with garlic and basil. Chill overnight.

- Bring to room temperature before serving.

You may leave the cheese rounds whole and serve as a garnish for a green salad. Or serve with French bread rounds as an appetizer.

Praline Brie

1 (2.2-pound) Brie round

½ pound butter or margarine

½ pound brown sugar

1 teaspoon vanilla extract

1 cup pecan halves

- Preheat oven to 350°.

- Bake Brie on a baking sheet at 350° for 10 minutes or until gooey and irresistible.

- Melt butter in a heavy saucepan over medium heat; add brown sugar; cook, stirring constantly, until bubbly. Stir in vanilla and pecans.

- Transfer Brie to a serving plate.

- Pour sauce over warm Brie, and serve immediately with bland crackers that won't break easily.

Layered Brie and Pesto

1 cup firmly packed
chopped fresh basil

¾ cup grated Parmesan
cheese

½ cup firmly packed
chopped fresh parsley

¼ cup pine nuts or walnuts

2 garlic cloves, quartered

⅓ cup olive oil

1 (8-ounce) package cream
cheese, softened

4½ ounces Brie, with rind
removed, softened

½ cup whipping cream

Garnish: fresh parsley or
basil sprigs

- Process first 5 ingredients in a food processor until pasty. With machine running, gradually pour oil through food chute. Process until consistency of soft butter.

- In small bowl, beat cream cheese and Brie at medium speed with an electric mixer until smooth.

- Beat whipping cream in a separate bowl at high speed with a handheld mixer until soft peaks form.

- Fold whipped cream into cheese mixture.

- Spread one-fourth of cheese mixture in a plastic-wrap-lined 4-cup bowl or mold. Top with one-third of pesto.

- Repeat layers twice, ending with cream cheese. Cover and chill overnight.

- Invert onto a serving platter, removing plastic wrap.

- Garnish, if desired. Serve with crackers.

1 (4-cup) cheese mold.

Celebrate

Find a reason to throw a party. Make it spontaneous. Celebrate something or someone— perhaps the first snow, the arrival of an out-of-town friend or the first flower in your garden. Never lose sight of the real celebration: that your family and friends are gathered together.

Brie with Cranberry Marmalade

12 ounces dried cranberries

¾ cup firmly packed light brown sugar

⅓ cup dried currants

⅔ cup water

2 teaspoons lemon juice

¼ teaspoon dry mustard

¼ teaspoon ground ginger

¼ teaspoon ground cloves

¼ teaspoon ground allspice

1 tablespoon cornstarch

2 tablespoons cold water

1 (8-inch) Brie round

- Cook first 9 ingredients in a heavy nonaluminum saucepan over medium-high heat, stirring often, 5 minutes or until most cranberries burst.

- Combine cornstarch and 2 tablespoons cold water, stirring to make a paste. Add paste to cranberry mixture; cook until thickened.

- Remove from heat, and let cool to room temperature. Cover and chill up to 3 days, if desired.

- Cut a circle in top of Brie rind; place Brie on an aluminum foil-lined baking sheet, and spread with cranberry marmalade. Cover and chill up to 6 hours.

- Bake at 300° for 12 minutes or just until softened.

- Serve Brie on a platter with crackers and fresh fruit.

Serves 12.

Peanuts in a Pepsi

It's a wonder. Why didn't more of us die? Remember when we put salted peanuts in our Pepsi and drank away? Amazingly, none of the goobers were ever inhaled, choking us half to death. But wasn't it good?

Goat Cheese and Sun-Dried Tomato Torte

1 (8-ounce) package cream cheese, softened

12 ounces goat cheese

½ pound butter or margarine, softened

1 cup basil pesto

1 cup sun-dried tomatoes in oil, drained and minced

½ cup pine nuts

- Beat first 3 ingredients at medium speed with an electric mixer until fluffy.

- Line an 8-inch round cakepan with dampened cheesecloth, leaving enough extra to fold over top.

- Layer one-third of cheese mixture in prepared pan; spread with half of pesto. Repeat layers once.

- Spread remaining one-third of cheese mixture on top, and cover with tomatoes.

- Cover with plastic wrap, and fold cheesecloth over. Chill at least 1 hour.

- When ready to serve, invert torte onto a plate, and remove cheesecloth. Invert again onto a serving plate, and remove plastic wrap.

- Sprinkle with pine nuts. Serve with assorted crackers.

Serves 25.

This attractive torte can be frozen for impromptu entertaining.

Italian Torte

2 (8-ounce) packages cream cheese, softened

6 ounces mild goat cheese

2 garlic cloves, minced

6 teaspoons minced fresh oregano

1/8 teaspoon ground pepper

1/2 cup sun-dried tomatoes in oil, drained and chopped

1/2 cup marinated artichoke hearts, drained and chopped

1/2 cup finely chopped hearts of palm

3/4 cup pesto

1 sun-dried tomato, sliced

2 tablespoons toasted slivered almonds

Garnishes: fresh oregano sprigs, fresh parsley sprigs

- Beat first 5 ingredients at medium speed with an electric mixer until smooth.

- Combine 1/2 cup dried tomato, artichoke, and hearts of palm in a separate bowl.

- Spread one-third of the cheese mixture in the bottom of a plastic-wrap-lined soufflé dish. Spread pesto evenly over cheese mixture.

- Top with half of remaining cheese mixture and dried tomato mixture. Spread with remaining cheese mixture. Cover and chill.

- Uncover torte, and invert onto a serving platter, removing plastic wrap.

- Fan dried tomato slices on top. Cover sides with almonds.

- Garnish, if desired. Serve with melba toast, pita toasts, crackers, baguettes, or fruit.

Serves 18.

> *Perhaps at our table with family and friends we can slow down long enough to revive the joy of eating and drinking together. Perhaps, in recalling again the sacred connection with food, we can make place within our hurried lives for mystic pleasure.*
>
> —Edward Hayes, Monk

Blue Cheese Mousse

¾ pound unsalted butter, softened

1 pound blue cheese, softened

3 tablespoons brandy

2 tablespoons chopped fresh parsley

1 tablespoon freshly cracked pepper

1 bunch radishes, chopped

1 large red onion, chopped

Vinaigrette

- Beat butter at medium speed with an electric mixer until creamy; gradually beat in blue cheese. Beat mixture until fluffy. Add brandy, parsley, and pepper, beating well.

- Spoon mixture into an oiled 5-cup mold, smoothing top. Chill until firm.

- Combine radish, onion, and vinaigrette.

- Invert cheese mold, and garnish with radish mixture. Serve with crackers.

Serves 20.

Any blue-veined cheese may be substituted for blue cheese, if desired.

Tomato and Herb Bruschetta

1 long French or Italian bread loaf, sliced diagonally

1 to 2 tablespoons olive oil

2 tablespoons minced garlic

6 kalamata olives, minced (optional)

¼ cup balsamic vinegar

3 tomatoes, seeded and chopped

2 to 3 tablespoons minced onion

⅓ cup olive oil

2 garlic cloves, crushed

1 tablespoon shredded fresh basil

- Brush bread slices evenly with 1 tablespoon oil; rub with minced garlic.

- Grill or toast until golden brown.

- Combine olives and next 5 ingredients. Let this mixture ripen 1 hour at room temperature.

- Spread on toasted bread; top with basil, and serve immediately.

Serves 6; more if used to accompany soup.

Hot Onion Soufflé ✓ Carrons

16 ounces frozen chopped onion, thawed and well drained

3 (8-ounce) packages cream cheese, softened

1½ cups freshly grated Parmesan cheese

½ cup mayonnaise

Hot sauce to taste

- Preheat oven to 425°.

- Combine all ingredients, stirring well.

- Bake in a 2-quart soufflé dish at 425° for 15 minutes or until golden brown.

Serves 8.

Tapenade

½ cup pitted kalamata olives

3 ounces dry-packed sun-dried tomatoes, reconstituted

2½ tablespoons capers, drained

3 tablespoons olive oil

1 garlic clove

3 tablespoons chopped canned artichoke hearts

- Process all ingredients in a food processor until blended.

- Serve with crostini.

Serves 12.

Leftovers may be used in pasta dishes.

Crostini

Crostini, Italian for little crusts, originated as a clever way of using the last bit of bread from yesterday's loaf. These small toasts are grilled either over an open wood fire or under the broiler, drizzled with good olive oil, and topped with a variety of mixtures from simple to complex.

Mushroom Pâté *Try*

2 (8-ounce) packages fresh mushrooms	• Pulse mushrooms in a food processor until semi-coarsely chopped.
4 tablespoons butter	• Melt butter in a large heavy saucepan over medium heat; add mushrooms, and sauté, stirring occasionally, 7 to 10 minutes or until liquid has evaporated. Add garlic, and cook, stirring constantly, 1 minute.
2 garlic cloves, minced	
1 (8-ounce) package cream cheese, softened	
2 tablespoons white wine or vermouth	
2 teaspoons fresh lemon juice	• Beat mushrooms, garlic, cream cheese, and next 5 ingredients at medium speed with an electric mixer until blended.
6 to 8 dashes hot sauce	• Spoon into a plastic wrap-lined mold or bowl. Chill at least 4 hours.
¼ teaspoon salt	
¼ teaspoon pepper	
Garnish: fresh parsley sprigs	• Invert onto a serving platter, removing plastic wrap.
	• Garnish, if desired. Serve with black pepper crackers.

Serves 12.

Mushroom mixture may also be piped into mushroom caps before chilling. Chill as directed, and serve.

Cocktail Tomato Rounds *similar to Whiskey Chute Tomatoes*

18 bread slices	• Cut bread into circles the size of cherry tomatoes; let stand at room temperature until hardened.
1 pound cherry tomatoes, sliced	
Salt	• Sprinkle tomato slices with salt, and let drain on paper towels.
1 cup mayonnaise	
⅓ cup lemon juice	• Combine mayonnaise, lemon juice, and seasoned salt. Spread evenly on bread rounds; top each with a tomato slice, and sprinkle with Parmesan cheese.
½ teaspoon seasoned salt	
Parmesan cheese	
	• Bake at 375° until browned around edges.
	• Broil 30 seconds or less.

Asparagus Rollups

24 fresh asparagus spears

24 sandwich bread slices,
with crusts removed

½ cup butter, softened

1 (8-ounce) package cream
cheese, softened

4 ounces blue cheese,
softened

¼ cup butter or margarine,
melted

- Preheat oven to 400°.

- Boil asparagus in salted water to cover 5 to
  6 minutes or until crisp-tender. Drain, and
  place in cold water until cool.

- Flatten bread slices using a rolling pin. Combine ½ cup butter and cheeses, stirring until
  well blended.

- Spread cheese mixture evenly on bread slices,
  and top each with an asparagus spear.

- Roll up, jellyroll fashion, and dip in melted
  butter. Cut each roll into fourths, and freeze.

- Bake at 400° for 15 minutes.

Serves 12.

Elegant Eggplant Spread

1 large eggplant, cut into
1-inch cubes

10 tablespoons vegetable or
olive oil, divided

2½ cups chopped onion

1 cup diced celery

2 (8-ounce) cans tomato
sauce

¼ cup red wine vinegar

2 tablespoons sugar

2 tablespoons capers,
drained

½ teaspoon salt

Pepper

12 pitted black olives,
sliced

- Sauté eggplant in 8 tablespoons (½ cup) hot oil
  in a skillet until tender. Remove eggplant from
  skillet.

- Sauté onion and celery in remaining 2 tablespoons hot oil in skillet until tender.

- Return eggplant to skillet; stir in tomato sauce,
  and bring to a boil. Cover, reduce heat, and
  simmer 15 to 20 minutes.

- Stir in vinegar and next 5 ingredients. Simmer,
  stirring occasionally, 15 minutes. Cover and
  chill overnight.

- Serve warm or chilled with crackers or toast
  points.

This appetizer freezes well.

Christ Church Spanakopita

1 (10-ounce) package frozen spinach, thawed and well drained

⅓ cup minced onion

4 ounces freshly grated Parmesan cheese

3 tablespoons feta cheese

2 tablespoons soft breadcrumbs

¼ teaspoon salt

¼ teaspoon ground nutmeg

3 tablespoons butter or margarine, melted

½ (16-ounce) package frozen phyllo pastry

- Combine first 7 ingredients; chill at least 1 hour.

- Cut a 2-inch-wide strip through all layers of pastry. Cover remaining pastry with a damp cloth to keep from cracking.

- Separate dough into stacks of 2 strips. Brush each stack of strips with melted butter, and spoon 1 rounded teaspoon spinach mixture onto the top of each strip. Fold over filling like folding a flag.

- Place on a buttered baking sheet, and brush with melted butter.

- Repeat procedure with remaining spinach mixture, pastry, and melted butter.

- Bake at 375° for 20 minutes. Serve warm.

Serves 25.

To freeze triangles, brush both sides with melted butter, and wrap well. Thaw and bake as directed.

Quesadilla Squares

2 cups (8 ounces) shredded
Cheddar cheese

2 cups (8 ounces) shredded
Monterey Jack cheese

2 (4-ounce) cans chopped
green chiles, drained

2 cups milk

1 cup biscuit mix

4 large eggs

¼ cup salsa

Toppings: sour cream, salsa

- Preheat oven to 425°.

- Sprinkle cheeses in the bottom of a 13- x 9-inch baking dish coated with vegetable cooking spray. Top with chiles.

- Combine milk, biscuit mix, and eggs in a large bowl, whisking until smooth; pour over chiles. Top with ¼ cup salsa. Bake at 425° for 25 to 30 minutes or until puffed.

- Cut into squares, and serve with desired toppings.

Black Bean Hummus

3 cups canned black beans,
rinsed and drained

4 tablespoons tahini

¼ cup lemon juice

3 tablespoons olive oil

1 teaspoon ground black
pepper

2 tablespoons minced garlic

1 tablespoon paprika

1½ teaspoons ground cumin

1½ teaspoons chili powder

½ teaspoon cayenne pepper

- Process all ingredients in a food processor until smooth, adding water if necessary to reach desired spreading consistency.

- Serve with pita chips or tortilla chips.

It seems to me that our three basic needs, for food and security and love, are so entwined that we cannot think of one without the other.

—M.F.K. Fisher

Baked Santa Fe Dip *– make day ahead*

2 cups (8 ounces) shredded
  Cheddar cheese
1 cup (4 ounces) shredded
  Monterey Jack or
  mozzarella cheese
½ cup mayonnaise
1 (8-ounce) can whole
  kernel corn
1 (4-ounce) can chopped
  green chiles
2 teaspoons minced
  jalapeño pepper
¼ teaspoon garlic powder
1 medium tomato, seeded
  and chopped
¼ cup sliced green onions
2 tablespoons chopped
  fresh cilantro

• Combine first 7 ingredients; spread into a
  shallow 1-quart baking dish or 9-inch pieplate.
  Cover and chill up to 24 hours.

• Combine tomato, green onions, and cilantro;
  cover and chill up to 24 hours.

• Bake cheese mixture at 350° for 25 minutes or
  until thoroughly heated.

• Spoon tomato mixture into center.

• Serve with raw vegetables or tortilla chips.

Serves 28.

BLT Dip

1 cup sour cream
1 cup mayonnaise
1 pound bacon, cooked and
  crumbled
1 medium tomato, chopped *or more or tiny tom. quartered*
1 cup lettuce, shredded

• Combine first 3 ingredients in a serving dish,
  stirring well. Sprinkle with tomato and lettuce.

• Serve with crackers or desired bread toasted.

Southwestern Cheesecake

1½ cups crushed tortilla chips

4 tablespoons butter, melted

2 (8-ounce) packages cream cheese, softened

2 large eggs, at room temperature

1 cup (4 ounces) shredded Monterey Jack cheese

1 cup (4 ounces) shredded colby or sharp cheddar cheese

1 (4-ounce) can chopped green chiles, drained

1 cup sour cream

1 cup chopped yellow or red bell pepper

1 cup thinly sliced green onions

⅔ cup chopped tomato

½ cup sliced pitted black olives

½ cup minced fresh jalapeño pepper (optional)

- Preheat oven to 325°.

- Pulse tortilla chips in a food processor until finely crushed.

- Combine chips and melted butter; press into the bottom of a 9-inch springform pan.

- Bake at 325° for 12 minutes.

- Beat cream cheese and eggs at medium-low speed with an electric mixer until well blended. Add shredded cheese and chiles, beating well; pour over prepared crust.

- Bake at 325° for 30 minutes.

- Remove from oven, and let cool on a wire rack. Remove sides of springform pan, and spread top of cake with sour cream.

- Decorate with bell pepper, next 3 ingredients, and, if desired, jalapeño.

- Serve with crackers or corn chips.

Serves 35.

The cheesecake will freeze without toppings for 2 months. Thaw in refrigerator, and let stand at room temperature 1 hour and 30 minutes before serving.

Mexican Cheese and Chips

1 (2-pound) round longhorn cheese

1 (15-ounce) can refried beans

1 (4-ounce) can chopped green chiles, drained

1 medium tomato, seeded and chopped

2 garlic cloves, minced

1/4 teaspoon ground oregano

1/4 teaspoon ground coriander

1/4 teaspoon hot sauce

Vegetable oil

5 corn tortillas

- Using a grapefruit knife and spoon, hollow out cheese, leaving a 1/2-inch-thick shell. Shred scooped out cheese.

- Cook beans and next 6 ingredients in a saucepan over medium heat until thoroughly heated. Set aside.

- Heat 1/2-inch-deep oil in a large skillet to 375°; fry tortillas, 1 at a time, for a few seconds. Drain and pat dry.

- Line a quiche dish with tortillas, overlapping slightly.

- Place cheese shell in center, and fill with bean mixture. Cover with reserved cheese.

- Bake at 375° for 45 minutes.

- Serve with tortilla chips.

Serves 8.

Bacon Cheese Spread Trey

2 (8-ounce) packages cream cheese, softened

10 bacon slices, cooked and crumbled

1 medium-size green bell pepper, chopped finely

1 (4-ounce) can chopped green chiles, drained

1/2 cup mayonnaise

1 tablespoon lemon juice

1/4 teaspoon garlic salt

1/4 teaspoon seasoned salt

1 1/2 cups (6 ounces) shredded sharp Cheddar cheese, divided

- Beat cream cheese at medium speed with an electric mixer until creamy; add bacon, next 6 ingredients, and 1/2 cup Cheddar cheese, beating well.

- Press mixture firmly into a plastic wrap-lined 4-cup bowl. Cover and chill overnight.

- Invert and remove plastic wrap.

- Top with remaining 1 cup Cheddar cheese. Serve with crackers.

Serves 40.

Prosciutto Palmiers

1 (17¼-ounce) package frozen puff pastry sheets, thawed and divided

⅔ cup Dijon mustard, divided

¾ pound prosciutto, thinly sliced and divided

2 cups grated Parmesan cheese

- Preheat oven to 425°.

- Roll out 1 pastry sheet on a lightly floured surface to a 14-inch square. Brush with a thin layer of mustard.

- Cover with half of prosciutto, slightly over-lapping and leaving a ½-inch border around edges. Sprinkle with 1 cup cheese.

- Roll up pastry, jellyroll fashion; pinch seams to seal, and tuck ends under.

- Cut into ½-inch slices.

- Bake slices, cut side up and 1 inch apart, on a greased baking sheet at 425° for 10 to 15 minutes or until lightly browned.

- Repeat procedure with remaining pastry sheet, mustard, prosciutto, and cheese.

Work with 1 sheet of puff pastry at a time. Keep remaining sheets wrapped, cold and moist. Work quickly.

Caviar Pie

10 hard-cooked eggs

1 stick butter, softened, no substitutions

1 (8-ounce) package cream cheese, softened

1 (8-ounce) container sour cream

1 bunch green onions, chopped

4 ounces black caviar, well drained

- Process eggs and butter in a food processor; press into a tart pan with removable bottom. Chill.

- Beat cream cheese, sour cream, and green onions at medium speed with a handheld mixer until well blended; spread over prepared egg mixture.

- Top with caviar. Serve with unsalted wafers.

Serves 12.

Country Pâté

1 pound chicken livers
Bay leaf
Chicken broth
2 sticks butter
1 onion, coarsely chopped
1 tablespoon curry powder
1½ ounces cognac
Salt
Pepper
1 (8-ounce) package cream
cheese, softened
Paprika (optional)
Sliced onion (optional)

- Bring chicken livers, bay leaf, and chicken broth to cover to a boil; cook until chicken livers are barely done. Remove and discard bay leaf.

- Melt butter in a skillet over medium heat; add onion, and sauté until tender.

- Process liver mixture, onion, curry powder, and next 3 ingredients in a food processor or blender until creamy.

- Chill until firm, and shape into a ball.

- Spread cream cheese evenly over ball.

- Dust with paprika or cover with sliced onion, if desired.

- Serve with wafers or melba toast.

Serves 25 for cocktails.

Crab Crostini

8 ounces fresh lump
crabmeat, drained
½ cup diced red bell pepper
2 tablespoons mayonnaise
2 tablespoons chopped
fresh parsley
1 tablespoon chopped fresh
chives
1 tablespoon lime juice
1 tablespoon Dijon mustard
2 teaspoons grated
Parmesan cheese
½ teaspoon hot sauce
16 Italian bread slices

- Combine all ingredients except bread, stirring until well blended.

- Spread 1 tablespoon crab mixture on each bread slice.

- Broil on an aluminum foil-lined broiler pan 4 inches from heat 5 to 6 minutes or until lightly browned.

Serves 8.

Crabmeat Crescents *[handwritten]*

1 (3-ounce) package cream
 cheese, softened

½ cup butter, softened

3 drops hot sauce

¼ teaspoon salt

1 tablespoon sesame seeds,
 toasted

¼ cup grated Parmesan
 cheese

1 cup all-purpose flour

1 cup finely chopped
 crabmeat

⅓ cup sour cream

2 teaspoons Dijon mustard

- Beat first 5 ingredients at medium speed with an electric mixer until creamy; beat in cheese and flour. Chill.

- Combine crabmeat, sour cream, and mustard. Roll chilled dough out thinly on a lightly floured surface; cut into circles using a 2½-inch round cookie cutter.

- Place ½ teaspoon filling on 1 side of each circle. Moisten edges, and fold over filling, pressing firmly to seal.

- Bake on a baking sheet at 450° for 8 to 10 minutes or until lightly browned.

- Serve warm.

[handwritten] Could make larger for luncheon

Serves 50.

May also be filled with chopped turkey or ham.

Gourmet Oysters and Chicken *[handwritten: try for supper club or brunch]*

6 tablespoons unsalted
 butter or margarine

1 (8-ounce) package fresh
 mushrooms, sliced

4 tablespoons all-purpose
 flour

2 cups heavy cream

2 cups diced cooked
 chicken

2 cups oysters, drained and
 cut in half

¼ cup dry sherry

¼ teaspoon salt

Freshly ground white
 pepper

- Melt butter in a skillet over medium heat; add mushrooms, and sauté 5 minutes. Stir in flour, and cook 2 to 3 minutes.

- Gradually stir in cream; cook, stirring often, until thickened. Stir in chicken and next 4 ingredients.

- Pour mixture into a chafing dish, and serve with patty shells or toast points.

Serves 6.

Smoked Oyster Cheese Ball

10-27-99
Supper club

1 can smoked oysters,
drained slightly and
chopped

1 (8-ounce) package cream
cheese, softened

½ teaspoon Worcestershire
sauce

¼ teaspoon curry powder
or garlic powder

½ cup chopped pecans,
lightly toasted

• Combine first 4 ingredients; chill.

• Form into a ball, and roll in chopped pecans.

1 cheese ball.

Just O.K

Christ Church Salmon Mousse

1 envelope unflavored
gelatin

¼ cup cold water

½ cup boiling water

½ cup mayonnaise

1 tablespoon lemon juice

1 tablespoon grated onion

1 dash of hot sauce

¼ teaspoon sweet paprika

1 teaspoon salt

2 tablespoons minced fresh
dill

2 cups canned salmon,
skinned, boned, and
finely flaked

1 cup heavy cream

Sliced pimiento-stuffed
olive

• Sprinkle gelatin over ¼ cup cold water in a
large bowl; add ½ cup boiling water, whisking
until gelatin dissolves. Let cool to room
temperature.

• Whisk in mayonnaise and next 6 ingredients
until well blended. Chill 20 minutes or until
mixture begins to thicken.

• Fold in flaked salmon.

• Beat cream in a separate bowl at high speed
with an electric mixer until stiff peaks form;
fold into salmon mixture.

• Spoon mixture into a 6-cup fish mold. Chill at
least 4 hours.

• Invert onto a serving platter, and place sliced
olive on mold as fish eye.

• Serve with black bread.

Serves 12.

Smoked Trout Spread

2½ pounds smoked trout, boned and skinned

1 tablespoon prepared horseradish, drained

1 small onion, chopped

Juice of 1 lemon

¼ teaspoon ground white pepper

2 tablespoons heavy cream

1 (3-ounce) package cream cheese, softened

• Process first 5 ingredients in a food processor 2 minutes or until fluffy.

• With machine running, add cream and cream cheese through food chute. Process until smooth.

• Chill.

Serves 12.

Shrimp for a Crowd

2 cups vegetable oil

1 cup tarragon vinegar

1 jar Durkee sauce

1 teaspoon salt

5 pounds medium-size boiled shrimp, peeled and deveined

5 or 6 Vidalia or purple onions, sliced

• Combine first 4 ingredients in a large bowl; stir in shrimp and onion.

• Chill overnight.

Serves 24.

For perfect boiled shrimp,

•*Don't add salt to the water.*
•*Season the water with a can of beer and 2 tablespoons pickling spices.*
•*Don't overcook! Shrimp are done when they JUST turn pink.*
•*Shrimp are easily peeled under cold running water.*
•*And to make shrimp sauce, blend well and chill:*
  1 cup ketchup
  2 tablespoons horseradish
  2 teaspoons fresh lemon juice

Summertime Iced Tea

6 regular-size tea bags

4 cups boiling water

1½ cups sugar

1 (6-ounce) can frozen orange juice or limeade concentrate, thawed and undiluted

1 (6-ounce) can frozen lemonade concentrate, thawed and undiluted

10 cups water

- Combine tea bags and 4 cups boiling water; let stand 5 minutes.

- Remove and discard tea bags.

- Stir in sugar and next 3 ingredients.

Serves 16 (1 gallon).

Berry Sherbet Punch

16 ounces cranberry juice drink

1½ cups fresh lemon juice (no substitutions)

1 cup sugar

2 (28-ounce) bottles ginger ale

1 quart raspberry sherbet

- Combine first 3 ingredients, stirring well. Chill until ready to serve.

- Stir in ginger ale and sherbet just before serving.

- Serve in a punch bowl with an ice ring.

Serves 16.

Sherbet will remain in chunks in punch. Cranberries and lemon slices may be frozen into ice ring.

Governor's Mansion Punch

1 large can grapefruit juice

1 large can pineapple juice

1 large can apple juice

2 cups sugar

1 cup water

1 (12-ounce) can frozen orange juice concentrate, undiluted

6 cups cold water

2 quarts ginger ale

- Freeze first 3 ingredients in cans. Let stand at room temperature 1 hour and 30 minutes, so juice will be slightly frozen.

- Cut out both ends of cans, and combine juices in a large punch bowl.

- Combine sugar and 1 cup water, stirring until dissolved; add to juice mixture.

- Combine orange juice and 6 cups cold water, stirring well.

- Pour orange juice into punch bowl; stir in ginger ale.

Serves 30.

For a pink punch, substitute cranberry juice for grapefruit juice.

Mexican Coffee

4 cups whole milk

1 teaspoon ground cinnamon

1 teaspoon vanilla extract

⅔ cup instant cocoa mix or ⅓ cup chocolate syrup

½ cup instant coffee granules

8 cups boiling water

⅓ cup Kahlúa (optional)

Whipped cream

Cinnamon sticks

- Combine first 5 ingredients, stirring well. Chill until ready to serve.

- Bring milk mixture to a simmer in a large Dutch oven over medium-low heat just before serving.

- Stir in 8 cups boiling water and Kahlúa.

- Serve with whipped cream and cinnamon sticks.

3 quarts.

Be sure to taste and adjust flavoring!

Coffee Cream Punch

½ envelope unflavored gelatin

1 pint whipping cream, divided

5 cups strong-brewed coffee

1 cup sugar

- Sprinkle gelatin in a medium bowl; cover with ½ cup cream.

- Bring remaining cream, coffee, and sugar to a boil in a medium saucepan. Add gelatin mixture, stirring well.

- Bring to a boil again.

- Pour mixture into a bowl, and let cool completely, stirring occasionally.

Serves 5.

This punch is even better when you use your favorite combinations of gourmet flavored coffees.

Coffee Bar

For a nice ending to a dinner or dessert party, set out several pots of gourmet roasted coffee:
- *Amaretto*
- *Kahlúa*
- *brandy*
- *Irish whiskey*
- *Grand Marnier*
along with sugar, cream and several garnishes:
- *cinnamon sticks*
- *shaved chocolate*
- *ground cinnamon*
- *ground nutmeg*
- *lots of fresh whipped cream*
Fill coffee cups 2/3 full of coffee and let each person add his own liqueur and garnishes.

Hot Spiced Cider

1 gallon apple cider

1 (12-ounce) can frozen
   lemonade concentrate,
   undiluted

2 teaspoons ground cinnamon

1 teaspoon ground cloves

1 teaspoon ground nutmeg

2 cups applejack brandy
   (optional)

- Combine first 5 ingredients in a large saucepan; cook over medium heat until hot (do not boil).
- Stir in brandy, if desired.

Serves 16.

Citrus Julius — *Orange Caesar?*

1 (6-ounce) can frozen orange
   juice concentrate, undiluted

1 cup water

½ cup sugar

1 cup milk

15 ice cubes

1 teaspoon vanilla extract

- Process all ingredients in a blender until smooth.
- Serve immediately.

Serves 4.

Berry, Berry Frosty Smoothie

1½ cups orange juice
1 banana
1 cup frozen strawberries
1 cup frozen raspberries

Pour the orange juice in blender. Add all the fruit and blend.

The Classic Frosty Smoothie

1 cup orange juice
½ cup vanilla yogurt
1 banana
1½ cups frozen strawberries

Pour the orange juice and yogurt in blender. Add banana and strawberries and blend. Milk may be used in place of orange juice for a creamier drink.

Juice with a Kick

1 (32-ounce) bottle
cranberry juice

1 quart orange juice

½ cup fresh lemon juice (no
substitutions)

1 cup sugar

1 bottle Chablis or white
zinfandel, chilled

2 bottles Champagne, chilled

Garnishes: orange slices,
strawberries, or
raspberries

- Combine first 4 ingredients. Chill until ready to
serve.

- Add wines just before serving.

- Garnish, if desired.

Serves 24.

Christmas Eve Eggnog

24 large eggs, separated

2 cups sugar

1 quart whipping cream

1 fifth Old Forester bourbon
or applejack brandy

Ground nutmeg

- Beat yolks at medium speed with an electric
mixer until light and pale; gradually add sugar,
beating until well blended. Very slowly add
bourbon, to taste.

- Beat egg whites in a separate bowl at high speed
with an electric mixer until stiff peaks form.

- Fold in bourbon mixture.

- Whip cream at high speed with a handheld
mixer; fold into egg mixture.

Serves 24.

*On Christmas Eve morning, four generations gather
'round Grandma's formica-top kitchen table. It is a
family tradition to concoct Papa's eggnog and each
member from age 2 to 82 has a job. Mothers beat
the eggs, children slowly add too much sugar, and
the menfolk sneak in an extra ounce or two of
brandy. Nothing is ever measured and the eggnog
tastes a little different every year. What has
remained the same, however, for generations, is the
main immeasurable ingredient—love.*

Eye Opening Bloody Marys

make up to 2 weeks ahead

1 (32-ounce) bottle
Beefamato juice

1 (5.5-ounce) can spicy
vegetable juice

1 (5.5-ounce) can tomato juice

1 tablespoon
Worcestershire sauce

½ to 1 teaspoon hot sauce

½ teaspoon dried dillweed

½ teaspoon celery salt

1 cup vodka (optional)

Celery sticks (optional)

• Combine first 7 ingredients; stir in vodka, if desired.

• Serve with celery sticks, if desired.

Serves 6.

This drink is best when made several days in advance. It will keep in the refrigerator up to four weeks. For extra zing, serve with a dill pickle spear instead of a celery stick.

Glencoe Champagne Punch

2 (750-ml) bottles
Champagne, chilled

1 cup brandy

1 cup Cointreau

1 liter club soda, chilled

• Combine all ingredients in a large punch bowl; add ice.

1 gallon.

For many years our family gathered on the banks of the York River at Glencoe Farm in Virginia for a skeet shoot, traditionally held the Saturday after Thanksgiving. From miles around, friends and family would come together to celebrate the season and enjoy this signature drink. Although Glencoe Farm has since been sold, the family still gathers and partakes of this punch every Thanksgiving. For the best results, use the highest quality ingredients.

BACK TO THE TABLE
Breads & Sandwiches

Margaret Hill

The staff of life

It's been said that bread is the staff of life. Everybody knows macaroni and cheese is the staff of life, of course, but that's another subject.

Imagine an early summer afternoon on the back porch — or veranda, if you prefer. The air is sweet with the bouquet of a thousand flowers. Butterflies dance among the blossoms like miniature ballerinas. The honeybees linger on golden petals. Songbirds offer up sweet serenades to a bright blue firmament. The world is at peace. Love is in the air.

Imagine, too, a glass and wrought iron table. A jug of good wine, full-bodied, deep red. Fresh-baked bread, a wedge of sharp cheese. A crock of chilled gazpacho, topped with toasty croutons. A basket of fruit. A perfect lunch. A perfect day.

One of the small and exquisite pleasures of life in the South is enjoyment of simple things. Simple fare. Warm and rosy times, when the world around seems to teem with the blessings of life. Bathed in the golden light of summer sun, and cooled by the slight breath of a breeze which moves across the shade almost whisper-like, these are the magic days filled with the wonders of the place we call home.

On these gentle zephyrs are carried the cozy memories of the good times. Of family. Of friends. Of Sunday afternoons on the farm. Of warm, lazy mornings drinking dark coffee in a bathrobe in the company of a good dog. Of children and cereal. And flip-flops and fat pancakes. And the smell of fresh-picked tobacco. And the laugh of sea-gulls. And somewhere, off in the distance, the faint reminder that rain will come in the afternoon.

Yes, these are the gentle, simple summer days made even better by the gifts of food and drink and the presence of God. They are moments to be savored and, like the summer days, lengthened. They are moments forever with us, recaptured from time to time at the table in soup and bread.

We invite you, again, to come back. To eat and drink well. To enjoy. To remember. To live.

Cranberry-Lemon Scones

2 cups unbleached all-
   purpose flour

¼ cup sugar

2 teaspoons baking powder

½ teaspoon salt

6 tablespoons butter,
   chilled and cut up

½ cup dried cranberries

2 teaspoons grated lemon
   rind

⅔ cup buttermilk

2 teaspoons milk

1 teaspoon sugar

- Preheat oven to 425°.

- Combine first 4 ingredients; cut in butter with a pastry blender until crumbly. Stir in cranberries and lemon rind. Add buttermilk, stirring until mixture holds together.

- Form into a ball, and knead gently on a floured surface.

- Shape into 2 (8-inch) circles; cut each into quarters or fifths, and place on a lightly greased baking sheet 2 inches apart.

- Brush with milk, and sprinkle with sugar.

- Bake at 425° for 15 to 20 minutes or until golden.

Serves 8.

For a tall, fluffy scone, make only 1 (8-inch) circle, and cut into eighths.

A feast requires only simple things, such as people who love one another, some food and drink, and a sense of magic. It should have a few rituals — prayer, silence, a toast, the breaking of a piece of bread, the glow of candlelight—anything that will touch our consciousness of the sacred nature of the gift before us.
   —Edward Hayes, Monk

Orange-Currant Scones

6 cups all-purpose flour

¾ cup sugar

⅓ cup baking powder

1 cup plus 2 tablespoons
unsalted butter

1 cup less 3 tablespoons
buttermilk

2 teaspoons grated orange
rind

6 tablespoons fresh orange
juice

1¼ cups currants

2 egg yolks, lightly beaten

- Preheat oven to 350°.

- Combine first 3 ingredients in a bowl; cut in butter using a pastry blender until crumbly.

- Add buttermilk, orange rind, and juice, stirring just until blended (dough will be sticky).

- Turn out onto a floured surface, and knead in currants. Divide dough into 4 portions; roll each into a 6-inch circle, ½ inch thick.

- Cut each circle into 8 wedges. Place ⅛ inch apart on floured baking sheets. Brush with egg yolk.

- Bake at 350° for 12 to 18 minutes.

32 scones.

The dough can also be cut into shapes with a cookie cutter.

Applesauce Spice Muffins

1 cup margarine, softened

2 cups sugar

2 large eggs

2 cups applesauce

4 cups all-purpose flour

2 teaspoons baking soda

1 teaspoon salt

1 tablespoon ground
cinnamon

2 teaspoons ground allspice

½ teaspoon ground cloves

1 cup pecans, chopped

Powdered sugar

- Preheat oven to 350°.

- Beat butter at medium speed with an electric mixer until creamy; gradually add sugar, beating well.

- Add eggs, 1 at a time, beating well after each addition. Beat in applesauce.

- Combine flour and next 5 ingredients; add to creamed mixture, beating well. Stir in pecans.

- Fill greased miniature muffin cups ¾ full.

- Bake at 350° for 14 minutes. Sprinkle with powdered sugar.

7 dozen.

Batter will keep in the refrigerator up to 2 weeks.

July '01 — made day ahead
July's other minute. + Jr.
almost same as Em's cousin

Decadent French Toast

2 tablespoons dark corn
  syrup
5 tablespoons butter
1 cup firmly packed brown
  sugar
Chopped pecans
6 (1½-inch-thick) French
  bread slices *or*
5 large eggs
1½ cups milk
1 teaspoon vanilla extract
Whipped cream
Strawberries or other fruit

See Casserole French Toast — R (Em's Baby Shower)

- Preheat oven to 350°.

- Cook first 3 ingredients in a small saucepan over medium heat until bubbly. Immediately remove from heat.

- Pour mixture into a *well* greased 13- x 9-inch baking dish; generously sprinkle with pecans. Arrange bread over pecans.

- Whisk together eggs, milk, and vanilla; pour over bread, and chill overnight.

- Bake at 350° for 45 minutes. Invert onto a serving platter immediately.

- Serve immediately with whipped cream and strawberries. *or orange syrup - p. 38*

Serves 6.

Egg substitute may be used instead of all or part of eggs.

Yummy Pecan Coffee Cake

Try — do not let rise overnight

2 cups pecans, divided
1 package frozen yeast rolls
1 (3.4-ounce) package
  butterscotch pudding
  mix
1 teaspoon ground
  cinnamon
1 cup firmly packed brown
  sugar
1 stick butter, melted

- Place half of pecans on the bottom of a greased (9-inch) tube or Bundt pan. Arrange rolls, evenly spaced, over pecans.

- Let rise in a warm place, free from drafts, 1 to 2 hours.

- Sprinkle with pudding mix.

- Combine cinnamon, brown sugar, and butter; pour over top. Sprinkle with remaining half of pecans.

- Bake at 350° for 30 to 35 minutes.

Serves 10.

For Yummy Pecan-Raisin-Apple Coffee Cake, add raisins and chopped apple to the dough. Proceed as directed.

Pecan French Toast with Orange Syrup

4 large eggs

⅔ cup orange juice

⅓ cup milk

¼ cup sugar

½ teaspoon vanilla extract

¼ teaspoon ground nutmeg

8 (½-inch-thick) French or
  Italian bread slices

¼ cup butter

½ cup chopped pecans

Orange Syrup

- Beat first 6 ingredients in an electric mixer until well blended.

- Arrange bread slices in a single layer in a 13- x 9-inch baking dish. Pour egg mixture over bread. Cover and chill 2 to 24 hours.

- Place butter in a 15- x 10-inch jellyroll pan; place in a 350° oven until butter melts.

- Remove from oven, and tilt pan to cover evenly with butter.

- Remove bread from egg mixture, and place in a single layer in prepared jellyroll pan.

- Bake at 350° for 20 minutes. Sprinkle with pecans.

- Bake 10 more minutes or until evenly browned. Broil 1 to 2 minutes, if desired.

- Serve immediately with Orange Syrup.

Orange Syrup

½ cup butter or margarine

½ cup sugar

⅓ cup frozen orange juice
  concentrate, thawed and
  undiluted

- Cook all ingredients in a saucepan over low heat, stirring often, until butter melts.

- Remove from heat, and let cool 10 minutes. Beat at medium speed with a handheld mixer until thickened.

- Serve warm.

Serves 8.

Because this must rest in the refrigerator for a period of time, it is a great breakfast for overnight guests.

Cranberry-Orange Bread

1 orange (plus orange juice)

2 tablespoons butter

2 cups all-purpose flour

½ teaspoon baking soda

1½ teaspoons baking powder

½ teaspoon salt

1 teaspoon ground cloves or cinnamon

¼ teaspoon ground nutmeg (optional)

1 cup sugar

1 to 2 large eggs

1 cup cranberries, halved

- Preheat oven to 350°.

- Combine grated rind from orange, butter, and enough orange juice to equal ¾ cup in a 1-cup glass liquid measuring cup.

- Combine flour, next 4 ingredients, and, if desired, nutmeg in a bowl.

- Remove butter from orange juice mixture; beat butter and sugar at medium speed with a handheld mixer in a large bowl until creamy; add egg, beating well.

- Add dry ingredients to egg mixture alternately with juice mixture, beginning and ending with dry ingredients and beating well after each addition.

- Stir in cranberries, and pour into 1 greased and floured (9- x 5-inch) loaf pan or 3 (5- x 3-inch) loaf pans.

- Bake at 350° for 45 minutes (large loaf) or 35 minutes (small loaves) or until a wooden pick inserted in center comes out clean.

1 (9- x 5-inch) or 3 (5- x 3-inch) loaves.

Best Banana-Nut Bread Ever!

⅔ cup butter

1½ cups sugar

2 large eggs

1 cup banana, mashed

½ cup buttermilk

2 cups all-purpose flour

1 teaspoon baking soda

1 cup nuts, chopped

1 teaspoon vanilla extract

- Preheat oven to 350°.

- Beat butter and sugar at medium speed with an electric mixer until creamy. Add eggs, beating well. Beat in banana and buttermilk.

- Sift together flour and soda in a large bowl; add ½ cup nuts and vanilla.

- Stir banana mixture into flour mixture, and pour into 2 greased and floured 9- x 5-inch loaf pans or muffin cups. Sprinkle with remaining ½ cup nuts.

- Bake at 350° for 1 hour (loaves) or 35 to 45 minutes (muffins).

2 (9- x 5-inch) loaves or 18 muffins.

Freezes well.

Harvest Pumpkin Bread

3 cups sugar

1 cup vegetable oil

4 large eggs

1 can pumpkin

2 cups all-purpose flour

1½ cups whole wheat flour

1 teaspoon baking powder

2 teaspoons salt

2 teaspoons baking soda

½ teaspoon ground cloves

1 teaspoon ground allspice

1 teaspoon ground cinnamon

1 teaspoon ground nutmeg

⅔ cup apple juice

- Preheat oven to 350°.

- Beat first 3 ingredients at medium speed with an electric mixer until fluffy. Stir in pumpkin.

- Combine all-purpose flour and next 8 ingredients; stir into pumpkin mixture. Stir in apple juice.

- Pour mixture into 2 (9- x 5-inch) or 5 (5- x 3-inch) loaf pans.

- Bake at 350° for 1 hour and 5 to 15 minutes (large loaves) or 1 hour (small loaves).

2 (9- x 5-inch) or 5 (5- x 3-inch) loaves.

Cinnamon Swirl Bread

6¾ to 7¼ cups all-purpose
  flour, divided

2 (¼-ounce) envelopes
  active dry yeast

1¼ cups sugar, divided

2 cups milk

⅓ cup butter or margarine

2 teaspoons salt

2 large eggs

1 egg yolk

4 teaspoons ground
  cinnamon

½ cup raisins, chopped
  pecans, or chopped apple
  (optional)

- Combine 3 cups flour and yeast in a large bowl.

- Cook ¼ cup sugar, milk, butter, and salt in a saucepan over medium heat, stirring constantly, just until butter is almost melted. Add to flour mixture; add eggs and yolk, and beat at high speed with an electric mixer 3 minutes. Stir in as much remaining flour as possible.

- Turn dough out on a lightly floured surface, and knead in enough remaining flour to make a moderately stiff dough, kneading 6 to 8 minutes or until smooth and elastic.

- Shape into a ball, and place in a lightly greased bowl, turning to grease top. Cover and let rise in a warm place (85°), free from drafts, 1 hour and 15 minutes or until doubled in bulk.

- Punch down, and divide dough in half. Cover and let rest 10 minutes.

- Roll each portion into a 15- x 7-inch rectangle on a lightly floured surface. Brush dough lightly with water.

- Combine remaining 1 cup sugar, cinnamon, and, if desired, raisins, nuts, or apple; sprinkle evenly over dough.

- Roll up, jellyroll fashion, beginning with a short end. Press seams to seal. Place rolls, seam side down, in 2 greased 9- x 5-inch loaf pans.

- Bake at 375° for 35 to 40 minutes or until done, covering with aluminum foil during last 15 minutes to prevent excessive browning.

- Remove from pans, and let cool on wire racks.

2 (9- x 5-inch) loaves.

"He that is of a merry heart hath a continual feast."
—Proverbs 15:15

Cinnamon-Pecan Buns

⅓ cup firmly packed light brown sugar

⅓ cup light corn syrup

⅔ cup butter, divided

1 cup pecans

6½ cups all-purpose flour, divided

⅓ cup granulated sugar

2 (¼-ounce) envelopes rapid-rise yeast

1½ teaspoons salt

¾ cup warm water

¾ cup warm milk

2 large eggs

1 tablespoon ground cinnamon

¼ cup granulated sugar

- Cook brown sugar, corn syrup, and 3 tablespoons butter in a saucepan over medium heat, stirring often, until dissolved.

- Pour into a greased 13- x 9-inch baking dish. Arrange pecans over mixture.

- Combine 2 cups flour, ⅓ cup granulated sugar, yeast, and salt in a large bowl; stir in ⅓ cup butter, ¾ cup warm water, and milk. Stir in remaining flour and eggs.

- Knead dough on a floured surface 8 minutes or until smooth. Roll dough out into a 24- x 8-inch rectangle.

- Melt remaining 2 tablespoons butter, and brush over dough. Sprinkle with cinnamon and ¼ cup granulated sugar.

- Roll up, jellyroll fashion, beginning at a short end. Pinch seams to seal. Cut into 1½-inch-thick slices, and place, cut side up, in prepared pan.

- Cover tightly. Chill 2 to 24 hours.

- Uncover and let stand at room temperature 10 minutes before baking.

- Bake at 375° for 40 to 45 minutes, covering with aluminum foil to prevent excessive browning if necessary.

- Invert onto a serving platter.

Serves 8.

You may also use regular yeast in this recipe. Dissolve in liquid, and proceed as directed. To freeze buns, place dough in prepared pan. Wrap tightly with plastic wrap. Freeze up to 4 weeks. Unwrap and thaw at room temperature 1 to 2 hours. Let rise in a warm place (85°), free from drafts, 1 hour and 30 minutes or until doubled in bulk. Bake as directed.

Raspberry-Cream Cheese Coffee Cake

2¼ cups all-purpose flour

¾ cup sugar

¾ cup margarine, cut up

½ cup almonds, sliced

2 large eggs, divided

¾ cup sour cream

½ teaspoon baking soda

½ teaspoon baking powder

¼ teaspoon salt

1 teaspoon almond extract

1 (8-ounce) package cream
cheese, softened

¼ cup sugar

½ cup raspberry preserves

- Preheat oven to 350°.

- Combine first 3 ingredients in a bowl, mixing with a pastry blender until crumbly.

- Combine 1 cup flour mixture and almonds in a separate bowl, reserving remaining flour mixture. Add 1 egg, sour cream, and next 4 ingredients to reserved flour mixture; spread over bottom and up sides of a greased and floured springform pan.

- Beat remaining egg, cream cheese, and sugar at medium speed with an electric mixer until creamy. Pour over prepared pan.

- Carefully spoon preserves over cream cheese mixture. Sprinkle with almond mixture.

- Bake at 350° for 45 to 50 minutes or until set.

- Remove from oven, and let cool 15 minutes before removing sides of pan. Let cool at least 2 hours before cutting.

Serves 8.

There's something festive about using every table in the house for a holiday feast or other special meal. It doesn't matter that the linens don't match or that the plates are different. Somehow the delight of bringing loved ones together makes the loaves and fishes bountiful all over again.

Angel Biscuits

1 (¼-ounce) envelope active
    dry yeast
2 tablespoons warm water
2½ cups all-purpose flour
½ teaspoon baking soda
1 teaspoon baking powder
1 teaspoon salt
2 tablespoons sugar
½ cup solid shortening
1 cup buttermilk

- Dissolve yeast in 2 tablespoons warm water.

- Combine flour and next 4 ingredients in a bowl; cut in shortening using a pastry blender until crumbly. Add yeast mixture and buttermilk, stirring until blended.

- Transfer to a large bowl, and cover. Chill at least 1 hour or for up to several days.

- Roll dough out to ¼-inch thickness on a lightly floured surface. Cut with a cutter, and place on a greased baking sheet.

- Let rise 1 hour to 1 hour and 30 minutes.

- Bake at 425° for 10 to 12 minutes.

24 biscuits.

These are indeed angelically light, but their greatest advantage is that the dough can be made ahead; ready to cut and bake right from the fridge. One cup sweet milk and 1 teaspoon vinegar may be combined and substituted for buttermilk, if desired.

*The pine float
and other mysteries*

There are people who will actually walk into a local eatery down our way and order up a "pine float." What's a pine float? Why, a glass of water and a toothpick. It's low in calories and easy on the pocketbook. Ketchup and water makes passable tomato juice. A couple of lemon slices and sugar, in water, yields faux lemonade. Add grape jelly to a sausage biscuit and you've got a three course breakfast.

Herb-Cheese Biscuits *Try w/ Herbed Butter (below)*

2½ cups biscuit mix

¼ teaspoon ground white pepper

2 tablespoons butter or margarine, cut up

1 cup (4 ounces) shredded Swiss cheese

1 teaspoon dried basil *or 4 t. fresh*

1 teaspoon dried thyme

1 teaspoon dried oregano

1 (8-ounce) container plain yogurt

• Preheat oven to 450°.

• Combine biscuit mix and pepper in a medium bowl; cut in butter with a pastry blender until crumbly. Add cheese and herbs, tossing to blend. Add yogurt, stirring just until dry ingredients are moistened.

• Turn dough out onto a surface dusted with biscuit mix; knead lightly 3 or 4 times. Roll to ½-inch thickness.

• Cut with a 2½-inch round cutter, and place on ungreased baking sheets.

• Bake at 450° for 8 to 10 minutes or until golden.

Serves 12.

☆ Four teaspoons fresh herbs may be substituted for 1 teaspoon dried, if desired.

Herbed Butter Try

Helpful Hint

Dried herbs are more concentrated than fresh herbs. To substitute, use three times more fresh than dried.

Herbed butter

Soften 1 cup of unsalted butter
add ¼ teaspoon salt
and ½ teaspoon white pepper
add 2 tablespoons minced fresh parsley
Shape into a roll on waxed paper. Chill until firm.

Melvin Biscuits *Try*

1½ c — 3 cups all-purpose flour

1½ c — 3 cups self-rising flour

¾ c — 1½ cups solid shortening

2 T — 4 tablespoons sugar

1 C — 2 cups cold milk

↓ 4 doz   ↓ 8 doz

- Preheat oven to 400°.
- Stir together first 4 ingredients, using a fork or dough hooks until crumbly. Add milk, stirring well.
- Roll half the dough out thinly on a floured surface. Carefully fold in half to make a double layer.
- Roll out, and cut with a round cutter.
- Repeat procedure with remaining half of dough.
- Bake at 400° until golden brown, or bake lightly and freeze.

About 8 dozen.

These biscuits are great for stuffing because they just pop open. You may stuff them with ham, brush with melted butter, and wrap in aluminum foil to freeze. When reheating, leave them wrapped in foil, so they won't dry out.

Quick Butter Biscuits - *similar to sour cream minatures*

2 cups biscuit mix

1 stick butter, melted

1 cup sour cream

Ground country ham (optional)

Chopped green onions (optional)

Shredded Cheddar cheese (optional)

- Preheat oven to 425°.
- Combine first three ingredients, and, if desired, ham, green onions, or cheese, mixing by hand (do not overmix; batter will be lumpy).
- Fill miniature muffin cups, coated with vegetable cooking spray, two-thirds full.
- Bake at 425° for 10 minutes or until golden.

2 dozen.

Pesto Biscuits

2 cups all-purpose flour

3 teaspoons baking powder

½ teaspoon baking soda

1 teaspoon salt

½ tablespoon chopped fresh chives

½ tablespoon chopped fresh rosemary

½ tablespoon chopped fresh parsley

2 garlic cloves, chopped

½ teaspoon pepper

¼ cup grated Romano cheese

3 tablespoons solid shortening

1 cup buttermilk

• Preheat oven to 450°.

• Combine first 4 ingredients in a large bowl; stir in chives and next 5 ingredients. Cut in shortening using a pastry blender until crumbly. Stir in buttermilk.

• Knead on a lightly floured surface; roll out to ½-inch thickness.

• Cut, using a round cutter, and place on baking sheets.

• Bake at 450° for 8 to 10 minutes or until golden brown.

2 dozen biscuits.

Biscuits freeze well. For an hors d'oeuvre, split the biscuits, and fill with a dried tomato in oil and mozzarella cheese.

Heavenly Rolls

1 cup vegetable oil

1 cup hot water

½ cup sugar

2 (¼-ounce) envelopes active dry yeast

1 cup tepid water

2 large eggs, well beaten

1 tablespoon salt

7 to 8 cups Southern Biscuit plain flour (no substitutions)

1 (¼-pound) stick butter, melted

- Combine first 3 ingredients in a large bowl.

- In another bowl, mix next 2 ingredients. Combine with first mixture. Add eggs and salt, and stir well.

- Sift flour, and add 7 cups or more (enough to make a firm dough).

- Put dough in a buttered bowl, and turn to grease top. Cover bowl with aluminum foil, and chill overnight.

- Roll dough out on a lightly floured surface to ¼-inch thickness. Cut with round cutter; dip 1 side in melted butter, and fold over into pocketbook shape.

- Cover with damp cloth, and let rise in a warm place (85°), free from drafts, 2 hours.

- Bake at 425° for 5 to 8 minutes or until nearly done.

- Freeze and reheat in foil.

5 dozen rolls.

Dough may be mixed with Mixmaster and bread hook.

During Spring, Fall and on a sunny Winter day, put your bread in your car to rise. It rises better and makes your car smell really great! Don't try in the summer — too hot.

Dilly Casserole Bread *Try*

1 (¼-ounce) envelope active dry yeast

¼ cup warm water

1 cup creamed cottage cheese, lukewarm

2 tablespoons sugar

1 tablespoon instant minced onion

1 tablespoon butter

2 teaspoons dill seed

1 teaspoon salt

¼ teaspoon baking soda

1 large egg

2½ cups all-purpose flour

- Dissolve yeast in warm water.

- Combine yeast mixture, cottage cheese, and next 7 ingredients in a large bowl. Gradually add flour, beating well at medium speed with an electric mixer after each addition.

- Cover and let rise in a warm place (85°), free from drafts, 50 minutes to 1 hour or until doubled in bulk.

- Punch down, and place in a well-greased 1½-quart baking dish. Let rise in a warm place 40 minutes.

- Bake at 350° for 40 to 50 minutes. ✱

Serves 8.

This bread can be prepared ahead of time. It freezes well.

✱ *Check after 15 min. Browns fast. May have to cover top w/ foil for rest of time —*

Herb Focaccia

1 (11-ounce) package refrigerated French bread dough

2 tablespoons olive oil

1 teaspoon kosher salt

1 teaspoon pepper

1 teaspoon dried oregano

1 teaspoon dried basil

½ teaspoon dried thyme

- Preheat oven to 375°.

- Unroll dough into a 15- x 10-inch jellyroll pan; flatten slightly. Make indentions at 1-inch intervals, using wooden spoon handle.

- Drizzle with oil, and sprinkle with salt and next 4 ingredients.

- Bake at 375° for 10 minutes or until lightly browned.

- Cut into rectangles, and serve with warm marinara sauce.

Serves 8.

Christ Church Newcomer Bread

1½ cups milk, scalded

2 tablespoons sugar

1 tablespoon salt

¼ cup butter

1 teaspoon dried oregano

6 cups sifted all-purpose flour, divided

2 cups (8 ounces) shredded sharp Cheddar cheese

3 (¼-ounce) envelopes active dry yeast

1 cup lukewarm water

1 large egg, lightly beaten

1 teaspoon water

- Combine first 5 ingredients in a large bowl; let cool to lukewarm.

- Add 2 cups flour, beating at medium speed with an electric mixer until smooth. Stir in cheese.

- Dissolve yeast in 1 cup lukewarm water in a large warm bowl. Add milk mixture, stirring well. Stir in enough remaining flour to make a soft dough.

- Turn out onto a lightly floured surface, and knead 10 minutes or until smooth and elastic.

- Place in a greased bowl, turning to grease top. Cover and let rise in a warm place (85°), free from drafts, 45 minutes or until doubled in bulk.

- Punch down. Turn out onto a lightly floured surface, and knead gently 1 to 2 minutes.

- Divide into 2 portions, and shape each portion into a loaf. Place each portion into a greased 9- x 5-inch loaf pan.

- Cover and let rise in a warm place 30 minutes or until doubled in bulk.

- Whisk together egg and 1 teaspoon water; brush over loaves.

- Bake at 400° for 30 to 40 minutes or until dark golden brown. Loaves should sound hollow when tapped on bottom.

2 (9- x 5-inch) loaves.

Add 1 cup chopped pepperoni to this bread for a yummy change.

Fried dough and other delectables

The State Fair down our way has its own brand of culinary delights. Cotton candy. Italian sausage, garnished with green peppers and fried onions. Real, sure enough bar-b-que that never heard of tomato sauce. Funnel cakes. And, yep, fried dough—one of the real mysteries of cooking. And all of it good for you, of course. Ask your doctor.

Sausage and Spinach Bread

½ pound spicy Italian pork
sausage

⅓ cup coarsely shredded
carrot

¼ cup chopped onion

1 (8-ounce) container chive
and bacon soft cream
cheese

½ (10-ounce) package
frozen spinach, thawed
and drained

⅓ cup chopped toasted
pecans

¼ cup fine, dry
breadcrumbs

1 (16-ounce) frozen bread
dough loaf, thawed

2 teaspoons butter or
margarine, melted

German-style mustard
(optional)

- Cook first 3 ingredients in a skillet over medium heat until sausage is browned and onion is tender. Drain. Stir in cream cheese; stir in spinach, pecans, and breadcrumbs.

- Roll bread dough into a 12- x 9-inch rectangle on a lightly floured surface. Carefully transfer to a greased baking sheet.

- Spoon filling lengthwise down center of dough in a 3-inch-wide strip to within 1-inch of ends. Make 3-inch cuts at 1-inch intervals on both long sides, from edges toward center.

- Moisten the end of each dough strip. Starting at 1 end, alternately fold opposite strips at an angle across filling, slightly pressing in the center to seal.

- Cover and let rise in a warm place (85°), free from drafts, 30 minutes or until doubled in bulk.

- Bake at 350° for 25 to 30 minutes or until golden brown.

- Remove from oven, and brush with melted butter. Let cool slightly on a wire rack. Serve with mustard, if desired.

- Cover and chill leftover bread.

Serves 10 to 12.

Tomato-Herb Bread

1 (¼-ounce) envelope active
dry yeast

¼ cup warm water

6¼ teaspoons sugar,
divided

1½ cups milk

3 tablespoons butter,
softened

2 teaspoons salt

7 to 9 cups all-purpose
flour, divided

2 large eggs, lightly beaten

1 cup peeled, seeded, and
chopped tomato

1 tablespoon dried minced
onion

1 teaspoon dried basil

¼ teaspoon dried marjoram

¼ teaspoon dried thyme

- Dissolve yeast in ¼ cup warm water; stir in ¼ teaspoon sugar. Let stand in a warm place (85°) 10 minutes or until bubbly.

- Heat milk and butter in a saucepan until warm.

- Combine remaining 6 teaspoons sugar, salt, and 2 cups flour in a large bowl. Gradually add milk mixture, beating with a wooden spoon 50 strokes.

- Add yeast mixture and ½ cup flour, beating 50 strokes. Stir in eggs and next 5 ingredients. Stir in enough remaining flour to make a soft dough.

- Turn dough out onto a lightly floured surface, adding flour to make workable. Knead 10 minutes or until smooth and elastic.

- Transfer to a greased bowl, turning to grease top. Cover and let rise in a warm place (85°), free from drafts, until doubled in size.

- Punch down. Knead 3 minutes on a lightly floured surface. Divide into 2 portions, and shape into loaves.

- Place in 2 greased 9- x 5-inch loaf pans. Let rise in a warm place 45 minutes or until doubled in bulk.

- Bake at 350° for 30 minutes.

Serves 24.

Blue Cornbread

1½ cups blue cornmeal

¼ teaspoon salt

1 tablespoon baking powder

1 medium onion, chopped

2 large eggs, lightly beaten

1 cup sour cream

½ cup butter or margarine, melted

1½ to 2 cups (6 to 8 ounces) shredded Cheddar cheese

¼ cup canned chopped green chiles

• Preheat oven to 350°.

• Combine first 4 ingredients in a large bowl, making a well in center of mixture. Add eggs and next 4 ingredients, stirring well.

• Bake in a greased 9-inch square pan at 350° for 40 minutes or until a knife inserted in center comes out clean.

• Serve warm with lots of butter.

Serves 6 to 8.

For a hotter flavor, jalapeño peppers may be substituted for green chiles.

Uptown Cornbread

2 cups yellow cornmeal

2 cups all-purpose flour

2 tablespoons baking powder

¼ cup sugar

1 jalapeño, seeded and diced

1 cup (4 ounces) shredded Cheddar cheese

½ cup dried tomatoes in oil, drained and chopped

2 large eggs

2 cups milk

⅔ cup peanut oil

• Preheat oven to 400°.

• Combine first 4 ingredients in a medium bowl; stir in jalapeño, cheese, and tomato.

• Whisk together eggs and milk in a separate bowl; add to flour mixture, stirring just until dry ingredients are moistened. Stir in oil.

• Heat a lightly greased 8-inch cast-iron skillet in a 400° oven until hot.

• Pour batter into prepared skillet.

• Bake at 400° for 40 minutes.

Serves 8.

If using an 8-inch baking pan, add 20 minutes to baking time.

Bet you never knew the word pone, as in cornpone, came from the Indians who were the first Southern cooks. It meant to them what it does to us: a fried or baked bread.

Southern Spoonbread

1 cup water

½ teaspoon salt

1 cup cornmeal

1½ cups milk

½ teaspoon honey or sugar

2 tablespoons butter

3 large eggs, separated

Kernels from 1 ear of corn
(optional)

1 jalapeño pepper, minced
(optional)

- Preheat oven to 350°.

- Bring water to a boil in a heavy saucepan or the top of a double boiler; stir in salt, and gradually add cornmeal, stirring constantly with a wooden spoon. Stir in milk, and cook over low heat, stirring often, 10 to 15 minutes or until thickened and smooth.

- Remove from heat, and stir in honey and butter. Add eggs yolks, 1 at a time, stirring well after each addition.

- Beat egg whites at high speed with an electric mixer 2 minutes or until stiff peaks form. Stir one-fourth of egg whites into cornmeal mixture just until mixed.

- Gently fold in remaining egg whites and, if desired, corn and jalapeño.

- Bake in a 2-quart baking dish lightly coated with vegetable cooking spray at 350° for 30 minutes or until puffed and lightly browned.

Serves 4.

Great with a light soup, vegetables, and a salad. Wonderful cold, and cut into slices.

Growing up in a small town in eastern North Carolina in the 60's, the entertainment opportunities were limited. My parents' bridge club would often organize a traditional cook-out at a local park. There would be sixteen adults and lots of children. We would put up a volleyball net, play hide and seek, tag, and croquet. The day was always capped off with roasting marshmallows by the fire. To this day, when we visit with these childhood friends, we still talk about those simple but fun times together.

Try

Bacon, Avocado, and Blue Cheese Sandwiches

8 ounces blue cheese

2 tablespoons mayonnaise

1 tablespoon milk

12 whole wheat bread slices, toasted

1 avocado, peeled and sliced

12 bacon slices, cooked *or Real Bacon Bits*

- Combine first 3 ingredients; spread evenly on bread slices.

- Layer 6 bread slices evenly with avocado and bacon; top with remaining 6 bread slices.

Serves 6.

Curried Pork Sandwiches

1 medium onion, minced

2 garlic cloves, minced

4 tablespoons vegetable oil

2 pounds lean ground pork

¾ teaspoon ground ginger

1 teaspoon curry powder

2 tablespoons soy sauce

⅓ cup sweet pickle relish

4 drops Tabasco

1½ teaspoons sugar

1 teaspoon white vinegar

Salt

¾ cup plain yogurt

10 pita bread rounds, halved

2 tomatoes, chopped (optional)

1 cup plain yogurt (optional)

- Sauté onion and garlic in hot oil in a skillet until tender. Add pork, and cook over low heat, stirring occasionally, 20 minutes or until meat crumbles and is no longer pink.

- Drain, discarding drippings.

- Stir ginger and next 7 ingredients into pork mixture; cook over low heat 10 to 15 minutes. Stir in ¾ cup yogurt, and bring almost to a boil.

- Fill pita halves with pork mixture. Top evenly with tomato and 1 cup yogurt, if desired.

Serves 10.

Picnic Sandwiches

4 ounces thinly sliced ham

4 ounces thinly sliced cotto salami

4 ounces thinly sliced turkey breast

8 ounces ricotta cheese

1½ cups (6 ounces) shredded provolone or Monterey Jack cheese

1 medium onion, chopped

½ cup chopped green bell pepper

½ cup chopped red bell pepper

1 teaspoon dried oregano

1 (1-pound) loaf frozen bread dough, thawed

1 large egg (optional)

1 tablespoon water (optional)

Sesame or poppy seeds (optional)

- Preheat oven to 350°.

- Cut meats into ¼-inch-wide strips. Combine meat strips, ricotta, and next 5 ingredients.

- Roll dough into a 10- x 14-inch rectangle on a lightly floured surface. Place on a lightly greased baking sheet.

- Spread filling over center third of dough. Bring edges to the center, and seal.

- Turn dough, seam side down; make slits in top of loaf.

- Combine egg and 1 tablespoon water, and, if desired, brush over loaf. Sprinkle with sesame seeds, if desired.

- Bake at 350° for 25 minutes or until golden brown.

- Let cool on a wire rack so that underside will be crisp.

Serves 4.

Smoked Turkey Sandwiches with Chutney and Alfalfa Sprouts

Try

½ cup mayonnaise

3 tablespoons Major Grey chutney, minced

24 thin whole wheat bread slices

Thin slices smoked turkey

Alfalfa sprouts

- Combine mayonnaise and chutney, stirring well.

- Spread evenly on half of bread slices; top with turkey and alfalfa sprouts.

- Top with remaining bread slices.

Serves 12.

Could add soft brie or Fontina or other soft cheese.

Festive Rye Sandwiches

1 cup (4 ounces) shredded Swiss cheese

½ pound bacon, cooked and crumbled

½ cup pimiento-stuffed olives, chopped

½ cup minced green onions

1 teaspoon Worcestershire sauce

¼ cup mayonnaise

36 party rye bread or pumpernickel slices

- Preheat oven to 375°.

- Combine first 6 ingredients; spread evenly on bread slices.

- Bake at 375° for 15 minutes or until browned.

Serves 36 sandwiches.

These sandwiches may be frozen after baking and reheated when ready to serve. Can also be served as an appetizer.

Tuna-Stuffed Pita Pockets

8 ounces mozzarella cheese slices, cut in half

1 (6½-ounce) can albacore tuna, drained

1 cup cherry tomatoes, quartered

1 small red onion, halved and sliced

2 celery ribs, minced

¼ cup olive oil

3 tablespoons red wine vinegar

1 tablespoon dried basil, crumbled

½ teaspoon salt

¼ teaspoon sweet red pepper flakes, crushed, or cayenne

Ground black pepper to taste

4 whole wheat pitas, halved and heated

- Combine first 5 ingredients in a large bowl.

- Whisk together oil and next 5 ingredients; pour over tuna mixture, tossing to coat.

- Cover and chill at least 1 hour.

- Spoon salad evenly into pita halves.

Serves 4.

Tomato sandwiches

There's nothing quite like a tomato sandwich. Sliced beefsteak tomatoes. Duke's mayonnaise. White bread. Salt and pepper. That's all. Best thing you ever put in your mouth. A lot of folks grew up on 'mater sandwiches. A lot of folks depend on 'em to get through the day. Add a glass of sweet tea, and, kazaam, you're in heaven.

Stroganoff Sandwiches

4 French rolls, halved

1 pound ground beef

¼ cup chopped onion

1 cup sour cream

2 tablespoons milk

Garlic powder

1 tomato, sliced

1 green bell pepper, sliced

1 cup (4 ounces) shredded
  Cheddar cheese

• Preheat oven to 350°.

• Bake rolls, wrapped in aluminum foil, at 350° for 15 minutes.

• Cook beef and onion in a skillet over medium heat, stirring until meat crumbles and is no longer pink. Stir in sour cream, milk, and garlic powder; cook, stirring often, until thoroughly heated. Do not boil.

• Spoon mixture onto bottom half of each roll, and top with tomato and bell pepper.

• Top evenly with cheese, and broil until cheese is melted.

• Place top half of rolls on sandwiches. Serve warm.

Serves 4.

Christ Church Vegetable Spread for Sandwiches

2 carrots, peeled and sliced

2 onions, peeled and sliced

2 cucumbers, peeled and
  sliced

2 bell peppers, seeded and
  sliced

2 tomatoes, peeled and
  sliced

1 package unflavored
  gelatin

1 cup mayonnaise

1 teaspoon hot sauce

• Process first 5 ingredients in a blender; drain, reserving juice.

• Combine reserved juice and gelatin in the top of a double boiler; bring water to a boil. Cook, stirring constantly, until syrupy. Stir in mayonnaise and hot sauce.

• Combine pureed vegetables and gelatin mixture, stirring well.

• Store in an airtight container in the refrigerator.

Serves 4 to 6.

This spread will keep in the refrigerator for several weeks.

Pimiento Cheese

1 pound process cheese
spread loaf, shredded

2½ cups shredded sharp
Cheddar cheese

1 (8-ounce) package cream
cheese, softened

8 ounces mayonnaise

1 (4-ounce) jar diced
pimientos, undrained

2 tablespoons vinegar

1 teaspoon sugar

1 tablespoon prepared
mustard

½ teaspoon ground red
pepper

½ teaspoon salt

can minced green chilies

- Combine shredded cheeses in a bowl.

- Stir together cream cheese and mayonnaise in a
separate bowl; stir in pimientos and next 5
ingredients. Add cheeses, stirring well. Chill.

- Serve on bread or with crackers.

4 cups.

Best if chilled several hours or overnight.

Ode to pimiento cheese

*It's gooey. It's ugly.
Nobody's quite sure what
it's made of. But, man, is it
go-o-o-d. How many of us
made it through grade
school on pimiento cheese,
with, of course, an
occasional peanut butter
and Welch's grape jelly on
white bread to break the
monotony? A five-course
meal in the third grade?
Pimiento cheese, carrot
sticks, hard-boiled egg, a
Twinkie and chocolate
milk. Whoa!*

BACK TO THE TABLE
Soups & Salads

JoAnn Wainright

Salad days

Let first onion flourish there,
Rose among roots, the maiden-fair
Wine-scented and poetic soul
Of the capacious salad bowl.

–Robert Louis Stevenson
A Child's Garden of Verse

There is something about springtime in the country, when geraniums burst forth and the last frosts are gone and the sky is azure tinged with rose. There is a sweet smell in the air. And buds on the vine. And the unfamiliar sound of a distant lawn mower.

You know spring is finally here when the first watermelons begin to show up. Round and sweet. The kind that make a solid "thunk" when you thump their sides. The roadside stands proclaim their arrival with gaudy hand-lettered signs with "cantaloupe" persistently misspelled. And that's when you know that cucumbers, and home-grown squashes and Vidalia onions can't be far behind. And, later on, peaches and silver queen corn and summertime green tomatoes. And peppers, green and red, and snap beans and juicy Beefsteak tomatoes.

The salad days are finally here.

Now, nothing befits a table quite like a salad. The melange of color: the bright greens, reds, yellows and oranges. The scents of vinaigrette and balsamic vinegar and bright green olive oil, and chives and lemon, and garlic and spring onions and fresh-ground pepper waft across the room like a cool springtime breeze.

Ah, and the sounds of a salad. That healthy snap and crunch like the crackle of a new American flag hoisted out back on Memorial Day. Like the almost imperceptible rustle of lace curtains, or the flutter of an awning at the beach on a still-chilly spring morning.

Yes, the salad days. The days we are reminded that life is a continuing love affair with nature. That out of the gloom and death of withered winter comes newness and vitality and the recurring reminder of God's promises of eternal life.

To make and taste a salad is truly to touch the spirit of the earth, and a reminder that life, in every form, is precious and good and forever.

Onion Soup

4 tablespoons unsalted
   butter

6 cups thinly sliced yellow
   onion

2 tablespoons all-purpose
   flour

6 cups beef broth

½ cup dry white wine

½ teaspoon salt

½ teaspoon freshly ground
   pepper

3 tablespoons brandy

6 French bread slices,
   toasted

6 Gruyère cheese slices

½ cup freshly grated
   Parmesan cheese

- Melt butter in a Dutch oven; add onion, and sauté until lightly browned. Add flour, stirring until blended. Add broth and next 3 ingredients; bring to a boil.

- Reduce heat, and simmer 10 minutes.

- Remove from heat, and stir in brandy.

- Spoon into 6 ovenproof bowls. Top evenly with bread and cheeses.

- Broil 1 to 2 minutes or until lightly browned. Serve immediately.

Serves 6.

> *We always held hands to say the blessing at dinner time in our family. We explained to guests it was our custom and they always joined in. It gave us a moment to quiet down from the day, to connect—to link up, as an aunt called it—and to become, for a few moments, a circle, a single entity, a family.*

Fat-Free Curried Squash Soup

2 to 3 large potatoes, peeled and cubed

2 to 3 pounds butternut squash, peeled and cubed

3 to 5 celery stalks, chopped

Carrots, chopped

1 sweet potato, peeled and cubed

4 cups water or chicken stock

2 teaspoons tomato paste or puree

2 teaspoons ground cumin or curry powder

Salt

Pepper

• Bring first 6 ingredients to a boil in a large Dutch oven (make sure water or stock covers vegetables).

• Reduce heat, and simmer 40 minutes or until potatoes are tender. Remove from heat, and let cool.

• Process vegetable mixture in batches in a blender until pureed; return to Dutch oven. Cook over medium heat until thoroughly heated.

• Stir in tomato paste and next 3 ingredients, adding additional water if necessary to reach desired consistency (soup should be thick).

Serves 6.

For added flavor stir in 1 to 2 tablespoons heavy cream or sour cream before serving. Or garnish with cream and top with chopped fresh parsley.

Pilgrimage Soup

3 pounds frozen broccoli

4 (10¾-ounce) cans condensed chicken broth, undiluted

2 quarts half-and-half

2 cups heavy cream

4 cups blue cheese

• Bring broccoli and chicken broth to a boil in a saucepan; boil 10 minutes.

• Puree mixture in a food processor. Return to pan, and stir in half-and-half and cream.

• Cook over medium heat until thoroughly heated (do not boil).

• Stir in blue cheese, and cook, stirring often, until melted.

Serves 12 servings (3 quarts).

This soup was served to a group of Christ Church parishioners on a pilgrimage in Scotland at a remote fishing lodge.

Book Club Soup

1 pound fresh asparagus, trimmed

¼ cup minced onion

4 cups chicken broth

1½ cups firmly packed fresh spinach, stemmed

2 tablespoons chopped fresh dill

⅛ teaspoon ground cayenne pepper

⅛ teaspoon ground nutmeg

½ to 1 cup heavy cream

Salt

Pepper

Freshly grated Parmesan cheese

Sour cream

- Cut tips off asparagus, and reserve.

- Bring asparagus stalks, onion, and chicken broth to a boil in a large Dutch oven. Cover, reduce heat, and simmer 25 minutes. Stir in spinach and next 3 ingredients; simmer 5 minutes.

- Process soup in batches in a food processor until pureed; return to Dutch oven. Stir in reserved asparagus tips, and simmer 5 minutes or until crisp-tender. Stir in cream.

- Season with salt and pepper. Serve in individual bowls; top each serving with Parmesan cheese and sour cream.

Serves 4.

To make this soup fat-free, omit the heavy cream and use nonfat sour cream and fat-free Parmesan cheese.

Lentil Soup

5 bacon slices

2 cups chopped Vidalia onion

2 carrots, chopped

2 to 3 garlic cloves, pressed

7 cups chicken stock

1 teaspoon dried thyme

2 bay leaves

Pepper

1½ cups dried brown lentils

Salt

- Cook bacon in a Dutch oven over medium heat until crisp; remove bacon, reserving drippings.

- Add onion, carrot, and garlic to drippings, and sauté over low heat 15 minutes or until tender. Stir in chicken stock and next 3 ingredients; add lentils, and bring to a boil.

- Cover, reduce heat, and simmer 40 minutes or until lentils are tender. Remove and discard bay leaves.

- Process half of soup and bacon in a food processor until smooth. Return to Dutch oven.

- Season with salt and pepper.

Serves 8.

Tomato-Dill Soup

½ cup butter

1 cup minced onion

1 cup minced celery

1 cup minced carrot

2 teaspoons minced garlic

1 teaspoon dried basil

1 teaspoon dried thyme

1 teaspoon dried tarragon

½ cup all-purpose flour

3 cups chicken broth

1 (35-ounce) can chopped
tomatoes, undrained

2½ cups tomato juice

1 cup heavy cream

1 teaspoon sugar

1 tablespoon chopped fresh
dill

- Melt butter in a large skillet over medium heat; add onion, celery, and carrot. Sauté 8 to 10 minutes or until tender.

- Stir in garlic and next 3 ingredients; cook 1 minute. Stir in flour, and cook 4 to 5 minutes.

- Stir in chicken broth, tomatoes, and tomato juice; bring to a boil. Reduce heat, and simmer 10 minutes.

- Stir in cream and sugar; cook 5 minutes or until thoroughly heated (do not boil).

- Stir in dill just before serving.

Serves 12.

Fat-Free Black Bean Soup

1 (15-ounce) can black
beans

1 (19-ounce) can black bean
soup

1½ cups water

½ to ¾ cup medium or hot
chunky salsa

¼ cup sliced green onions

¼ cup nonfat sour cream

Chopped fresh cilantro

- Bring first 5 ingredients to a boil in a saucepan; cover, reduce heat, and simmer 15 minutes.

- Serve topped with sour cream and cilantro.

Serves 4.

This recipe may also be served as a dip with tortilla chips.

Tuscany White Bean Soup

1 pound dried white beans,
rinsed

Bay leaves

2 to 3 quarts water

Freshly ground pepper

1 to 2 yellow bell peppers,
cubed

1 large onion, chopped

2 tablespoons minced garlic

2 tablespoons olive oil

1 cup chopped plum
tomatoes

1 teaspoon sugar or honey

3 to 4 bay leaves

8 fresh sage leaves

4 cups chicken broth

Salt

Freshly grated Parmesan or
Romano cheese

Balsamic vinegar

• Bring first 4 ingredients to a boil in a Dutch
oven; cover and turn off heat.

• Let stand 1 hour. Drain. Remove and discard
bay leaves.

• Sauté bell pepper, onion, and garlic in hot oil in
a large skillet over low heat 10 to 15 minutes.
Stir in beans, tomato, and next 4 ingredients.
Season with salt and pepper.

• Bring to a low boil; cover, reduce heat, and
simmer 30 to 45 minutes or until beans are
tender. Remove and discard bay leaves.

• Spoon into soup bowls; sprinkle with Parmesan
cheese, and add a splash of balsamic vinegar.

Serves 6.

> *The table is a meeting place, a gathering
> ground, the source of sustenance and
> nourishment, festivity, safety, and satisfaction.*
> —Laurie Colwin

Tomato Bisque

½ pound bacon

½ cup minced onion

½ cup minced celery

1 (28-ounce) can crushed tomatoes

1 teaspoon dried basil

1 teaspoon salt

½ teaspoon pepper

1 pint half-and-half

- Fry bacon in a skillet over medium heat until crisp. Remove bacon, reserving drippings. Crumble bacon.

- Add onion and celery to drippings, and sauté until tender; drain.

- Combine onion mixture and tomatoes in a saucepan; stir in bacon, basil, and next 3 ingredients.

- Cook over low heat until thoroughly heated (do not boil).

Serves 6.

You can use 1 cup half-and-half and 1 cup chicken broth in this recipe, if desired.

Chilled Chicken and Almond Bisque

¾ cup almonds

1 medium or 2 small onions, diced

6 garlic cloves, peeled

4 green onions, thinly sliced

2 tablespoons olive oil

2 (6-ounce) chicken breasts, cooked, diced, and divided

1 quart chicken stock

½ to ¾ cup coarsely chopped fresh cilantro

Salt

Pepper

- Sauté first 4 ingredients in hot oil in a large skillet until almonds are golden brown and garlic is tender.

- Process almond mixture and half of the chicken in a blender, adding enough stock to make a smooth puree. Add cilantro, and process until smooth.

- Pour into a serving bowl, and stir in remaining half of chicken. Season with salt and pepper.

- Chill slightly, and serve with chips.

Serves 4.

Corn Chowder

6 bacon slices

2 tablespoons unsalted butter

1 large onion, chopped

1 cup chopped celery

4 large potatoes, peeled and cut into ½-inch cubes

3 cups water

2 cups fresh corn kernels or 1 (10-ounce) package frozen corn

2 cups milk

1½ cups half-and-half

Pepper

- Cook bacon in a Dutch oven over medium heat until done. Remove bacon, reserving 1 tablespoon drippings. Chop bacon.

- Add butter to Dutch oven, and melt over medium heat. Add onion and celery, and sauté until tender.

- Add potatoes and 3 cups water, and bring to a boil. Cover, reduce heat, and simmer 10 minutes.

- Stir in chopped bacon, corn, and next 3 ingredients; bring to a boil. Reduce heat, and simmer 20 minutes or until potatoes are tender.

- Store in refrigerator up to 2 days.

- To serve, reheat and season with salt and pepper.

Serves 6 to 8.

Cream of Asparagus Soup

1 pound fresh asparagus, trimmed

4 tablespoons butter

2 cups chopped yellow onion

1 quart chicken stock

¼ cup heavy cream

Salt

Pepper

- Slice asparagus into ½-inch pieces, reserving tips.

- Melt butter in a Dutch oven over low heat; add onion, and simmer 20 minutes or until tender. Add chicken stock, and bring to a boil.

- Add ½-inch asparagus pieces to broth; cover, reduce heat, and simmer 40 to 45 minutes.

- Process mixture in a food processor until smooth. Return to Dutch oven, and stir in reserved asparagus tips. Simmer 5 to 10 minutes or until tender. Stir in cream, salt, and pepper.

- Serve immediately or chill and serve very cold.

The common bond of all people and all nations is— the table.

Serves 5.

Roasted Red Bell Pepper Soup

8 red bell peppers

2 tablespoons butter

1 large onion, chopped

3 garlic cloves, crushed

4 to 5 cups chicken stock

1 cup whipping cream

Salt

Freshly ground pepper

2 tablespoons cornstarch

Minced fresh basil or
    parsley

• Preheat oven to 425°.

• Prick bell pepper skin with a fork; bake on well-greased baking sheets at 425° for 30 to 40 minutes or until charred. Transfer immediately to a paper bag; close tightly, and let cool.

• Peel and seed peppers; cut into large pieces, and puree in a food processor.

• Melt butter in a heavy saucepan over medium heat; add onion and garlic, and sauté 3 minutes or until tender.

• Combine bell pepper puree, onion mixture, and chicken stock in a Dutch oven; bring to a boil. Reduce heat, and simmer 20 minutes.

• Reserve 3 tablespoons cream; stir remaining cream into soup.

• Season with salt and pepper, and simmer until thoroughly heated.

• Combine reserved cream and cornstarch, stirring until smooth. Stir into soup, and cook, stirring constantly, 3 minutes or until thickened.

• Spoon soup into warm bowls; sprinkle with parsley or basil.

• Serve immediately.

Serves 8.

Canned roasted sweet red peppers may be substituted for fresh bell peppers, if desired.

Baked Potato Soup

3 tablespoons butter or
   margarine, divided

½ cup chopped onion

½ cup chopped celery

4 cups milk

1 teaspoon salt

Pepper

3 tablespoons all-purpose
   flour

2 large potatoes, baked,
   peeled, and cut into
   ¾-inch cubes

1 cup (4 ounces) shredded
   Cheddar cheese

½ cup bacon bits

½ cup sour cream

Chopped fresh chives

• Melt 1 tablespoon butter in a large saucepan over medium heat; add onion and celery, and sauté until tender. Stir in milk, salt, and pepper; bring almost to a boil, stirring occasionally.

• Melt remaining 2 tablespoons butter in a small saucepan; whisk in flour. Cook 3 minutes, whisking constantly, until thickened; whisk into milk mixture.

• Cook, stirring constantly, until thickened. Stir in potato; cook, stirring often, until thoroughly heated.

• Spoon soup into serving bowls; top evenly with cheese, bacon, and sour cream.

• Garnish, if desired.

Serves 8.

Marion Cunningham,
creator of Fannie Farmer
Cookbook, believes that
home cooked meals are the
"magnets" that bring
families together.

Cream of Wild Mushroom Soup

2 tablespoons butter

1 cup minced onion

2 garlic cloves, crushed

1 pound button mushrooms, sliced

1½ pounds or more wild mushrooms, sliced

2 tablespoons olive oil

¼ cup all-purpose flour

1 pint half-and-half

4 (14½-ounce) cans chicken broth

1 teaspoon ground nutmeg

Salt

Ground white pepper

2 tablespoons sherry (optional)

- Melt butter in a large saucepan over low heat; add onion and garlic, and sauté until tender. Sauté mushrooms in hot oil in a separate saucepan until tender. Stir flour into onion mixture, and cook 1 minute.

- Gradually add half-and-half to onion mixture, stirring until smooth and thickened.

- Stir in mushrooms, chicken broth, and next 3 ingredients. Simmer 20 minutes.

- Stir in sherry, if desired.

Serves 10.

You can use cremini, shiitake, portobello, or other wild mushrooms in this recipe.

Cream of Brie Soup

4 tablespoons butter

½ cup chopped celery

½ cup chopped onion

¼ cup all-purpose flour

2 cups milk

2 cups chicken stock or low-sodium canned chicken broth

¾ pound Brie cheese, with rind removed and cubed

Salt

Pepper

Garnish: chopped fresh chives

- Melt butter in a saucepan over medium heat; add celery and onion, and sauté until tender. Stir in flour, and cook until bubbly.

- Remove from heat; gradually stir in milk and chicken stock. Return to heat, and cook, stirring constantly, until thickened.

- Add cheese, stirring until melted.

- Season with salt and pepper. Garnish, if desired.

Serves 4.

Christ Church Brunswick Stew

2 large whole chickens

½ pound streak-o-lean or fatback

2 large onions, chopped

6 large potatoes, peeled and cubed

½ gallon canned diced tomatoes with juice

2 pints canned butter beans

2 pints canned white shoepeg corn

1 to 2 teaspoons hot sauce

Salt

Pepper

1 to 2 tablespoons Worcestershire sauce

2 teaspoons prepared mustard

1 cup sherry

Juice of 2 lemons

- Boil chickens in water to cover in a large Dutch oven 1 hour or until falling off bone. Drain, reserving broth.

- Remove meat from bones, discarding bones and fat. Cut meat into bite-size pieces.

- Brown streak-o-lean in a skillet over medium heat. Drain, reserving drippings; chop meat into small pieces.

- Sauté onion in reserved drippings in skillet over medium heat until tender. Drain.

- Bring potatoes and reserved chicken broth to a boil in Dutch oven; cook until potatoes are tender. Stir in onion and tomatoes with their juices. Reduce heat, and simmer until thickened.

- Stir in chicken, butter beans, and corn, and bring to a simmer. Stir in hot sauce and next 6 ingredients. Bring to a simmer.

- Adjust seasoning to taste; cook until thickened.

Serves 20.

> "...Nature has a beautiful and perfect order of which we are all only a small part, and never lords. I want to be a subject to the mystery of this world, and I can do so, in part, by celebrating it at my table, with those I love."
>
> ...the late Bill Neal,
> in Southern Cooking

Daddy's Depression Soup   Try

1½ pounds lean stew beef

Soup Vegetables, divided

1½ quarts water

Diced potatoes, as many as you like

Salt

Pepper

Worcestershire sauce

- Cook beef and half of Soup Vegetables in 1½ quarts water in a Dutch oven over medium heat 1 hour and 30 minutes or until meat is tender.

- Remove meat, and let cool; chill. Remove and discard vegetables.

- Chill stock overnight; remove and discard fat.

- Add meat, remaining half of Soup Vegetables, and potatoes to stock. Cook until thoroughly heated and vegetables are done.

- Season with salt, pepper, and Worcestershire sauce.

Soup Vegetables

1 cabbage, cut into large pieces

4 onions, chopped, or 1 package French onion soup mix

2 cups coarsely chopped carrots

2 turnips

1 celery stalk, coarsely chopped

4 cans diced tomatoes

½ cup uncooked barley

Serves 8.

"My children call this daddy's depression soup because I began making it at night when I couldn't sleep. Frozen is okay, but fresh is divine, as we say in church."

Shrimp and Andouille Sausage Gumbo

½ cup vegetable oil

½ cup all-purpose flour

4 celery stalks, coarsely chopped

2 medium onions, coarsely chopped

2 green bell peppers, chopped

2 bay leaves

Salt

2 teaspoons dried crushed oregano

½ teaspoon cayenne pepper

5 (8-ounce) bottles clam juice

1 (28-ounce) can plum tomatoes, drained and chopped

1 pound smoked andouille or kielbasa sausage, halved lengthwise and cut into ¼-inch slices

½ pound okra, trimmed and sliced

2 pounds unpeeled medium-size fresh shrimp, peeled and deveined

Hot cooked rice

• Heat oil in a heavy Dutch oven over high heat until almost smoking; stir in flour, and cook, stirring constantly, 8 minutes or until dark brown.

• Stir in celery, onion, and bell pepper; cook, stirring often, 5 minutes. Stir in bay leaves and next 3 ingredients.

• Stir in clam juice, tomatoes, and sausage; bring to a boil, and cook 15 minutes. Stir in okra; reduce heat, and simmer 15 minutes or until okra is tender.

• Stir in shrimp, and simmer 3 minutes or until shrimp turn pink.

• Remove and discard bay leaf.

• Serve gumbo over hot cooked rice.

Serves 8.

Fran Stew

During that memorable post-hurricane week in 1996 when the power was off and freezers were a dim memory, folks around here got to know each other once again. Heck, there wasn't much of anything to do by candlelight but cook, and talk, and get to be friends again with people we hardly knew. But out of all this misery came "Fran Stew"—a concoction of whatever had thawed out in the Sub-Zero made useless by a big oak across the power line. There's no recipe for "Fran Stew," of course, other than imagination, a sense of adventure and rediscovered friendship.

Spinach-Oyster Soup

3 cups coarsely chopped onion

2 tablespoons clarified butter

3 cups chicken stock

1½ pounds fresh spinach or 2 (10-ounce) packages frozen spinach, thawed and drained

3 tablespoons butter or margarine

2 tablespoons unbleached all-purpose flour

3 cups milk

1½ teaspoons salt

1 teaspoon freshly ground pepper

½ teaspoon freshly grated nutmeg

1 pint oysters, drained

- Sauté onion in hot clarified butter in a heavy saucepan over low heat until tender (do not brown).

- Stir in chicken stock, and bring to a boil. Reduce heat, and simmer 10 minutes.

- Reserve 8 perfect spinach leaves; stir remaining spinach leaves into onion mixture. Bring to a boil, and remove from heat. Let cool.

- Melt 3 tablespoons butter in a separate heavy saucepan over medium heat; stir in flour, and cook 2 minutes. Gradually add milk, stirring constantly.

- Bring to a boil, and remove from heat.

- Puree spinach mixture in a food processor; add to milk mixture. Stir in salt, pepper, and nutmeg.

- Add oysters, and cook until curled.

- Top each serving with a fresh spinach leaf.

Serves 8.

Clarified Butter — the clear part

Also known as drawn butter. Melt unsalted butter, slowly, until the golden butter is clear on the top and the milk solids have sunk to the bottom. After the foam appears, skim it off. The clear (clarified) butter is poured into the dish.

Oyster Stew

6 country bacon slices

1 carrot, chopped

2 celery stalks, chopped

1 fennel stalk, peeled and diced

2 cups half-and-half

2 cups milk

24 fresh oysters, drained

Worcestershire sauce

Hot sauce

Salt

Ground white pepper

- Cook bacon in a skillet until crisp. Drain, reserving 2 tablespoons drippings.

- Cook carrot, celery, and fennel in drippings until tender.

- Combine vegetables, bacon, half-and-half, and milk in a Dutch oven. Simmer over medium heat.

- Add oysters, and cook 3 to 4 minutes or until done. Reduce heat to low, and add Worcestershire sauce and next 3 ingredients, to taste.

- Serve in warm bowls.

Serves 4.

Artichoke Soup with Mushrooms and Shrimp

3 tablespoons butter

½ cup thinly sliced fresh mushrooms

2 tablespoons minced onion

2 tablespoons all-purpose flour

2 cups chicken stock

2½ cups half-and-half

¼ cup white wine

½ teaspoon salt

2 (8½-ounce) cans water-pack artichoke hearts, drained and chopped

1 cup tiny cooked shrimp (½ pound)

- Melt butter in a 2-quart saucepan; add mushrooms and onion, and sauté 5 minutes. Stir in flour, and cook 2 to 3 minutes.

- Gradually stir in stock; cook, stirring often, until thickened.

- Stir in half-and-half, wine, and salt. Reduce heat, and cook until thickened.

- Stir in artichokes and shrimp; cook 1 to 2 minutes or until thoroughly heated.

Serves 6.

Fire and Ice Soup ✓ *food preview 2000*

4 ripe avocados, peeled and pitted

6 tablespoons lemon juice

1½ teaspoons ground cumin

4½ cups chicken broth

½ cup minced green onions

1 tablespoon canned diced jalapeño peppers

¼ cup sour cream

Salt

Pepper

Hot Tomato Ice

- Mash together first 3 ingredients in a bowl.

- Bring chicken broth to a simmer in a saucepan; whisk into avocado mixture. Stir in green onions and jalapeños.

- Puree mixture in 2 batches in a food processor. Pour into bowl.

- Whisk in sour cream, salt, and pepper. Cover and chill 2 hours.

- Spoon soup into chilled sherbet glasses, and top each serving with 1 Hot Tomato Ice cube.

Hot Tomato Ice

1 (14-ounce) can Italian plum tomatoes, undrained

½ cup chicken broth

1 tablespoon lemon juice

1 teaspoon sugar

½ teaspoon hot sauce

- Puree tomatoes in a food processor; pour through a wire-mesh strainer into a bowl, pressing hard on solids. Discard solids. Add chicken broth and next 3 ingredients to tomato juice, stirring well.

- Pour mixture into ice cube trays; freeze 3 hours or until not quite solid.

- Chop tomato cubes into pieces, and process in food processor until smooth.

- Return mixture to ice cubes trays, and freeze 2 hours or until firm.

Serves 12.

Cucumber Soup

1 cup chicken broth
¼ cup minced onion
½ teaspoon salt
½ teaspoon dried dill weed
Garlic powder, 1 dash
1 teaspoon grated lemon rind
3 tablespoons fresh lemon
   juice
1 cup plain yogurt
1 cup sour cream
3 cucumbers, seeded and
   chopped
Garnishes: thinly sliced
   lemon and cucumber

- Process first 7 ingredients in a food processor until smooth.

- Combine yogurt and sour cream; add to mixture, processing a few seconds.

- Add cucumber, pulsing a few times. Cucumber should be finely grated but not liquified. Chill 1 hour.

- Garnish each serving, if desired.

Serves 6.

White Gazpacho

3 cucumbers, peeled,
   seeded, and chopped
3 garlic cloves, minced
2¼ cups chicken stock
2½ cups yogurt
3 tablespoons white wine
   vinegar
2 teaspoons salt
2 teaspoons ground white
   pepper
2 red bell peppers, chopped
1 yellow and 1 green bell
   pepper, chopped
½ cup green or red seedless
   grapes, halved
½ cup heavy cream

- Process first 3 ingredients in a food processor 2 minutes.

- Combine yogurt and next 7 ingredients in a large bowl; add cucumber mixture, stirring well. Chill.

Find a time that's good for all family members for one meal a day—breakfast, lunch or dinner.

Gazpacho

6 large tomatoes

½ cup red wine vinegar

½ cup olive oil

1½ cups vegetable juice

2 red bell peppers, coarsely
chopped

2 onions, coarsely chopped

2 large shallots, coarsely
chopped

2 garlic cloves, crushed

1 tablespoon
Worcestershire sauce

Ground red pepper

Hot sauce, 1 dash

Salt

Ground black pepper

½ cup chopped fresh
parsley

Sour cream

Chopped fresh dill or
parsley

- Chop tomatoes, reserving juice.

- Combine reserved juice, vinegar, oil, and
vegetable juice.

- Process chopped tomato, bell pepper, and next
3 ingredients in batches in a food processor
until chopped. With machine running, gradually add vinegar mixture, processing until
almost smooth. Do not puree completely.

- Stir in Worcestershire sauce and next 5
ingredients. Cover and chill 4 to 6 hours.

- Top each serving with a dollop of sour cream,
and sprinkle with chopped fresh dill.

Serves 6.

Serve with homemade croutons.

*Peel garlic and store in a
covered jar of vegetable
oil. The garlic will stay
fresh and the oil will be
nicely flavored.*

A Colorful Salad

½ pound fresh snow peas,
trimmed

1 large yellow bell pepper,
sliced

1 large red bell pepper,
sliced

1 (8-ounce) package fresh
mushrooms, thinly sliced

Sweet and Sour Dressing

2 tablespoons sesame seeds,
toasted

- Plunge snow peas into boiling water for
1 minute. Drain and rinse with cold water.
Drain again. Pat dry with paper towels.

- Combine snow peas, bell peppers, and mushrooms in a large bowl.

- Toss with Sweet and Sour Dressing to coat.
Sprinkle with sesame seeds.

Serves 6.

Sweet and Sour Dressing

2 teaspoons sesame oil

3 tablespoons white wine
vinegar

2 tablespoons sugar

½ tablespoon salt

½ tablespoon freshly
ground pepper

¼ cup vegetable oil

- Whisk together all ingredients.

This salad is especially good after a day in the
refrigerator.

> *I was hungry and you gave me food,*
> *I was thirsty and you gave me drink,*
> *I was a stranger and you welcomed me.*
> John 25:35

Fontina Cheese-Sweet Red Pepper Salad

2 tablespoons red wine
    vinegar
2 teaspoons Dijon mustard
⅛ teaspoon freshly ground
    pepper
6 tablespoons olive oil
1 head lettuce, torn
1 bunch green onions,
    thinly sliced
¼ cup chopped fresh chives
¼ cup diced celery
4 or 5 diced anchovy strips
1 cup Danish fontina
    cheese, cubed
1 (8-ounce) jar roasted
    sweet red peppers, cut
    into ¼-inch-wide strips

- To make vinaigrette, combine first 3 ingredients in a small bowl; gradually add oil, whisking until emulsified.

- Toss together lettuce, next 4 ingredients, and vinaigrette in a large bowl.

- Serve on individual salad plates, and place cheese cubes in the center of each serving.

- Arrange pepper slices around cheese.

Serves 6.

A slightly different, milder flavored cheese may be substituted for fontina cheese.

Heart Ball Salad

⅓ cup raspberry vinegar
1 cup vegetable oil
¾ cup sugar
¼ cup minced purple onion
1 teaspoon salt
1 tablespoon
    Worcestershire sauce
  Mixed salad greens
Sliced mushrooms
Currants
Sunflower seeds
Chopped purple onion
Crumbled feta cheese

- Process first 6 ingredients in a blender until smooth.

- Arrange salad greens and next 5 ingredients on individual salad plates.

- Spoon dressing over each salad.

Serves 4.

Summer Salad

4 red bell peppers

1 large onion, thinly sliced

1 garlic clove

1 teaspoon coarse-grained salt

Pepper, 1 pinch

2 tablespoons red wine vinegar

6 to 8 tablespoons olive oil

Favorite salad greens

3 tomatoes, cut into bite-size pieces

4 hard-cooked eggs, sliced

Favorite fresh herbs

Favorite fresh edible flowers

- Char bell peppers over a flame; place in a paper bag, and let steam 10 minutes.

- Peel carefully; halve, seed, and tear into strips.

- Toss together bell pepper and onion in a large bowl.

- Mash together garlic, salt, and pepper in a small bowl; stir in vinegar and oil.

- Pour over pepper mixture, and chill 2 to 3 hours.

- Add salad greens and next 4 ingredients, tossing well.

Serves 4.

For salad greens, use arugula, sorrel, chicory, or red leaf, green leaf, or Boston lettuces.

Edible Flowers

Fresh edible flowers are the perfect addition to a summer salad or as a garnish on any plate. You will find many of them in your own yard. If you don't have any, befriend a neighbor whose garden abounds! Be certain not to use any flowers that have been treated with pesticides. Some of our favorites include nasturtiums, chive blossoms, pansies, lavender, violets and geraniums.

Market Salad

½ cup fresh asparagus tips, sliced diagonally

½ cup snow peas

¾ cup green beans, cut into 1-inch pieces

½ pound fresh broccoli florets

¾ cup fresh or frozen peas

¾ cup diagonally sliced celery

½ medium-size purple onion, thinly sliced

½ cup diced green bell pepper

½ cup diced red bell pepper

¼ cup chopped fresh parsley

1 small can chickpeas

1 small can pitted ripe or Greek olives

½ cup sliced artichoke hearts

Tarragon Dressing

Garnish: cherry tomatoes

• Plunge first 4 ingredients into boiling water to cover. Drain and rinse with cold water. Drain again.

• Combine blanched vegetables, peas, and next 8 ingredients in a large bowl.

• Pour Tarragon Dressing over mixture, tossing well. Cover and chill, tossing occasionally, for several hours.

Tarragon Dressing

¼ cup tarragon wine vinegar
½ cup vegetable oil
1½ teaspoons salt
1½ teaspoons sugar
½ teaspoon hot sauce
2 tablespoons capers
1 teaspoon dried tarragon
1 teaspoon dried basil
2 tablespoons chopped shallots
1 teaspoon dried oregano
2 tablespoons minced fresh basil

• Combine all ingredients in a jar; cover tightly, and shake vigorously.

Serves 12.

This salad will keep in the refrigerator for several days. You can substitute 1 (2-ounce) diced pimiento, drained, for red bell pepper.

Try for supper club

Mock Caesar Salad with Avocado

¾ cup olive oil, divided

¼ cup lemon juice, divided

2 garlic cloves, crushed

1 anchovy fillet

1 avocado, thinly sliced

Lemon juice

1 head romaine lettuce, torn

Freshly grated Parmesan cheese

Freshly ground pepper

- Using a pestle, mash together 1 tablespoon oil, 1 tablespoon lemon juice, garlic, and anchovy in a large wooden bowl.

- Whisk in remaining 3 tablespoons lemon juice and remaining olive oil.

- Brush avocado lightly with lemon juice. Add avocado slices, lettuce, cheese, and pepper to dressing, tossing well.

- Serve immediately.

Serves 6.

Zippy Cole Slaw

3 cups chopped green cabbage

1 cup chopped red cabbage

¼ cup chopped fresh dill

¼ cup mayonnaise

2 tablespoons champagne vinegar

2 tablespoons sugar

Celery seed

Salt

Pepper

- Combine all ingredients in a large serving bowl, tossing well.

- Let stand at room temperature up to 30 minutes before serving.

Serves 8.

Tomato and Mozzarella Salad with Balsamic Basil Vinaigrette

Try Kit's?

6 vine-ripened tomatoes, cut into ½-inch slices

1 pound mozzarella cheese, thinly sliced

½ cup thinly sliced Vidalia onion

Balsamic Basil Vinaigrette

Garnish: fresh basil sprigs

- Arrange tomato slices alternately with mozzarella on a deep platter. Top with onion slices.

- Pour Balsamic Basil Vinaigrette over salad, and let stand at room temperature 20 minutes.

- Garnish, if desired.

Balsamic Basil Vinaigrette

3 tablespoons balsamic vinegar

1 teaspoon chopped garlic

Salt

Pepper

¼ cup olive oil

⅓ cup chopped fresh basil

- Process first 4 ingredients in a blender until smooth.

- With machine running, add oil in a slow steady stream. Process until smooth. Stir in basil.

Serves 8.

Blue Cheese Dressing for Fresh Tomatoes

½ cup vegetable oil
¼ cup vinegar
1 garlic clove, crushed
4 ounces blue cheese
Fresh tomatoes, sliced

- Place oil in a small mixing bowl; add vinegar, 1 drop at a time, beating at medium speed with an electric mixer. Beat until thick and creamy.

- Stir in garlic and cheese. Pour dressing over tomato slices.

Serves 4.
Never refrigerate fresh tomatoes.

Cherry Tomatoes for a Tailgate

¼ cup minced fresh parsley

¼ cup vegetable oil

3 tablespoons vinegar

½ teaspoon dried basil

½ teaspoon dried oregano

½ teaspoon salt

½ teaspoon sugar

1 pint cherry tomatoes, halved

Lettuce leaves

Garlic clove, minced (optional)

Onion rings (optional)

Celery ribs (optional)

Sliced mushrooms (optional)

Beau Monde seasoning (optional)

• Combine first 7 ingredients in a bowl; stir in cherry tomatoes. Cover and chill, stirring occasionally, at least 3 hours.

• Serve on lettuce-lined plates.

• Top with garlic and next 4 ingredients, if desired.

Serves 6.

Balsamic Beet Salad

4 tablespoons balsamic
vinegar

1 garlic clove, minced

1 teaspoon Dijon mustard

1 tablespoon olive oil

4 large cooked beets,
peeled and coarsely
shredded

½ cup thinly sliced green
onions

Salt

Freshly ground pepper

• Whisk together first 4 ingredients in a bowl;
add beets and green onions, tossing well.

• Season with salt and pepper. Serve at room
temperature.

Serves 4.

Black-eyed Pea Salad

¼ cup balsamic vinegar

¼ cup corn oil

¼ cup sugar

2 (16-ounce) cans black-
eyed peas, rinsed and
drained

½ red bell pepper, chopped

½ green bell pepper,
chopped

½ yellow bell pepper,
chopped

1 bunch green onions,
chopped

• Combine first 3 ingredients in a small bowl,
whisking until sugar dissolves.

• Combine peas and next 4 ingredients in a large
bowl; add dressing, tossing to coat.

Serves 8.

This salad will keep in the refrigerator up to 2
weeks. For a low-fat version, omit balsamic
vinegar, corn oil, and sugar, and use 1
tablespoon olive oil, juice of 1 lemon, ½ cup
salsa, and ½ teaspoon ground cumin instead.
You can also substitute 1 (16-ounce) can black
beans, rinsed and drained, and 1 (16-ounce)
can white shoepeg corn, rinsed and drained, for
black-eyed peas, if desired.

Fresh Corn Salad

6 ears of white corn

1 green bell pepper, chopped

1 red bell pepper, chopped

2 zucchini, chopped

1 onion, chopped

1 bunch green onions, chopped

¼ cup chopped fresh parsley

1 garlic clove, chopped

¼ teaspoon salt

2 teaspoons sugar

⅛ teaspoon pepper

1 teaspoon ground cumin

2 teaspoons Dijon mustard

½ teaspoon hot sauce

⅔ cup vegetable oil

⅓ cup white vinegar

• Boil corn in water to cover in a large Dutch oven 10 minutes or until done. Drain and let cool. Cut corn from cob.

• Combine corn kernels, bell peppers, and next 4 ingredients in a large bowl.

• Combine garlic and next 8 ingredients in a separate bowl, whisking until blended; add to vegetable mixture, tossing well. Chill several hours.

Serves 6.

Wild Rice Salad ᴛʀʸ

(10 ounces wild and brown
    rice mix

2 quarts water

½ teaspoon salt

(⅓ cup red wine vinegar

) ¼ cup olive oil

3 scallions, chopped

½ cup slivered almonds,
    toasted

1 orange

1 cup seedless red grapes,
    halved

1 teaspoon salt

1 teaspoon pepper

• Bring first 3 ingredients to a boil in a saucepan. Cover, reduce heat, and simmer 25 minutes or until rice is al dente. Drain and transfer to a large bowl.

• Add vinegar and next 3 ingredients. Zest the orange, and add to rice mixture.

• Peel orange, and cut pulp into small pieces; stir pulp into salad. Add grapes, salt, and pepper, mixing thoroughly using your hands.

• Let stand at room temperature 30 minutes.

Serves 8.

Ten ounces brown rice can also be used in this recipe.

Spinach Salad Dressing

½ cup olive oil
¼ cup tarragon vinegar
1 (6-inch) strip anchovy paste
1 garlic clove, minced
Dry mustard, 1 pinch
¼ teaspoon paprika
¾ teaspoon salt
¼ teaspoon pepper
Dried oregano, 1 pinch
Dried thyme, 1 pinch

• Combine all ingredients in a jar; cover tightly and shake vigorously.

Tempting Tortellini Salad

2 ounces fresh pea pods, sliced diagonally into 1¼-inch pieces

1 (7-ounce) package refrigerated cheese-filled tortellini, cooked and chilled

½ cup freshly grated Asiago cheese

1 large tomato, chopped

Salt

Freshly ground pepper

Mustard-Basil Vinaigrette

- Plunge pea pods into boiling water to cover; drain. Rinse with cold water; drain again.

- Combine blanched pea pods, chilled tortellini, and next 4 ingredients in a large bowl.

- Add Mustard-Basil Vinaigrette, tossing to coat. Cover and let stand at room temperature at least 30 minutes.

- Serve at room temperature.

Mustard-Basil Vinaigrette

½ cup olive oil

3 tablespoons white wine vinegar

2½ tablespoons Dijon mustard

3 tablespoons minced fresh basil or dill

2 tablespoons minced shallots or green onions

1 garlic clove, minced

½ teaspoon sugar

- Whisk together all ingredients in a small bowl.

Serves 6 to 8.

Citrus Salad with Herbs

1 orange
1 grapefruit
1 lemon (optional)
½ purple onion, sliced
Olive oil
Chopped fresh mint
Chopped fresh basil
Salt
Pepper

• Peel citrus fruit, and cut into ¼-inch-thick slices.

• Layer fruit and onion on a serving plate. Drizzle with oil, and sprinkle with mint and next 3 ingredients.

• Serve at room temperature.

Serves 2.

Orange and Grapefruit Salad

2 oranges
1 grapefruit
3 tablespoons lemon juice
2 envelopes unflavored
    gelatin
½ cup cold water
¾ cup boiling water
¾ cup sugar
Lettuce leaves
Mayonnaise
Shredded cucumber for
    garnish

• Section oranges and grapefruit into a bowl, squeezing juice from rinds; stir in lemon juice.

• Sprinkle gelatin over ½ cup cold water; stir to dissolve.

• Combine gelatin mixture, ¾ cup boiling water, and sugar, stirring until sugar dissolves. Chill until mixture begins to set.

• Stir in orange mixture, and pour into a mold or individual molds coated with vegetable cooking spray. Chill until set.

• Unmold onto a lettuce-lined serving plate. Top with mayonnaise and shredded cucumber.

Serves 8.

Greens and Grapefruit Salad ~Try~

8 cups mixed salad greens, torn

2 heads radicchio, leaves separated

2 heads Belgian endive, leaves separated

1 medium-size purple onion, thinly sliced

2 tablespoons chopped fresh basil

2 pink grapefruit, sectioned

Dijon Vinaigrette

¼ cup pine nuts, toasted

- Combine first 6 ingredients in a large bowl; drizzle with ¾ cup Dijon Vinaigrette.

- Sprinkle with pine nuts, and serve with remaining vinaigrette.

Dijon Vinaigrette – *Blender*

½ cup red wine vinegar

¼ cup Dijon mustard

2 tablespoons lime juice

¼ teaspoon salt

¼ teaspoon freshly ground pepper

2 tablespoons sugar (optional)

¾ cup olive oil

- Process first 5 ingredients in a blender; add sugar, if desired, and process until smooth, stopping once to scrape down sides.

- With machine running, add oil in a slow steady stream. Process until well blended

Serves 10.

Fresh basil is a must.

A lot may happen under dinner tables. Lovers hold hands, children sneak food they dislike to the dog, siblings squabble and babies learn to crawl.

Pear-Walnut Salad ~~Try~~

Mixed salad greens, torn

6 red pears, sliced into wedges

2 ounces walnut pieces

4 ounces Gorgonzola cheese, crumbled *or blue cheese*

¼ teaspoon salt

1 tablespoon Dijon mustard

2 tablespoons balsamic vinegar

½ cup olive oil

Freshly ground pepper

Dressing

- Place mixed greens on individual salad plates; arrange pear wedges on top of greens. Sprinkle with walnuts and cheese.

- Whisk together salt, mustard, and vinegar. Add oil, 1 drop at a time, whisking constantly.

- Drizzle vinaigrette over each salad.

Serves 6.

Roquefort Waldorf Salad

½ cup Dijon mustard

1 cup Champagne vinegar

4 tablespoons minced shallots

1½ teaspoons sea salt

¾ teaspoon ground white pepper

3 cups olive oil

1½ cups arugula

¾ cup Bibb lettuce

4 Granny Smith apples, chopped

1 cup walnuts, chopped

1 celery stalk, minced

½ cup mayonnaise (optional)

½ bunch fresh parsley, minced

⅓ cup Roquefort cheese, crumbled

- Whisk together first 5 ingredients in a large bowl; add oil, 1 drop at a time, whisking until emulsified. Let this vinaigrette stand at room temperature.

- Combine arugula and lettuce; drizzle lightly with half of vinaigrette, reserving remaining vinaigrette.

- Toss to coat, and arrange on individual salad plates.

- Combine apple, walnuts, and celery; drizzle with vinaigrette, reserving remaining vinaigrette for another use. Toss to coat.

- Place evenly in center of greens.

- Top each with a dollop of mayonnaise, and sprinkle with parsley and cheese.

Serves 4.

Store vinaigrette in the refrigerator; bring to room temperature before serving.

Spinach-Strawberry Salad ✓ my recipe

½ cup sugar

1 tablespoon poppy seeds

2 tablespoons sesame seeds

1½ teaspoons minced onion

¼ teaspoon paprika

¼ cup cider vinegar

¼ cup wine vinegar

½ cup vegetable oil

¾ cup almonds, slivered
  and toasted

1 pound fresh spinach, torn

1 pint fresh strawberries,
  sliced

• Whisk together first 8 ingredients in a bowl.

• Combine almonds, spinach, and strawberries in
  a serving bowl; pour dressing over salad, tossing
  lightly.

• Serve immediately.

Serves 8.

Award-Winning Salad Dressing

2 tablespoons pure maple syrup
2 tablespoons cider vinegar
2 tablespoons balsamic vinegar
2 tablespoons soy sauce
2 garlic cloves, minced
1 large shallot, minced
1 teaspoon Dijon mustard
½ cup canola oil
½ cup olive oil

• *Combine first 7 ingredients in a bowl; add oils in
  a slow steady stream, whisking constantly.*
• *Chill in covered jar for up to 1 week.*
• *Let stand at room temperature 30 minutes before
  serving. Stir well.*

Salad Verte Aux Fruit

2 large avocados, peeled and cubed

Lemon juice

½ teaspoon dry mustard

1 teaspoon water

¼ cup white wine vinegar

2 teaspoons grated orange rind

½ cup fresh orange juice

¼ teaspoon lemon juice

¼ cup sugar

½ teaspoon salt

1 cup vegetable oil

¼ cup heavy cream (optional)

1 head romaine lettuce, torn

1 head iceberg lettuce, torn

1 cup orange sections

1 cup grapefruit sections

½ cup diced apple

2 green onions, chopped

- Sprinkle avocado with lemon juice.

- Stir together dry mustard and 1 teaspoon water.

- Whisk together dry mustard mixture, vinegar, and next 6 ingredients in a large serving bowl. Add cream, if desired, whisking well.

- Add lettuces to vinaigrette mixture; center avocado, orange, and next 3 ingredients over lettuces.

- Toss just before serving.

Serves 8.

Mandarin Orange Salad

¼ cup slivered almonds

1 tablespoon plus 1 teaspoon sugar

½ head Bibb lettuce, torn

½ head romaine lettuce, torn

1 cup chopped celery

3 green onions, thinly sliced

Orange Salad Vinaigrette

1 (11-ounce) can mandarin oranges, drained

• Cook almonds and sugar in a skillet over low heat, stirring constantly, until sugar is melted and almonds are coated. Remove to wax paper, and let cool; break apart.

• Combine Bibb lettuce and next 3 ingredients in a heavy-duty zip-top plastic bag; seal and chill.

• Pour Orange Salad Vinaigrette into plastic bag 5 minutes before serving; add oranges. Seal and shake to coat. Add sugared almonds; seal and shake well.

Orange Salad Vinaigrette

¼ cup vegetable oil

2 tablespoons white vinegar

2 tablespoons sugar

1 tablespoon chopped fresh parsley

½ teaspoon salt

Pepper

Dash of hot sauce

• Combine all ingredients in a jar; cover tightly, and shake vigorously. Chill at least 1 hour.

Serves 4.

Be honest about it.

Okay, you've enjoyed this cookbook so far, but now it's time to "'fess up." A simple show of hands will do. How many of you actually drank out of the milk carton? Or the orange juice container? How many of you ate peanut butter out of the jar? Or licked the centers out of the Oreos? Or ate peanut butter plain? Or stuck your actual finger in the mayonnaise jar? Or ate a spoonful of chocolate fudge ripple ice cream out of the carton, then put it back? Just thought we'd check.

Holiday Cranberry Salad

1 package unflavored
    gelatin
⅓ cup cold water
1 can whole-berry cranberry
    sauce
½ to ¾ cup sugar
1 (3-ounce) package cherry
    gelatin
1 cup hot water
1 cup ginger ale
1 cup crushed pineapple,
    well drained
¾ cup chopped pecans
1 cup finely diced celery

- Combine unflavored gelatin and ⅓ cup cold water in a bowl, stirring to dissolve; add cranberry sauce and sugar, stirring well.

- Combine cherry gelatin and 1 cup hot water in a separate bowl, stirring well to dissolve; stir in unflavored gelatin mixture and ginger ale. Chill until partially set.

- Stir in pineapple, pecans, and celery. Chill until firm.

Serves 12.

Scrumptious New Year's Day Salad

8 cups mixed salad greens,
    torn
2 red apples, chopped
1 cup diagonally sliced
    celery
¾ cup raisins
½ cup sugar
½ cup vinegar
1 cup vegetable oil
2 tablespoons
    Worcestershire sauce
1 medium onion, grated
⅓ cup ketchup
¾ cup toasted pecans,
    chopped
½ cup blue cheese, crumbled

- Combine first 4 ingredients in a large serving bowl.

- Combine sugar and next 5 ingredients in a jar; cover tightly, and shake vigorously.

- Pour dressing over apple mixture; add nuts and cheese, tossing to coat.

Serves 8.

Horseradish Aspic

1 (3-ounce) package lemon
gelatin
1 cup boiling water
¼ teaspoon salt
1 bottle prepared
horseradish
1 cup sour cream
Lettuce leaves
Garnishes: fresh chives,
fresh parsley sprigs, or
pimiento slices

- Sprinkle gelatin over 1 cup boiling water; stir to dissolve. Stir in salt. Add horseradish and sour cream, stirring until smooth.

- Pour into a mold, and chill.

- Serve on a lettuce-lined plate, and garnish, if desired.

Serves 4 to 6.

Creamy Tomato Aspic Ring

2 tablespoons unflavored
gelatin
½ cup cold water
2 (8-ounce) cans tomato
sauce
2 tablespoons lemon juice
1 cup sour cream
½ cup white wine
½ teaspoon salt
1 tablespoon instant minced
onion
3 tablespoons cold water
2 tablespoons minced fresh
parsley
1 cup thinly sliced celery
Potato or macaroni salad
Garnishes: pimiento-stuffed
olive, watercress

- Sprinkle gelatin over ½ cup cold water.

- Bring tomato sauce to a boil in a saucepan; add gelatin mixture, stirring well. Stir in lemon juice and next 3 ingredients. Chill until slightly thickened.

- Combine onion and 3 tablespoons cold water. Let stand until water is absorbed.

- Fold onion, parsley, and celery into gelatin mixture.

- Spoon into a 5-cup ring mold. Chill until set.

- Invert onto a serving plate, and fill center with potato or macaroni salad. Garnish, if desired.

Serves 6.

Layered Potato Salad

8 medium potatoes

1½ cups mayonnaise

1 cup sour cream

1½ teaspoons prepared horseradish

1 teaspoon celery seed

½ teaspoon salt

1 medium Vidalia or other sweet onion, minced

1 cup minced fresh parsley

Salt

- Boil potatoes in water to cover in a large Dutch oven 20 minutes or until done. Drain and let cool. Peel and cut into ⅛-inch slices.

- Combine mayonnaise and next 4 ingredients in a small bowl.

- Combine onion and parsley in a separate bowl.

- Place a layer of potato slices in the bottom of a large serving bowl; season lightly with salt. Cover with a layer of mayonnaise mixture. Sprinkle with a layer of onion mixture.

- Repeat layers using remaining ingredients, ending with onion mixture. Do not stir. Cover and chill 8 hours.

Serves 8.

You can substitute chopped fresh cilantro for chopped fresh parsley, if desired.

Blue Cheese Potato Salad

8 large potatoes, boiled, peeled, and cubed

½ cup diced celery

½ cup water chestnuts, drained and chopped

½ cup chopped scallions

2 tablespoons chopped fresh parsley

2½ teaspoons salt

¼ teaspoon pepper

½ teaspoon celery seed

2 cups sour cream

4 ounces blue cheese, crumbled

¼ cup white wine vinegar

Salt

Pepper

• Combine first 8 ingredients in a large bowl.

• Combine sour cream, cheese, and vinegar; pour over potato mixture, tossing lightly. Season with salt and pepper. Chill overnight.

Serves 8 to 12.

You can substitute toasted slivered almonds for water chestnuts, if desired.

Bride's Chicken Salad

2 pounds skinned and boned chicken breasts, cooked and chopped

4 celery stalks, sliced and halved

6 hard-cooked eggs, chopped

1 cup salad dressing

1 cup India relish, drained

1 cup Durkee sauce

½ cup toasted almonds

½ cup green grapes, halved

Lemon juice

• Combine all ingredients in a large bowl. Chill.

Serves 12.

This salad is best if prepared a day ahead.

Chicken-Chutney Salad ⟨ᵐ⟩

2 cups diced cooked chicken

1 (13½-ounce) can pineapple tidbits, drained

1 cup diced celery

½ cup sliced green onions

⅔ cup mayonnaise

2 tablespoons Major Grey's chutney

Grated rind of 1 lime

2 tablespoons fresh lime juice

½ teaspoon curry powder

½ teaspoon sea salt

Lemon pepper

Lettuce leaves

¼ cup almonds, slivered

• Combine first 4 ingredients in a large bowl.

• Combine mayonnaise and next 5 ingredients; stir into chicken mixture. Stir in lemon pepper to taste. Chill.

• Serve on lettuce-lined plates, and sprinkle with almonds or pass them separately.

Serves 4.

This delicious, pretty recipe can be prepared ahead of time. You can also double or triple it. You can substitute "Nellie and Joe's" Key lime juice for fresh and also use reduced-fat mayonnaise for half of mayonnaise, if desired.

Curried Tuna Salad

1 tablespoon curry powder

½ cup mayonnaise

2 (6½-ounce) cans white albacore tuna, drained

1 tablespoon chopped scallions

1 tablespoon chopped fresh parsley

1 celery stalk, minced

2 to 2½ tablespoons mango chutney

2 to 2½ tablespoons raisins

Salt

Pepper

• Combine curry powder and mayonnaise in a large bowl; add tuna and remaining ingredients, tossing to coat. Chill.

Serves 4.

You may increase the amount of chutney, if desired, and you might have to dice some of the larger chutney chunks. You also may substitute fat-free mayonnaise for regular, if desired.

Make 2-3 hrs. ahead

Chicken, Spinach, and Pasta Salad *Try -*

2 tablespoons sesame seeds

½ cup olive oil, <u>divided</u>

6 ounces uncooked tri-
colored rotini, cooked

⅓ cup soy sauce

⅓ cup white wine vinegar

2 tablespoons sugar

4 skinned and boned
chicken breast halves,
cooked and chopped

⅓ cup chopped fresh
parsley

½ cup sliced green onions

1 (14-ounce) can artichoke
hearts (optional)

Freshly ground pepper

1 (10-ounce) package fresh
spinach

Garnish: cherry tomatoes.

• Cook sesame seeds in ¼ cup hot oil in a skillet
over low heat, stirring constantly, until golden.

• Place hot cooked pasta in a large bowl.

• Combine sesame seeds, remaining ¼ cup oil,
soy sauce, vinegar, and sugar; pour over pasta.
Add chicken, parsley, green onions, and, if
desired, artichokes, tossing well. Season with
pepper. <u>Let stand at room temperature several
hours.</u>

• Add spinach just before serving, tossing well.
Garnish, if desired.

Serves 6.

Shrimp-Tarragon Salad *Try*

3 pounds unpeeled,
medium-size fresh
shrimp

½ cup sour cream

½ cup mayonnaise

1 tablespoon dried crushed
tarragon

Salt

Freshly ground pepper

2 celery stalks, finely diced

• Boil shrimp in water to cover 3 to 5 minutes or
just until pink. Drain. Peel and, if desired,
devein.

• Whisk together sour cream and mayonnaise in a
bowl. Add shrimp, tarragon, and next 3
ingredients, tossing well. Cover and chill at least
4 hours. Season with salt and pepper before
serving.

Serves 8 to 10.

Oriental Chicken Salad

1 medium cabbage, finely chopped

4 green onions, chopped

4 cups diced cooked chicken

1 cup vegetable oil

4 tablespoons sugar

6 tablespoons rice vinegar

2 teaspoons salt

1 teaspoon pepper

2 packages chicken-flavored ramen noodles, uncooked

4 tablespoons toasted sesame seeds

4 tablespoons toasted almond slivers

• Combine first 3 ingredients in a bowl; chill overnight.

• Combine oil, next 4 ingredients, and seasoning packets from ramen noodles, stirring well; add to cabbage mixture.

• Crush ramen noodles, and sprinkle over top of salad, tossing well. Top with sesame seeds and almonds before serving.

Serves 8.

You may omit chicken, and serve as a side salad, if desired.

BACK TO THE TABLE
Pasta, Eggs & Cheese

Nancy Pruden

Brave noodle world

When we were growing up, pasta meant spaghetti. Some of us knew about ravioli and Spaghettios and lasagna or that staple macaroni and cheese, but pasta was never much of anything special beyond cheese grits or Stove Top stuffing.

Then along about the 1970's somebody out in California proclaimed that pasta was "in," and before you could say "rigatoni" we were eating the stuff like mad.

Not that we gave up on shrimp and grits or anything, but almost overnight, pasta became THE go-with dish in all the restaurants, even those without names like Luigi's or Mario's or Mama Angelina's. Even at the family table, pasta has jumped out front as a mainstream entrée.

Our pasta vocabulary has grown from "spaghetti with meat sauce" to such tongue twisters as tagliarini, tortelloni, cappelletti in brodo, fusilli in insalata, mezzalune con melanzane, pappardelle, tagliatelle alle zucchine, fettuccine agli scampi, penne con carote, fedelini, farfalle alle noci and gemelli al quatro formaggi.

Mind you, this is good stuff, even if it is hard for someone who grew up in the rural South to pronounce. They're even serving pasta in middle school. So don't be surprised when one of your kids asks, "Hey mom, when are we gonna have some of that fedelini al fagioli like they serve at the food court?"

The good news is that most anything goes well with, beside, or on top of pasta. Tomatoes, clams, shrimp, mushrooms, cheeses, olive oil, beans, butter, eggs and bacon, chicken livers, even broccoli. Pasta hasn't made its way to pork chops or country ham yet, but stick around.

Without a doubt, pasta, as a food group, is perhaps the most versatile dish around. Even plain — with butter or olive oil with a hint of garlic — pasta promises a delectable and filling treat. Now, it's unlikely anybody's going to order "a cheeseburger with a side of rigatoni," but pasta has earned a well-deserved reputation as a major league player on our tables.

So even if you're not Italian, you're in for a real treat, and perhaps a new adventure, in the pages to come.

Prego, a tavola!

Eggs-ceptional Over Artichokes

4 egg yolks

1½ tablespoons cold water

1 cup butter, melted

2 tablespoons lemon juice

2 to 3 dashes hot sauce

½ teaspoon sweet red
   pepper flakes

½ teaspoon salt

⅛ teaspoon ground black
   pepper

8 artichoke bottoms

8 poached eggs

24 bacon slices, cooked and
   sprinkled with pepper

- Whisk together yolks and 1½ tablespoons cold water in the top of a double boiler; bring water to a boil. Reduce heat to low; cook, whisking constantly, until yolks thicken and pull away from the bottom of the pan.

- Gradually whisk in butter; whisk in lemon juice and next 4 ingredients.

- Top each artichoke bottom with a poached egg; top with sauce.

- Serve with bacon.

Serves 8.

Company Breakfast Casserole   *Easy Try*

4 cups (1 pound) shredded
   Monterey Jack cheese

1 tablespoon all-purpose
   flour

2 cups (8 ounces) shredded
   sharp Cheddar cheese

1 pound bacon, cooked and
   crumbled

12 large eggs

1 cup milk

- Toss together Monterey Jack cheese and flour; place in the bottom of a greased 13- x 9-inch baking dish. Top with Cheddar cheese. Sprinkle with bacon.

- Whisk together eggs and milk; pour over bacon. Cover and chill 8 hours or overnight.

- Let stand at room temperature 30 minutes before baking.

- Bake at 325° for 40 to 45 minutes or until a knife inserted in center comes out clean.

- Let stand at room temperature 5 minutes before serving.

Serves 12 to 16.

Breakfast for a King or Queen

3 tablespoons butter

¼ cup chopped green onions

1 dozen large eggs, lightly beaten

1 (4-ounce) can sliced mushrooms, drained

¼ teaspoon salt

⅛ teaspoon pepper

Cheddar Cheese Sauce

1 pound bacon, cooked and crumbled

- Melt butter in a saucepan over medium heat; add green onions, and sauté until tender. Add eggs, and cook until softly scrambled (do not overcook).

- Add mushrooms, salt, and pepper. Fold in Cheddar Cheese Sauce and bacon.

- Spoon mixture into a lightly greased 13- x 9-inch baking dish. Cover and chill.

- Bake at 350° for 30 minutes.

Serves 8.

Cheddar Cheese Sauce

2 tablespoons butter

2½ tablespoons all-purpose flour

2 cups milk

1 cup (4 ounces) shredded sharp Cheddar cheese

¼ teaspoon salt

⅛ teaspoon pepper

- Melt butter in a saucepan over medium heat; add flour, stirring until smooth. Allow to bubble 1 to 2 minutes.

- Stir in milk; cook, stirring constantly, until thickened. Add cheese, salt, and pepper, stirring until cheese is melted.

This dish can be prepared up to 2 days ahead.

If you shake an egg and you hear it rattle, you can be sure it's stale. A really fresh egg will sink and a stale one will float.

Blue Cheese and Egg Bake

6 tablespoons butter

6 tablespoons all-purpose flour

1 teaspoon salt

3 cups milk

2 ounces blue cheese, crumbled

½ cup chopped celery

¼ cup chopped pimiento

Salt

Pepper

12 hard-cooked eggs, quartered lengthwise

⅓ cup finely crushed saltine crackers

1 tablespoon butter or margarine, melted

- Preheat oven to 325°.

- Melt 6 tablespoons butter in a saucepan over low heat; stir in flour and salt. Add milk, and cook, stirring often, until mixture is bubbly and thickened. Stir in blue cheese, celery, and pimiento; season with salt and pepper.

- Place eggs in an 11- x 7-inch baking dish. Top with cream sauce.

- Combine cracker crumbs and 1 tablespoon melted butter; sprinkle around edges of casserole.

- Bake at 325° for 45 minutes or until bubbly and lightly browned.

Serves 8.

Crabmeat-Sherry Quiche

1 tablespoon butter

2 tablespoons minced green onions

4 large eggs

2 cups heavy whipping cream

¾ teaspoon salt

2 (6-ounce) packages frozen crabmeat, thawed and drained

1 cup (4 ounces) shredded Swiss cheese

2 tablespoons sherry

⅛ teaspoon ground red pepper (optional)

1 unbaked 9-inch deep-dish pastry shell

Garnish: tomato rose

- Preheat oven to 425°.

- Melt butter in a skillet; add green onions, and sauté until tender.

- Whisk together eggs, whipping cream, and salt in a large bowl. Stir in green onions, crabmeat, cheese, sherry, and, if desired, red pepper.

- Pour mixture into deep-dish pastry shell.

- Bake at 425° for 15 minutes.

- Reduce oven temperature to 325°, and bake 35 to 40 minutes.

- Garnish, if desired.

Serves 6.

Eight ounces fresh crabmeat may be substituted for frozen, if desired.

Wonderful Cheese Soufflé

8 French or egg bread slices, with crusts removed

4 tablespoons unsalted butter (mixed with 1 teaspoon prepared mustard, if desired)

4 cups (1 pound) shredded sharp Cheddar cheese

6 large eggs

2¾ cups milk

- Cut bread slices into triangles, and butter both sides.

- Layer half each of bread and cheese in a 9-inch soufflé dish. Repeat layers once.

- Whisk together eggs and milk; pour over cheese. Cover and chill 6 hours or overnight.

- Let stand at room temperature 1 hour before baking.

- Bake at 350° for 1 hour.

- Serve immediately.

Serves 6.

Company Gruyère Cheese Soufflé

4 tablespoons butter or
margarine, melted

½ teaspoon mustard

Ground red pepper

1 garlic clove, minced

¾ teaspoon dried tarragon

6 white bread slices, with
crusts removed

2 cups (8 ounces) shredded
Gruyère cheese

1 chicken bouillon cube

½ cup water

3 large eggs

1 cup dry white wine

- Preheat oven to 425°.

- Combine first 5 ingredients; spread mixture
evenly on bread slices.

- Place bread in a lightly greased 13- x 9-inch
baking dish. Top with cheese.

- Combine bouillon cube and ½ cup water,
stirring until dissolved.

- Whisk together bouillon mixture, eggs, and
wine; pour over cheese. Cover and chill
overnight.

- Bake at 350° for 45 minutes or until done.

- Serve immediately.

Serves 6.

Family Fun Fondue

6 cups (1½ pounds)
shredded sharp Cheddar
or Swiss cheese

3 tablespoons all-purpose
flour

2 teaspoons dry mustard

1 pint half-and-half

1 tablespoon
Worcestershire sauce

1 garlic clove, minced

Salt

Dippers: French bread
cubes, pear slices, apple
slices, broccoli flowerets,
cubed turkey

- Combine first 3 ingredients in a large saucepan;
add half-and-half, and cook over medium heat,
stirring constantly, until cheese is melted. Add
Worcestershire sauce, garlic, and salt, stirring
until smooth.

- Transfer mixture to a fondue pot, and serve
with desired dippers.

Serves 6.

This is a well-balanced, fun-filled meal for
families.

Cheese and Vegetable Strata

½ cup sliced mushrooms

¼ cup sherry

4 cups day-old white or French bread cubes

2 cups (8 ounces) shredded Cheddar cheese

10 large eggs, lightly beaten

1 quart milk

1 teaspoon dry mustard

¼ teaspoon onion powder

Freshly ground pepper

1 teaspoon salt (optional)

8 to 10 bacon slices, cooked and crumbled

½ cup tomatoes, peeled and chopped

• Sauté mushrooms in sherry in a saucepan until tender; drain.

• Arrange bread cubes in a buttered 13- x 9-inch baking dish, and sprinkle with cheese.

• Combine eggs, next 4 ingredients, and, if desired, salt; pour over cheese. Sprinkle mixture with bacon, mushrooms, and tomato. Sprinkle with additional pepper.

• Cover and chill up to 24 hours.

• Bake at 325° for 1 hour or until set. Cover loosely with aluminum foil to prevent overbrowning, if necessary.

Serves 10.

Baked Grits with Caviar

2 cups uncooked quick-cooking grits

1 cup milk

4 large eggs, lightly beaten

1 (3-ounce) package cream cheese

6 tablespoons butter

1 pound bacon, cooked and crumbled

1 cup sliced fresh mushrooms

1 (8-ounce) can sliced water chestnuts, drained

1 cup chopped pecans

3 (4-ounce) cans red caviar

• Preheat oven to 350°.

• Cook grits according to package directions in a saucepan; add milk and next 3 ingredients, stirring well. Add bacon and next 3 ingredients, stirring well.

• Spoon mixture into a lightly greased shallow 2-quart baking dish.

• Bake at 350° for 20 to 30 minutes.

• Spread caviar over top, and serve immediately.

Serves 12.

Gourmet Gruyère Grits

1 quart whole milk, no
substitutions

1½ sticks butter, divided

1 cup uncooked regular
grits

1 teaspoon salt

1½ teaspoons pepper

1 cup (4 ounces) shredded
Gruyère cheese

⅓ cup grated Parmesan
cheese

• Bring milk to a boil, stirring constantly, in a saucepan. Add 1 stick of butter; cook, stirring often,
until melted. Gradually add grits, stirring
constantly; cook over medium heat until
thickened.

• Remove from heat. Beat mixture with a
handheld mixer 5 minutes. Stir in salt and
pepper.

• Pour into a lightly greased 13- x 9-inch pan. Let
stand at room temperature until firm.

• Cut into squares, and layer in a separate lightly
greased 13- x 9-inch pan, overlapping domino
style.

• Melt remaining ½ stick of butter, and pour over
grits. Sprinkle evenly with cheeses.

• Bake at 350° for 30 minutes.

Serves 8.

Solving the grits mystery

*Folks who live up north do not understand grits.
In fact, they think grits is plural and that "grit" is
singular. They suffer under the delusion that in
order to taste good, grits have to have something
on them. Butter. Cheese. Red eye gravy. Sausage
gravy. Eggs. Shrimp. Truth is, grits are (is?) just
fine with plain old salt and pepper. And just
what are (is?) grits? Who cares.*

Red eye gravy

*Meat and potatoes. Bread and butter. Peanut
butter and jelly. Grits and (pause) red eye gravy.
How do you make it? Simple. Black coffee and the
juice from fried country ham. Tell this to your
friends from the North and watch 'em gag.*

Gougère with Mushrooms and Ham

4 tablespoons butter

2 medium onions, chopped

1 (8-ounce) package fresh mushrooms, sliced

1½ tablespoons all-purpose flour

1 tablespoon salt

1 teaspoon pepper

1 cup chicken broth

2 large tomatoes, peeled and quartered

6 ounces cooked ham, cut into thin strips

Pâte à choux

2 tablespoons shredded Cheddar cheese

2 tablespoons chopped fresh parsley

Pâte à choux

1 cup all-purpose flour

Salt

Pepper

1 cup water

½ cup butter, cut up

4 large eggs

½ cup diced Cheddar cheese

- Preheat oven to 400°.

- Melt butter in a large skillet; add onion, and sauté until tender. Add mushrooms, and cook 2 minutes. Stir in flour, salt, and pepper, and cook 2 minutes. Add chicken broth; reduce heat, and simmer, stirring constantly, 4 minutes. Remove from heat.

- Cut each tomato quarter into 4 strips; add tomato strips and ham to sauce, stirring well.

- Spoon Pâte à choux into a ring around the edge of a buttered 10-inch ovenproof skillet, leaving center open.

- Pour mushroom filling into center. Top evenly with Cheddar cheese.

- Bake at 400° for 40 minutes or until puffed and browned.

- Sprinkle with parsley, and cut into wedges.

- Sift together first 3 ingredients.

- Heat 1 cup water and butter in a large saucepan until butter melts. Bring to a boil; add flour mixture, and let boil 1 minute or until mixture forms a ball in the center of the pan.

- Remove from heat, and let cool 5 minutes.

- Add eggs, 1 at a time, beating with a wooden spoon after each addition.

- Stir in diced cheese.

Serves 6.

Six ounces cooked and crumbled bacon may be substituted for ham, if desired.

Orzo with Broccoli, Feta, and Olives

1½ cups uncooked orzo

1 pound broccoli, cut into flowerets

3 tablespoons pine nuts

¼ cup olive oil

½ teaspoon sweet red pepper flakes

¾ cup feta cheese

¾ cup kalamata olives, sliced

½ cup grated Parmesan cheese

¼ cup chopped fresh basil

Ground black pepper

• Cook orzo in boiling salted water to cover in a saucepan 8 minutes; add broccoli, and cook 2 minutes or until crisp-tender.

• Cook pine nuts in hot oil in a heavy skillet over medium heat 3 minutes. Add red pepper, and cook, stirring constantly, 30 seconds. Remove from heat.

• Drain orzo and broccoli, and transfer to a large bowl; add pine nut mixture, tossing to coat. Add feta and next 3 ingredients, tossing to coat.

• Season with black pepper.

Serves 6.

This orzo is great with grilled pork, chicken, or veal.

Angel Hair Pasta with Vegetables

1 pound fresh broccoli

6 tablespoons butter

11 ounces goat cheese, cubed

Freshly grated Parmesan cheese

1 quart heavy cream

¼ cup chopped fresh basil

Ground white pepper

Salt

1 pound uncooked angel hair pasta, cooked

12 cherry tomatoes, halved

• Arrange broccoli in a steamer basket over boiling water. Cover and steam 15 to 20 minutes or until crisp-tender.

• Melt butter in a skillet over medium heat; add goat cheese, and cook until melted. Add Parmesan cheese and heavy cream, and cook until reduced by half or until it has a light consistency. Add basil, and season with salt and pepper.

• Toss together broccoli, hot cooked pasta, and cherry tomato halves in a saucepan over high heat.

• Add cheese sauce; reduce heat, and cook until thoroughly heated.

Serves 4.

This pasta sauce is different from an Alfredo sauce. It has a light, mild goat cheese flavor.

Pasta with Fresh Tomatoes, Basil, and Cheese

3-4 7 tomatoes, cut into ½-inch cubes

½ c 1 cup chopped fresh basil

1 T 2 tablespoons chopped fresh parsley

1½ 3 garlic cloves, minced

¼ t. ¾ teaspoon dried crushed red pepper

½ lb. 1 pound reduced-fat mozzarella, cubed

⅙ c ⅓ cup vegetable oil

1 T 2 tablespoons olive oil

⅛ t ⅛ teaspoon salt (optional)

½ lb. 1 pound uncooked small pasta shells, cooked

2 tablespoons toasted pine nuts (optional)

- Combine first 8 ingredients, and, if desired, salt in a large bowl.

- Let stand at room temperature 1 hour.

- Add hot cooked pasta, tossing to coat. Sprinkle with pine nuts, if desired.

- Serve hot or cold.

Serves 6 to 8.

Gorgonzola Tortellini

1½ cups vermouth or dry white wine

2¼ cups heavy cream

Freshly ground pepper

Freshly grated nutmeg

1 pound sweet Gorgonzola cheese, crumbled

1½ tablespoons grated Parmesan cheese

1½ pounds uncooked fresh tortellini, cooked

- Boil vermouth in a small heavy saucepan until reduced by half. Add cream, and bring to a boil again. Reduce heat, and simmer.

- Season with pepper and nutmeg. Simmer 15 minutes or until reduced by one-third. Stir in half of cheeses.

- Combine hot cooked pasta and sauce in a large saucepan; cook over medium heat 7 minutes or until sauce thickens.

- Serve on individual plates, and top evenly with remaining half of cheeses.

Serves 6.

Pasta with Roasted Eggplant

3 large eggplants, cut into ½-inch-thick rounds

Salt

1 medium-size red onion, cut into ½-inch-thick rounds

¾ cup olive oil, divided

Freshly ground black pepper

1 cup chopped red onion

2 garlic cloves, minced

¼ cup lemon juice

¼ teaspoon dried sweet red pepper flakes

1½ pounds uncooked penne or other tubular pasta, cooked

3 large tomatoes, seeded and cut into ¼-inch-wide strips

½ cup plus 2 tablespoons toasted pine nuts

½ cup chopped fresh or 1 tablespoon dried oregano

½ cup chopped fresh basil

1½ cups freshly grated Romano cheese

- Arrange eggplant on a triple layer of paper towels on a baking sheet. Sprinkle both sides with salt. Cover with additional paper towels, and place cutting board over paper towels; weight with heavy objects. Let stand at room temperature 12 to 48 hours.

- Brush eggplant and onion rounds with ½ cup oil.

- Grill, covered with grill lid, over high heat (400° to 500°) 2½ minutes on each side.

- Transfer to a large pan; season with salt and black pepper. Let cool slightly.

- Cut grilled vegetables into ½-inch-wide strips.

- Combine vegetable strips, remaining ¼ cup oil, chopped red onion, and next 3 ingredients. Let stand at room temperature 1 hour.

- Add hot cooked pasta, tossing to coat. Stir in tomato and next 4 ingredients.

- Season with salt and black pepper.

Serves 12.

This recipe can be prepared ahead to the point of combining grilled vegetable strips with ¼ cup oil, chopped onion, and next 3 ingredients. Cover and chill overnight, if desired. Let stand at room temperature 2 hours, and proceed as directed.

> *That's something I've noticed about food: Whenever there's a crisis, if you can get people to eating, normally things get better.*
> —Madeleine L'Engle

Francisca Julian's Linguine and Pesto

2 cups loosely packed fresh
 basil

2 garlic cloves

½ teaspoon salt

3 ounces pine nuts

1 tablespoon freshly grated
 Romano cheese

1 tablespoon freshly grated
 Parmesan cheese

¾ cup olive oil

6 tablespoons unsalted
 butter

1¼ pounds uncooked
 linguine, cooked

- Process first 7 ingredients in a food processor until thick and pasty, stopping to scrape down sides.

- Toss together butter and hot cooked pasta. Add 6 tablespoons pesto sauce, tossing well. Reserve remaining pesto for another use.

Serves 6.

Pesto sauce may be frozen or kept in the refrigerator for weeks.

Pesto for Today

4 cups fresh spinach, with stems removed
1½ to 2 tablespoons low-sodium reduced-fat chicken broth
⅓ cup grated Parmesan cheese
2½ garlic cloves, minced
1 cup fresh basil
1 tablespoon olive oil
Pine nuts (optional)

- *Pulse spinach, a little at a time, in a food processor alternately with chicken broth until mixture is smooth.*
- *Add cheese and next 3 ingredients. Process until smooth.*
- *This keeps, covered, in the refrigerator up to 2 weeks. It also freezes well.*

Serves 6.

Double Fettuccine with Peas and Prosciutto

1 cup heavy cream

1 cup cooked peas

5 ounces prosciutto

1/2 cup grated Parmesan cheese

1/4 teaspoon salt

1/2 teaspoon pepper

6 ounces uncooked spinach fettuccine, cooked

6 ounces uncooked fettuccine, cooked

Grated Parmesan cheese

- Heat cream in a medium saucepan over medium heat (do not boil). Stir in peas and next 4 ingredients; cook, stirring occasionally, 5 minutes or until thoroughly heated.

- Place hot cooked pasta on a serving platter; top with sauce, tossing gently. Sprinkle with additional Parmesan cheese.

- Serve immediately.

Serves 4.

Pasta with Smoked Salmon Cream Sauce

1 tablespoon butter or olive oil

1 small red onion, thinly sliced

1/4 cup heavy cream

1/2 cup half-and-half

1/2 cup chicken or vegetable broth

1/4 teaspoon ground white pepper

4 ounces smoked salmon, thinly sliced strips

Dash of vermouth or dry white wine

1/4 cup green peas

2 tablespoons chopped fresh chives

Salt

Ground black pepper

1 pound uncooked pasta, cooked

Grated Parmesan cheese

- Melt butter in a skillet over medium heat; add onion, and sauté until tender. Stir in cream and next 3 ingredients; cook 10 minutes or until slightly reduced. Stir in salmon and next 3 ingredients.

- Season with salt and black pepper.

- Toss with hot cooked pasta, and sprinkle with Parmesan cheese.

Serves 8.

Pasta with Sun-Dried Tomatoes, Mushrooms, and Artichoke Hearts

¼ cup butter

1 (14½-ounce) can diced tomatoes, undrained

¾ cup half-and-half

½ cup vodka

¼ teaspoon dried crushed red pepper

Salt

Ground black pepper

6 ounces fresh shiitake mushrooms, stemmed and sliced

2 tablespoons olive oil

¾ cup sun-dried tomatoes in oil

1 (14-ounce) can artichoke heart quarters, drained

1 tablespoon chopped shallots

½ cup chopped fresh basil

1 pound uncooked penne

2 tablespoons chopped fresh basil

Freshly grated Parmesan cheese

- Melt butter in a large heavy skillet over medium-high heat; add diced tomatoes with their juices and next 3 ingredients. Reduce heat, and simmer 8 minutes or until thickened. Season with salt and black pepper.

- Sauté mushrooms in hot oil in a separate large heavy skillet 4 minutes. Add dried tomatoes, artichoke quarters, and shallots; cook, stirring constantly, 2 minutes. Add tomato mixture, and cook 5 minutes.

- Season with salt and black pepper. Stir in ½ cup basil.

- Cook pasta according to package directions in a Dutch oven; drain, reserving ½ cup cooking liquid.

- Return pasta to pot; add sauce and reserved ½ cup cooking liquid, tossing to coat.

- Transfer mixture to a serving bowl. Sprinkle with 2 tablespoons basil and Parmesan cheese.

Serves 4.

> *No one who cooks, cooks alone. A cook in the kitchen is surrounded by generations of cooks past, the advice and menus of cooks present, the wisdom of cookbook writers.*
>
> —*Laurie Colwin*

Low-fat Penne in Vodka Sauce

4 garlic cloves, minced

2 tablespoons olive oil

1½ pounds tomatoes, peeled, seeded, and chopped

1½ cups low-fat milk

¼ cup vodka

1 tablespoon cornstarch

Salt

Pepper

1 pound uncooked penne, cooked

Freshly grated Parmesan cheese (optional)

Chopped fresh basil or parsley (optional)

- Sauté garlic in hot oil in a large skillet until tender. Add tomato; reduce heat, and simmer 30 to 45 minutes.

- Reserve 3 tablespoons milk; add vodka and remaining milk to tomato mixture.

- Combine reserved 3 tablespoons milk and cornstarch in a small bowl, stirring until smooth; add to tomato mixture.

- Cook, stirring often, over medium heat until thickened. Season with salt and pepper.

- Spoon sauce over hot cooked pasta. Top with Parmesan cheese and basil or parsley, if desired.

Serves 8.

Tomato Vodka Shrimp and Pasta

1 tablespoon butter

1 (28-ounce) can Italian
plum tomatoes,
undrained

¼ cup chopped fresh or
2 teaspoons dried basil

½ cup vodka

6 tablespoons whipping
cream

Salt

Pepper

1 pound unpeeled medium-
size fresh shrimp, peeled
and deveined

1 pound uncooked penne,
cooked

Freshly grated Parmesan
cheese

Garnish: fresh basil sprigs

- Melt butter in a large heavy skillet over medium heat; add tomatoes, and bring to a boil, crushing tomatoes with the back of a spoon. Reduce heat, and add chopped basil, vodka, and cream. Simmer 15 minutes (do not boil).

- Season with salt and pepper. Add shrimp, and simmer, turning occasionally, 3 minutes or until shrimp turn pink.

- Add hot cooked pasta, and cook, stirring often, until thoroughly heated.

- Serve on individual plates.

- Top with Parmesan cheese, and garnish, if desired.

Serves 4.

Brie and Tomato Pasta — *could try Fontina or other soft cheese —*

4 tomatoes, cubed

1 cup olive oil

1 pound Brie, rind removed,
torn into pieces

Fresh basil leaves, torn into
pieces

½ teaspoon pepper

3 garlic cloves, chopped

Freshly grated Parmesan
cheese

2½ teaspoons salt

1½ pounds uncooked linguini

- Combine first 7 ingredients in a large bowl; stir in ½ teaspoon salt. Cover let stand at room temperature 2 hours.

- Cook pasta in water with 2 teaspoons salt; drain.

- Add hot cooked pasta to tomato mixture, stirring well.

- Serve at room temperature.

Serves 6.

Herbed Chicken Pasta

Try

1 teaspoon butter

2½ cups fresh sliced mushrooms

1½ cups chopped onion

1 garlic clove, minced

1 pound skinned and boned chicken breasts, cut into 1-inch cubes

½ teaspoon salt

2 teaspoons dried basil

1 teaspoon coarsely ground pepper

2 cups coarsely chopped tomato

8 ounces uncooked fettuccine, cooked

¼ cup freshly grated Parmesan cheese

- Melt butter in a large nonstick skillet over medium-high heat; add mushrooms, onion, and garlic, and sauté 2 minutes.

- Add chicken and next 3 ingredients, and sauté 5 minutes or until chicken is done. Add tomato, and sauté 2 minutes.

- Serve over hot cooked pasta. Sprinkle with cheese.

Serves 4.

Penne Pasta with Shrimp and Broccoli

Try

¼ cup olive oil

3 tablespoons butter

3 or 4 garlic cloves, minced

1 pound broccoli, cut into flowerets

1 pound medium-size fresh shrimp, peeled and deveined

Salt

Pepper

1 pound uncooked penne, cooked

Freshly grated Parmesan cheese

- Heat oil and butter in a large skillet until butter is melted; add garlic and broccoli, and sauté several minutes. Add shrimp, salt, and pepper, and sauté until shrimp turn pink and broccoli is tender.

- Combine shrimp mixture and hot cooked pasta in a large serving bowl, tossing well. Add Parmesan cheese, tossing well.

- Serve immediately with additional Parmesan cheese.

Serves 6.

Shrimp with Feta Cheese on Vermicelli

1 pound medium-size fresh
shrimp, peeled and
deveined

Dried crushed red pepper

¼ cup olive oil, divided

4 ounces feta cheese,
crumbled

½ teaspoon crushed garlic

1 (14½-ounce) can tomato
wedges, undrained

¼ cup dry white wine

¾ teaspoon dried basil

½ teaspoon dried oregano

¼ teaspoon salt

¼ teaspoon ground black
pepper

8 ounces uncooked
vermicelli, cooked

Garnish: fresh basil sprigs

- Preheat oven to 400°.

- Sauté shrimp and red pepper in 2 tablespoons
  hot oil in a skillet 1 to 2 minutes or until
  shrimp are slightly pink.

- Arrange mixture in a 10- x 6-inch baking dish,
  and sprinkle with feta.

- Sauté garlic in remaining 2 tablespoons hot oil
  in a skillet over low heat until tender. Stir in
  tomato wedges, and cook 1 minute. Stir in wine
  and next 4 ingredients; simmer uncovered for
  10 minutes.

- Spoon tomato mixture over shrimp mixture.

- Bake at 400° for 10 minutes.

- Serve over hot cooked pasta. Garnish, if desired.

Serves 4.

BACK TO THE TABLE

Poultry, Meat and Seafood

Elizabeth High

We've got to stop meating like this

No one knows for sure when homo sapiens began cooking meat. Maybe it was when our ancestors decided they couldn't stomach one more tuber. Or it could have been on the occasion of man's first backyard bar-b-que 50 million years ago when an errant sabre-tooth blundered into a campfire and became history's first rack of ribs.

We've come a long way. And over the millennia, man has managed to concoct myriad ways to prepare and adorn meat—cheese sauces, cream sauces, tomato sauces, gravies, marinades, breadings, garnishes, herbs, and of course bar-b-que of every description. We have managed to elevate the preparation of meat, fish and poultry to an art form. Volumes have been devoted to ways to enhance choice cuts of beef and pork and free-range chicken and fresh-caught mahi-mahi (in the south we know it as "dolphin," and while we're on the subject, just what is "orange roughy" anyway?).

We have poked and prodded and guessed and read the cookbooks. We have stuck in makeshift meat thermometers, slathered on cheese, stir-fried and sautéed and broiled and baked and poached and grilled and roasted and deep-fat fried and stewed and smoked our way into thousands of meat entrées. Each of us, on the average, can expect to devour over 54,000 helpings of something-with-meat-in-it over our lifetimes. And this doesn't count Big Macs eaten between meals as teenagers or Vienna (pronounced VI-enna) sausages consumed in duck blinds.

This being a short book and all, we can't promise the full gamut of unforgettable meat cookery in these pages. But there are plenty of mouth-watering recipes guaranteed to get your crowd back around the dinner table quicker than you can say "pot roast." So, if you like the sound of such meaty treasures as "curried shrimp over green rice," "herbed apricot pork tenderloin," "Reuben pie," "stayabed stew" and "cold steak parisienne," read on. You're in for a treat.

Capital City Chicken

4 (2½-pound) whole chickens, quartered

1 garlic head, pureed

¼ cup dried oregano

Coarse-grain sea salt

Freshly ground pepper

½ cup red wine vinegar

½ cup olive oil

1 cup pitted prunes

¾ cup pitted green olives

¼ cup capers, slightly drained

6 bay leaves

1 cup firmly packed brown sugar

1 cup white wine

¼ cup minced fresh parsley or cilantro

- Combine first 11 ingredients in a large bowl; cover and chill overnight.

- Remove chicken from marinade, reserving marinade.

- Arrange chicken in 1 or 2 large shallow baking pans; top evenly with marinade. Sprinkle with brown sugar; add wine.

- Bake at 350° for 50 minutes to 1 hour or until done, basting often with pan juices. Remove and discard bay leaves.

- Using a slotted spoon, transfer chicken, prunes, olives, and capers to a serving platter. Top with several spoonfuls of pan juices; sprinkle with parsley.

- Serve remaining pan juices on the side.

Serves 12.

Marinating the chicken overnight is essential for it to be moist. This dish can be stored in the refrigerator several days. The flavor improves with time. It also travels well and makes excellent picnic fare. The amount of garlic used may be tailored to the amount of chicken marinated. Herb vinegar may be substituted for red wine vinegar and cranberry juice for white wine. Chicken is done when thigh juices run yellow when pricked with a fork at their thickest portion. This recipe may also be served cold: Let cool to room temperature before transferring chicken, prunes, olives, and capers to a serving platter. If chicken has been covered and refrigerated, allow to return to room temperature before serving. Spoon reserved pan juices over chicken.

Chicken and Artichoke Casserole *in Cheese Sauce*

Try

2 (14-ounce) cans artichoke heart quarters, drained

½ cup butter

2 (8-ounce) packages or 1 pound fresh mushrooms, sliced

½ cup all-purpose flour

3 cups chicken stock

4 cups (16 ounces) shredded Cheddar cheese, divided

Salt

Pepper

4 to 5 cups chopped cooked chicken

½ to ¾ cup soft breadcrumbs from day-old French bread

- Preheat oven to 350°.

- Place artichokes in a lightly greased 13- x 9-inch baking dish.

- Melt butter in a saucepan; add mushrooms, and sauté until tender. Remove mushrooms with a slotted spoon, and sprinkle over artichoke.

- Add flour to saucepan; cook, whisking constantly, 3 minutes. Add chicken stock, and cook, stirring often, until thickened. Stir in 3 cups cheese, and season with salt and pepper.

- Top mushrooms and artichokes with chicken, and pour sauce over top. Sprinkle with breadcrumbs and remaining 1 cup cheese.

- Bake at 350° for 30 minutes or until lightly browned.

Serves 8.

Chicken Mahanani

Try

4 skinned and boned chicken breasts, flattened to 1-inch thickness

1 teaspoon salt

¼ teaspoon pepper

2 cups (8 ounces) shredded Cheddar cheese

1 (8-ounce) package cream cheese, softened

¼ cup corn oil

1 (10-ounce) jar Major Grey chutney

- Preheat oven to 350°.

- Season chicken with salt and pepper.

- Combine Cheddar and cream cheese; spoon cheese mixture evenly in the center of each chicken breast.

- Roll up, jellyroll fashion, tucking in ends; secure with wooden picks. Place in a baking pan, and brush all sides with oil.

- Bake at 350° for 40 minutes.

- Spoon chutney evenly over chicken, and bake 20 more minutes or until done.

Serves 4.

Chicken Gourmet

12 skinned and boned chicken breasts, flattened to ¼-inch thickness

12 thin prosciutto slices

¾ pound provolone cheese slices

36 asparagus spears

3 cups (12 ounces) Parmesan-Romano cheese mix

Olive oil

2 pounds fresh mushrooms, sliced

¾ cup dry Marsala

6 cups whipping cream

½ cup minced fresh parsley

Salt

Pepper

- Preheat oven to 350°.

- Place chicken breasts shiny side down; top breasts evenly with prosciutto and provolone cheese. Top each with 3 asparagus spears and 3 tablespoons Parmesan-Romano cheese mix.

- Roll up, jellyroll fashion, and secure with wooden picks.

- Brown rolls, seam side down, in hot oil in a skillet. Transfer to a baking sheet; pour oil over rolls.

- Bake at 350° for 15 minutes.

- Cook mushrooms and Marsala in skillet over high heat; tilt skillet, and ignite. Boil until reduced by half. Add cream and parsley to skillet, and season with salt and pepper.

- Remove wooden picks from chicken.

- Pour sauce over chicken, and serve immediately.

Serves 12.

Chicken in Sun-Dried Tomato Cream Sauce

1 tablespoon butter or
margarine

1 garlic clove, minced

1 cup chicken stock, divided

½ cup dry-packed sun-dried
tomatoes, cut into bite-
size pieces

1 cup heavy cream or half-
and-half

1 pound skinned and boned
chicken breasts

Salt

Freshly ground pepper

2 tablespoons vegetable oil

2 tablespoons chopped
fresh basil

8 ounces fettuccine, cooked

• Melt butter in a saucepan over low heat; add
garlic, and sauté 30 seconds. Add ¾ cup
chicken stock and tomatoes; bring to a boil.
Reduce heat, and simmer 10 minutes or until
tomatoes are tender.

• Add cream, and bring to a boil. Simmer over
medium heat until thickened.

• Season chicken with salt and pepper; sauté in
hot oil in a heavy skillet until done. Transfer to
a plate; cover and keep warm.

• Wipe skillet clean; add remaining ¼ cup stock,
and bring to boil. Boil until reduced by half.
Reduce heat; stir in tomato sauce and basil.

• Toss pasta with 3 to 4 tablespoons cream sauce.

• Cut each chicken breast into 2 or 3 diagonal
slices.

• Place pasta on serving plates; top evenly with
chicken and sauce.

Serves 4.

This dish, though delicious, is not suitable for
a formal dinner party because it requires
constant attention during preparation. It can't
be made ahead. It's a great recipe for a dinner
with friends who stand in the kitchen and
prepare a salad while the cook prepares the
chicken and sauce.

*Call it a clan, call it a
network, call it a tribe,
call it a family. Whatever
you call it, whoever you
are, you need one.*
—Jane Howard

Chicken Pie on a Diet

Fry

Easy

Can make ahead + freeze

6 skinned and boned
  chicken breasts

1 (10¾-ounce) can reduced-
  fat cream of celery soup,
  undiluted

1 cup skim milk

1 tablespoon vinegar

1 cup self-rising flour

1 stick light margarine,
  melted

Salt

Pepper

- Preheat oven to 375°.

- Boil chicken breasts in water to cover in a Dutch oven 1 hour or until done; drain, reserving 1 cup broth.

- Cube chicken, and place in a lightly greased 11- x 9-inch baking dish.

- Combine reserved 1 cup broth and soup; pour over chicken.

- Combine milk and vinegar; let stand at room temperature 5 minutes. Stir flour and butter into milk mixture; pour over chicken. Season with salt and pepper.

- Bake at 375° for 40 minutes.

- Let stand at room temperature 5 minutes before serving.

Serves 6.

This casserole can be prepared ahead to the point of seasoning with salt and pepper; do not bake. Freeze, if desired. If frozen, bake casserole 30 additional minutes. Two cups frozen mixed vegetables may be added to chicken cubes, if desired.

The most important ingredient in the family dinner is togetherness.

Chicken with Cashews and Snow Peas

1 skinned and boned chicken breast, cut into 1-inch cubes

2 garlic cloves, minced

1 tablespoon soy sauce

1 tablespoon dry sherry

2 tablespoons cornstarch

1 teaspoon hoisin sauce

1 tablespoon peanut oil

20 snow peas, trimmed

½ cup water chestnuts, sliced

½ cup chicken stock, heated

½ teaspoon salt

½ cup raw unsalted cashews

• Combine first 6 ingredients; chill 15 minutes.

• Remove chicken from marinade, discarding marinade.

• Stir-fry chicken in hot oil in a wok over medium-high heat 3 minutes. Add snow peas and water chestnuts, and stir-fry 30 seconds. Add chicken stock and salt; stir-fry until slightly thickened.

• Stir in cashews, and serve over rice.

Serves 4.

If unsalted cashews cannot be found, use salted cashews, and omit ½ teaspoon salt.

Chicken with Wine and Shallots

3 skinned and boned chicken breasts, trimmed and cut into 1½-inch-thick pieces

Salt

Freshly ground pepper

¼ cup flour

2 tablespoons vegetable oil, divided

1 tablespoon butter

1 tablespoon minced garlic

1 tablespoon minced shallots

¼ cup chicken broth

⅓ cup dry white wine

Juice of half a lemon

¼ cup chopped fresh parsley

• Season chicken with salt and pepper; dredge in flour.

• Sauté half of the chicken in 1 tablespoon hot oil in a skillet for 3 minutes.

• Melt butter in a separate large skillet. Transfer cooked chicken to butter.

• Repeat procedure with remaining chicken and 1 tablespoon oil.

• Sprinkle all of chicken with garlic and shallots, tossing well. Add broth and next 3 ingredients; cover, reduce heat, and simmer 2 to 3 minutes.

Serves 6.

Back To The Table

Try

Party or Dinner

Sweet and Sour Chicken

1¼ cups pineapple juice

1 (1-ounce) envelope Ranch-style dressing mix

½ cup soy sauce

½ cup sherry

¾ cup red wine vinegar

1½ teaspoons garlic, minced

¼ cup sugar

12 boneless chicken breast halves, cut into bite-size pieces

- Combine first 7 ingredients.

- Place chicken in a shallow baking dish, and pour marinade over top. Chill overnight.

- Bake at 350° for 30 to 40 minutes.

Serves 8 to 12.

Can also be used as an appetizer and served in chafing dish with cocktail wooden picks.

Chicken with a Twist

3 tablespoons butter

4 skinned and boned chicken breast halves

1 tablespoon Dijon mustard

1 garlic clove, crushed

1 tablespoon minced fresh parsley

1 tablespoon lemon juice

¼ cup fine, dry breadcrumbs

½ cup grated Parmesan cheese

- Melt butter in a large skillet over medium heat; add chicken, and cook 10 minutes or until lightly browned. Stir in mustard and next 3 ingredients; cook 3 to 4 minutes or until done.

- Sprinkle with breadcrumbs and Parmesan cheese.

Serves 4.

Think of the secrets imparted, victories celebrated, information exchanged, hurts comforted, laughs shared, flavors relished and new tastes discovered. And all this happened at the dinner table.

Christ Church Chicken Pie

1 whole chicken

1 stick butter, divided

1 cup chopped onion

1 cup chopped celery

1 cup sliced carrot

1 cup diced potato

1 can English peas

4 tablespoons all-purpose flour

2 cups milk

Salt

Pepper

1 teaspoon lemon juice

1 teaspoon ground mace

Quick Butter Biscuits

• Simmer chicken in salted water to cover until meat falls off the bone. Drain chicken, reserving broth. Bone chicken, and discard bones. Tear meat into large pieces.

• Melt ½ stick butter in a skillet; add onion and celery, and sauté until tender.

• Cook carrot, potato, and reserved chicken broth in a saucepan over medium heat until tender. Drain vegetables, reserving broth.

• Combine chicken, cooked vegetables, and peas in a 13- x 9-inch baking dish.

• Melt remaining ½ stick butter in skillet; stir in flour. Cook, stirring constantly, until browned. Stir in 2 cups reserved broth and milk; cook, stirring often, until thickened. Add salt and next 3 ingredients to gravy; pour over chicken mixture.

• Top with homemade or Quick Butter Biscuit dough.

• Bake at 400° until biscuits are lightly browned and casserole is thoroughly heated.

Quick Butter Biscuits

2 cups sour cream

2 sticks butter or margarine

4 cups biscuit mix

• Combine all ingredients, stirring just until moistened.

Serves 4.

Lemon juice cuts the grease and adds a fresh taste to meat pies and stews. Your favorite homemade biscuit recipe may be substituted for Quick Butter Biscuits, if desired.

Louisville Party Chicken

8 chicken breast halves

Salt

Pepper

Butter, cut up

½ cup lightly packed brown sugar

1 tablespoon Worcestershire sauce

1 bottle chili sauce

1 (15-ounce) can dark, sweet pitted cherries

¾ cup sherry

- Preheat oven to 350°.

- Place chicken breast halves in a 13- x 9-inch baking dish; season with salt and pepper, and dot with butter.

- Bake at 350° for 30 minutes.

- Combine brown sugar, Worcestershire sauce, and chili sauce; pour over chicken. Bake 30 more minutes.

- Combine cherries and sherry; spoon over chicken. Bake 15 more minutes.

Serves 8.

Pastor's Aide Chicken, Sausage, and Rice Casserole

2 pounds hot sausage

2 to 3 pounds chicken

1 large onion

2 packages long-grain and wild rice mix, cooked

1 (10¾-ounce) can cream of celery soup, undiluted

3 (10¾-ounce) cans cream of mushroom soup, undiluted

- Preheat oven to 350°.

- Brown sausage in a skillet over medium heat; drain, reserving drippings.

- Boil chicken in water to cover in a Dutch oven 1 hour or until tender; remove chicken from pot, discarding broth. Bone chicken, and discard bones; cut up meat.

- Sauté onion in reserved drippings in skillet until tender.

- Combine sausage, chicken, onion, rice, and soups; spoon into a 13- x 9-inch baking dish.

- Bake at 350° for 1 hour.

Serves 12.

Freezes well.

Oriental Grilled Chicken Breasts

3 garlic cloves, crushed

1½ teaspoons salt

½ cup firmly packed brown sugar

3 tablespoons coarse-grained mustard

¼ cup cider vinegar

Juice of 1 lime

Juice of 1 lemon

6 tablespoons olive oil

Pepper

6 small or 3 large chicken breasts, boned and halved

• Combine first 7 ingredients; whisk in oil, and add pepper.

• Place chicken in a shallow dish; add marinade. Cover and chill overnight, turning once.

• Let chicken stand at room temperature 1 hour before preparing. Remove chicken from marinade, discarding marinade.

• Grill chicken, covered with grill lid, over medium heat (300° to 350°) 4 minutes on each side or until done. Do not overcook.

Serves 6.

These chicken breasts may also be broiled. Cook for the same amount of time.

Mother's Chicken Imperial

8 chicken breast halves

1 cup sherry

1 cup slivered almonds, divided

1 cup seasoned breadcrumbs

1 teaspoon salt

¼ teaspoon freshly ground pepper

1 cup freshly grated Parmesan cheese

2 tablespoons chopped fresh parsley

1 garlic clove, crushed

¾ cup butter or margarine, melted

• Combine chicken and sherry; chill 3 hours.

• Remove chicken from sherry, discarding sherry; pat dry with paper towels.

• Combine ¾ cup almonds, breadcrumbs, and next 5 ingredients in a shallow dish. Dip chicken in melted butter, and dredge in breadcrumb mixture. Discard remaining butter and breadcrumb mixture.

• Arrange chicken in a 13- x 9-inch baking dish, and top with remaining ¼ cup almonds.

• Bake at 350° for 45 minutes to 1 hour.

Serves 8.

Spicy Garlic Chicken

1 bunch cilantro with roots
1 garlic head
2 tablespoons coarsely
   ground black pepper
1 teaspoon curry powder
¼ teaspoon crushed red
   pepper
¼ cup peanut oil
⅓ cup soy sauce
1 whole chicken

• Cut off roots of cilantro, and process roots, some cilantro leaves, a few cilantro stems, and garlic in a food processor until coarsely chopped.

• Combine garlic mixture, remaining whole cilantro, black pepper, and next 4 ingredients, stirring well.

• Combine garlic mixture and chicken in a shallow dish, and chill overnight.

• Remove chicken from marinade, discarding marinade.

• Bake chicken in a baking dish at 350° for 1 hour.

Serves 4.

The flavor of this dish is best if barbecued on the grill. If grilling, have water handy to douse flames.

No Place to Go

The happiest nights
   I ever know
Are those when I've
   No place to go,
And the missus says
   When the day is through:
"Tonight we haven't
   A thing to do."…
Needn't hurry
   My evening meal
Nor forces the smiles
   That I do not feel,
But can grab a book
   From a nearby shelf,
And drop all sham
   And be myself.
Oh, the charm of it
   And the comfort rare;
Nothing on earth
   With it can compare
And I'm sorry for him
   Who doesn't know
The joy of having
   No place to go.
        —Edgar Guest

Sautéed Chicken Breasts in Brandy

8 skinless boneless chicken breast halves, flattened to 1/4-inch thickness

Salt

Ground white pepper

6 tablespoons butter

1/2 cup Madeira

2 tablespoons cognac or brandy

3/4 cup chicken stock or canned chicken broth

• Season chicken with salt and pepper.

• Melt butter in a skillet over low to medium heat; add chicken, and cook 1 to 2 minutes on each side or until lightly browned.

• Remove chicken from skillet; keep warm.

• Add Madeira to skillet; cook, stirring to loosen browned particles. Add cognac and chicken stock; bring to a boil, and cook until reduced by half. Return chicken to skillet, stirring to coat.

• Reduce heat, and simmer 2 to 3 minutes.

Serves 8.

Southwest Chicken Casserole

8 skinless boneless chicken breasts

3 cups cooked rice

1 (16-ounce) container sour cream

1/2 cup mayonnaise

3 (4.5-ounce) cans chopped green chiles

4 cups (16 ounces) shredded Monterey Jack cheese

3 teaspoons minced garlic

Dash of hot sauce

2 cups (8 ounces) shredded sharp Cheddar cheese

• Preheat oven to 350°.

• Pound chicken using a meat mallet or rolling pin to tenderize.

• Cook chicken in boiling water to cover in a saucepan 15 to 20 minutes. Remove chicken from saucepan, discarding broth. Cut chicken into bite-size pieces.

• Combine chicken, rice, and next 6 ingredients.

• Spoon mixture into a 13- x 9-inch baking dish. Top with Cheddar cheese.

• Bake at 350° for 30 minutes.

Serves 8.

Gourmet Upside-down Turkey

½ to 1 cup chicken stock

Herb-seasoned stuffing mix (optional)

1 (15- to 20-pound) turkey

Butter for rubbing

1 garlic clove, minced

1 teaspoon dried basil

1 teaspoon salt

½ teaspoon pepper

¼ teaspoon dried rosemary, crushed

¼ teaspoon dried marjoram

⅛ teaspoon dried thyme

1½ cups white wine, at room temperature

1½ sticks sweet butter, melted

- Preheat oven to 325°.

- Pour ½ cup chicken stock into a roasting pan; spoon stuffing into turkey, if desired.

- Combine garlic and next 6 ingredients; sprinkle over turkey.

- Bake turkey, breast side down, on a buttered rack in roasting pan at 325° for 20 minutes.

- Combine wine and butter. Baste turkey generously with butter mixture, and bake 15 to 18 more minutes per pound, basting every 30 minutes. Add additional stock, if needed, to keep breast from sticking to rack. Cover loosely with aluminum foil, if necessary, to keep from overbrowning.

- Turn turkey breast side up during last hour of cooking.

- Transfer to a large heated platter. Cover loosely with aluminum foil, and let stand in a warm place (85°) 15 minutes before serving.

Cooking the turkey upside-down makes the breasts much juicier.

Turkey Spaghetti Casserole

1 (5- to 6-pound) turkey breast

¼ cup butter or margarine

¼ cup olive oil

2 onions, chopped

2 green bell peppers, chopped

16 ounces uncooked thin spaghetti

1½ quarts chicken broth

2 (10-ounce) cans RoTel tomatoes, crushed

2 tablespoons Worcestershire sauce

1 (10¾-ounce) can cream of mushroom soup, undiluted

1 (16-ounce) package frozen tiny green peas

1 pound process cheese spread loaf, shredded

1 cup slivered almonds, toasted

• Cook turkey according to package directions until done. Cut meat into bite-size pieces, discarding bones.

• Heat butter and oil in a skillet; add onion and bell pepper, and sauté until tender.

• Bring spaghetti and chicken broth to a boil in a large saucepan; cook until tender. Do not drain.

• Mash tomatoes with their juice. Combine tomatoes, onion, bell pepper, Worcestershire, and soup.

• Layer spaghetti (do not drain), chicken, peas, and tomato mixture in a buttered 13- x 9-inch baking dish. Sprinkle with cheese. Top with almonds.

• Bake at 350° for 30 minutes.

Serves 12.

One five year old parishioner shares how to cook a turkey:
"Wash the turkey off. Stab it with a fork. Put on a tray and put in oven at 20 degrees for about 20 seconds. Wait for it to beep."

Country-Style Barbecue Ribs

July 01
C, K, K v RA

4 pounds country-style ribs
(beef or pork)

¾ teaspoon salt, divided

½ cup chopped onion

2 garlic cloves, minced

1 tablespoon olive oil

⅔ cup ketchup

⅓ cup apricot preserves

2 teaspoons chili powder

good flavor, but be sure ribs are lean

- Cook ribs and ½ teaspoon salt, covered, in boiling water to cover in a 6-quart Dutch oven 30 minutes or until tender.

- Sauté onion and garlic in hot oil in a small skillet 5 minutes or until golden; stir in remaining ¼ teaspoon salt, ketchup, preserves, and chili powder. Heat until boiling.

- Drain ribs, and brush with sauce, reserving remaining sauce.

- Grill ribs, covered with grill lid, over medium heat (300° to 350°) 5 to 7 minutes on each side, basting often with reserved sauce.

Serves 6.

Sunday Lunch Pork Tenderloin

3 pounds pork tenderloin

Freshly ground pepper

½ cup Dijon mustard

½ cup firmly packed brown
sugar

1 teaspoon dried rosemary

- Preheat oven to 475°.

- Line a baking dish with enough aluminum foil to wrap tenderloins; place tenderloins on foil, and sprinkle with pepper.

- Combine mustard, sugar, and rosemary; pour over tenderloins. Sprinkle with more pepper.

- Wrap tenderloins tightly in foil, and bake at 475° for 40 minutes.

Serves 4.

Summertime corn on the cob

- *Place shucked corn in a steamer over cold water.*
- *Bring to a rolling boil.*
- *Cover and remove from heat.*
- *Let sit for at least 10 minutes.*
- *Smother with butter, salt and pepper and enjoy!*

Grilled Pork Tenderloin

Bacon slices

2 pounds center cut pork tenderloin

1½ cups vegetable oil

¾ cup soy sauce

2 tablespoons dry mustard

1 tablespoon pepper

⅓ cup lemon juice

½ cup white wine vinegar

1 to 2 garlic cloves, crushed

Minced fresh parsley

- Wrap bacon slices around each tenderloin, covering meat completely. Secure bacon with wooden picks.

- Combine oil and next 7 ingredients; pour over tenderloin. Cover and chill 24 hours.

- Remove tenderloin from marinade, reserving marinade.

- Grill tenderloin, covered with grill lid, over medium heat (300° to 350°) 45 to 50 minutes or until a meat thermometer inserted into thickest portion registers 150° to 160°, basting frequently.

- Remove wooden picks, and slice.

Serves 4.

Douse flames with water when grilling. Be sure to cook the meat slowly. The meat will be slightly pink in the center. You may want to reserve some of the marinade before marinating the pork to serve with it once grilled.

Mango-Black Bean Salsa

2 mangos, diced
1 can black beans, rinsed
  and drained
¼ fresh pineapple, cubed
1 teaspoon brown sugar
Juice of 1 lime
2 tablespoons chopped
  fresh cilantro
1 garlic clove, minced
½ jalapeño pepper, finely
  chopped

- Combine all ingredients in a bowl. Chill until ready to serve.

This salsa is great with fish and pork.

Herbed Apricot Pork Tenderloin

¼ cup olive oil

4 garlic cloves, crushed

3 tablespoons balsamic vinegar

2 teaspoons dried thyme

2 teaspoons dried tarragon

½ teaspoon coarsely ground pepper

¾ cup apricot jam

3 (2-pound) packages pork tenderloins

1 large onion, halved and thinly sliced

¾ cup chopped dried apricots

- Combine first 7 ingredients in a large bowl; add tenderloins, tossing to coat. Chill 4 to 6 hours or overnight.

- Remove tenderloins from marinade, reserving marinade and scraping any bits off tenderloins.

- Grill tenderloins, covered with grill lid, over medium-high heat (350° to 400°) until seared on all sides.

- Transfer tenderloins to a roasting pan; combine reserved marinade, onion, and apricots, and pour over tenderloins, covering well.

- Bake at 350° for 25 minutes or until a meat thermometer inserted into thickest portion registers 150°.

- Let stand at room temperature a few minutes before slicing.

Serves 8.

Tenderloins may also be fully prepared on the grill. Omit onion and dried apricots. Continue grilling once seared, basting with reserved marinade, until meat thermometer inserted into thickest portion registers 150°. Proceed as directed.

Indonesian Pork Saté

¼ cup creamy peanut butter

2 tablespoons ground coriander

1 garlic clove

½ small onion, minced

1 teaspoon ground red pepper

¾ teaspoon salt

3 tablespoons lemon juice

¼ cup soy sauce

1 tablespoon brown sugar

2 pounds lean pork, cubed

2 zucchini

3 pints cherry tomatoes

¼ cup butter, melted

• Combine first 9 ingredients; place pork in a shallow pan, and add marinade. Chill, covered tightly, 3 hours or overnight.

• Soak bamboo skewers in water 30 minutes.

• Cut zucchini in half lengthwise; cut halves into ½-inch slices.

• Remove pork from marinade, discarding marinade. Thread pork, zucchini, and tomatoes onto skewers.

• Grill, covered with grill lid, over medium heat (300° to 350°), basting occasionally with butter, until desired degree of doneness.

Serves 6.

For appetizers, cut pork into small cubes. Prepare recipe as directed using 4-inch bamboo skewers, and threading 1 piece each of pork, zucchini, and tomato onto each skewer. Grill as directed. Kabobs may also be microwaved on a tray on HIGH 1 minute and 45 seconds, turning after 1 minute.

Three-Onion Marmalade

4 tablespoons butter
1 medium-size purple onion,
  thinly sliced
1 medium-size yellow onion,
  thinly sliced
2 leeks, thinly sliced
½ cup red wine vinegar
1 cup sugar
Fresh thyme sprigs

• Melt butter in a heavy
  saucepan; add onions, and
  sauté until they begin to
  caramelize.

• Add leeks, and cook until
  caramelized. Add sugar and
  vinegar; reduce heat, and
  simmer. Add thyme. Do not
  overcook or onions will be
  too soft.

This marmalade is wonderful
with pork and beef.

Pork Chops with Pecan Crust

½ cup light soy sauce

¼ cup lemon juice

2 tablespoons brown sugar

3 green onions, chopped

2 teaspoons prepared
horseradish

¼ teaspoon grated fresh
ginger

4 (8-ounce) pork chops

¼ cup all-purpose flour

½ cup finely chopped
pecans

¼ cup white cornmeal

1 teaspoon salt

½ teaspoon white pepper

¼ cup olive oil

• Combine first 6 ingredients in a shallow dish; add pork chops, turning to coat. Cover and chill 1 hour.

• Remove pork chops from marinade, discarding marinade.

• Combine flour and next 4 ingredients; dredge pork chops in mixture, coating well.

• Brown pork chops in hot oil in a large skillet 5 to 7 minutes on each side or until done.

Serves 4.

Pork Chops aux Preserves

¼ cup black currant,
damson plum, or
blackberry preserves

1½ tablespoons Dijon
mustard

6 (1- to 1½-inch-thick)
center-cut pork chops

Salt

Freshly ground pepper

⅓ cup white wine vinegar

• Combine preserves and mustard.

• Brown pork chops on both sides in a nonstick skillet. Season with salt and pepper, and top evenly with preserve mixture. Reduce heat, cover, and simmer 20 minutes or until done.

• Transfer to a serving platter, and keep warm.

• Remove excess fat from skillet; add vinegar, and bring to a boil over medium heat, stirring to loosen browned particles. Cook until reduced by one-third.

• Pour sauce over chops, and serve immediately.

Serves 4.

Pork Roast with Bulgur Stuffing

⅓ cup bulgur

4 tablespoons dried tomatoes

3 green onions, sliced

2 tablespoons chopped fresh parsley

2 tablespoons olive oil

2 tablespoons lemon juice

¾ teaspoon dried mint leaves, crushed

¼ teaspoon salt

1 (4 to 5-pound) pork loin center rib roast, with backbone loosened

Salt

Pepper

- Preheat oven to 325°.

- Combine bulgur and water to cover, and let stand 10 minutes; drain well.

- Combine tomatoes and boiling water to cover, and let stand 5 minutes. Drain and chop.

- Combine bulgur, tomatoes, green onions, and next 5 ingredients in a bowl, tossing well.

- Turn roast rib side down. Cut a 3½-inch-long, 1-inch-deep pocket on the meaty side above each rib, making 8 to 10 pockets.

- Spoon bulgur mixture evenly into pockets. Season with salt and pepper.

- Bake roast, rib side down, in a shallow roasting pan at 325° for 1 hour and 30 minutes to 2 hours and 30 minutes or until a meat thermometer inserted into thickest portion registers 160°.

- Cover loosely with aluminum foil after 1 hour to prevent stuffing from browning.

- Slice roast between ribs to serve.

Serves 8.

Bulgur is a nutritious staple grain from the Middle East.

Sweet and Sour Pork

1 tablespoon dry sherry

1 tablespoon soy sauce

1 teaspoon salt

1 pound lean boneless pork, trimmed and cut into 1-inch cubes

1 large egg, lightly beaten

¼ cup all-purpose flour

¼ cup cornstarch

Vegetable oil

Sweet and Sour Sauce

- Combine first 3 ingredients; pour over pork, and let stand 10 minutes.

- Remove pork from marinade, discarding marinade. Add egg to pork; add flour, stirring to coat. Add enough cornstarch for batter to cover pork.

- Heat oil to 375° in a deep fryer. Add half of pork, 1 cube at a time.

- Fry 5 to 6 minutes, turning to brown on all sides.

- Remove pork, and drain. Keep warm.

- Repeat procedure with remaining pork.

- Combine pork and Sweet and Sour Sauce.

Sweet and Sour Sauce

4 ounces tomato sauce

½ cup sugar

½ cup vinegar

½ cup pineapple juice

3 tablespoons cornstarch

3 tablespoons water

1 cup crushed pineapple

1 green bell pepper, cut into 1-inch squares

1 onion, quartered

- Bring first 4 ingredients to a boil in a saucepan.

- Combine cornstarch and 3 tablespoons water, stirring until smooth. Add to tomato mixture, and cook until thickened and clear.

- Add pineapple, bell pepper, and onion just before serving. Cook until thoroughly heated.

Serves 4.

Southern Baked Smithfield (Virginia) Ham

1 Smithfield, Virginia, ham

2 to 3 cups water

3 to 4 teaspoons light brown sugar

2 to 3 tablespoons all-purpose flour

Apple cider vinegar

- Cut off ham hock using a saw, and reserve for another use. Soak ham in warm water to cover in a sink or dishpan several hours. Scrape off pepper for curing, using a kitchen brush and knife.

- Place ham, rind side up, in a shallow baking pan; add 2 to 3 cups water.

- Bake at 250° for 2 hours and 30 minutes or until rind begins to loosen. Ham is done when meat pulls away from the bone.

- Remove from oven; cut rind, and peel it off. Trim excess fat from ham. Pour off pan drippings, reserving for another use; add enough water to pan to keep ham from scorching.

- Combine brown sugar, flour, and enough vinegar to make a thin paste; spread evenly over ham.

- Bake at 250° for 30 minutes or until slightly brown.

1 ham.

Smithfield ham is a delicacy. To enjoy the flavor best, carve thin slices. For appetizers, serve with Heavenly Rolls (page 48).

Come, my Light, my feast, my Strength:
such a light as shows a feast;
such a feast as mends in length;
such a strength as makes his guest.

George Herbert, Priest (1593–1633)
Hymn 487, verse 2

Grilled Butterflied Leg of Lamb

1 boned leg of lamb,
  butterflied and trimmed
3 tablespoons coarsely
  ground pepper, divided
1½ teaspoons dried
  rosemary
5 teaspoons minced garlic
½ cup raspberry vinegar
¼ cup soy sauce
½ cup dry red wine
2 tablespoons Dijon
  mustard

• Place lamb flat in a large roasting pan.

• Combine 1 tablespoon pepper, rosemary, and next 4 ingredients. Pour over lamb, and chill at least 8 hours.

• Remove lamb from marinade, discarding marinade.

• Combine remaining 2 tablespoons pepper and mustard; spread thinly over lamb.

• Grill, covered with grill lid, over medium heat (300° to 350°) until meat thermometer inserted into thickest portion registers 150° (medium rare).

Serves 6.

Savory Mint Lamb Chops

¼ cup olive oil
¼ cup chopped fresh mint
4 garlic cloves, minced
2 teaspoons salt
2 teaspoons ground cumin
1 teaspoon ground
  coriander
1 teaspoon cayenne pepper
1 teaspoon ground black
  pepper
8 (1½-inch-thick) lamb
  chops

• Combine all ingredients except lamb chops. Spread mixture on both sides of lamb.

• Broil 5 minutes on each side or until brown and crusty on the outside and medium rare inside.

Serves 8.

Marinated Lamb with Mint

½ cup olive oil

¼ cup soy sauce

2 tablespoons chopped fresh rosemary

2 tablespoons chopped fresh oregano

Juice of 1 lemon

4 garlic cloves, minced

1 boned leg of lamb, butterflied

1 jar mint jelly

Chopped fresh mint or rosemary for garnish

- Spread lamb on a flat surface, and pound to an even thickness.

- Combine first 6 ingredients in a shallow dish; add lamb, and chill 4 hours or overnight.

- Prepare fire by piling charcoal on each side of grill, leaving center empty.

- Place a drip pan with a small amount of water in it between coals. Open vent in bottom of grill. Coat food rack with vegetable cooking spray, and place on grill.

- Remove lamb from marinade, discarding marinade.

- Arrange lamb over drip pan, and grill, covered with grill lid, over medium heat (300° to 350°) until meat thermometer inserted into thickest portion registers 125° or to desired degree of doneness.

- Melt jelly in a small saucepan over low heat; add chopped fresh mint or rosemary. Serve with lamb.

Serves 6.

Have the butcher bone and butterfly the leg of lamb. New Zealand or Australian lamb is best.

I thank you, Lord of the Feast,
for holidays and holy days,
for anniversaries and
  victory celebrations,
for homecomings and
  weddings,
for all these times and many
  more
when we can pray with food
  and drink,
in the company of candles
  and conversation.
    —Edward Hayes, monk

Grilled Lamb Kabobs

¾ to 1 cup soy sauce

½ cup olive oil

1⅛ teaspoons minced fresh garlic

1½ tablespoons dried rosemary

3 tablespoons grated fresh ginger

3 pounds leg of lamb, cut into bite-size pieces

- Combine first 5 ingredients in a jar; cover tightly, and shake vigorously.

- Place lamb in a shallow dish; add marinade. Chill overnight.

- Remove lamb from marinade, discarding marinade. Thread onto metal skewers.

- Grill, covered with grill lid, over medium heat (300° to 350°) until desired degree of doneness.

4 servings.

Do not use the stringy part of the ginger.

Lamb Sauté

1½ pounds lamb sirloin or chops, cut into strips

2 tablespoons olive oil, divided

1 medium onion, cut in half lengthwise and sliced

1 red bell pepper, thinly sliced

1 yellow bell pepper, thinly sliced

1 teaspoon minced garlic

1 pound fresh spinach

2 teaspoons dried red pepper flakes

Salt

Ground black pepper

- Stir-fry lamb in 1 tablespoon hot oil until browned.

- Transfer to a heated platter, and keep warm.

- Sauté onion in remaining 1 tablespoon hot oil in skillet over medium-high heat 1 minute. Add bell peppers and garlic, and sauté 2 minutes or until tender. Reduce heat to medium, and add spinach, 1 handful at a time, cooking until each handful is wilted.

- Return lamb to skillet; add red pepper flakes, salt, and black pepper. Cook 3 minutes or until thoroughly heated.

Serves 2.

Company Special Veal

2 tablespoons butter

1 (8-ounce) package fresh mushrooms, sliced

½ cup all-purpose flour

1½ teaspoons salt

¼ teaspoon pepper

1 teaspoon paprika

Garlic powder

1½ pounds veal, cut into ½- x 1-inch pieces

¼ cup butter or margarine

1 green bell pepper, cut into strips

1 onion, thinly sliced

1½ cups chicken broth, divided

⅓ cup pimiento-stuffed olives

1½ cups uncooked rice, cooked

- Melt 2 tablespoons butter in a skillet; add mushrooms, and cook until browned. Remove from skillet.

- Combine flour and next 4 ingredients in a zip-top plastic bag; add veal, and shake to coat. Reserve excess flour mixture.

- Melt ¼ cup butter in skillet; add veal, and brown. Add bell pepper, onion, and 1 cup broth. Cover, reduce heat, and simmer 30 minutes.

- Combine 3 tablespoons reserved flour mixture and remaining ½ cup broth, stirring until smooth. Add to veal, and cook, stirring often, until thickened.

- Add mushrooms, and cook until thoroughly heated.

- Combine olives and rice; serve veal over rice.

Serves 6.

Making dinner is about a lot more than getting food to the table—it is doing something with your family and friends.

Veal Parmigiana

2 (15-ounce) cans tomato sauce

1 tablespoon butter or margarine, melted

1 tablespoon brown sugar

2 teaspoons Worcestershire sauce

1 teaspoon dried oregano

1 teaspoon dried basil

¼ teaspoon garlic powder

1¼ teaspoons Season-All, divided

½ teaspoon pepper, divided

2 large eggs

2 pounds veal cutlets, cut into serving-size pieces

4 cups soft breadcrumbs

½ cup olive oil

¼ cup grated Parmesan cheese

8 ounces sliced mozzarella cheese

- Preheat oven to 350°.

- Cook first 7 ingredients, 1 teaspoon Season-All, and ¼ teaspoon pepper in a saucepan over medium heat, stirring occasionally, 5 minutes. Remove from heat.

- Combine eggs and remaining ¼ teaspoon Season-All and pepper, beating well.

- Dip cutlets in egg mixture, and dredge in breadcrumbs.

- Brown cutlets in hot oil in a skillet. Transfer to a lightly greased 13- x 9-inch baking dish.

- Pour sauce over cutlets, and sprinkle with Parmesan cheese.

- Bake, covered, at 350° for 30 minutes.

- Uncover and top with mozzarella cheese. Bake 5 more minutes or until cheese is melted.

Serves 6.

The dinner table is where children learn most of their values.

—Ann Landers

Veal Scaloppine with Tomatoes and Olives

½ cup all-purpose flour

Salt

Pepper

1 large egg

1 tablespoon water

8 veal scallops, flattened to
⅛-inch thickness

2 tablespoons vegetable oil

7 tablespoons butter or
margarine, divided

1 red bell pepper, thinly
sliced

2 teaspoons minced garlic

1 large onion, chopped

1 (15-ounce) can diced
tomatoes

24 pimiento-stuffed olives,
sliced

1 teaspoon dried oregano

2 tablespoons red wine
vinegar or dry red wine

Garnish: 3 tablespoons
chopped fresh parsley

- Combine flour, salt, and pepper in a shallow dish.

- Beat egg and 1 tablespoon water in a separate dish. Coat veal with flour mixture, and shake off excess; dip in egg mixture.

- Heat oil and 1 tablespoon butter in a large skillet; add veal, and sauté 2 to 3 minutes on each side or until lightly browned.

- Transfer to a warm serving platter; keep warm.

- Wipe skillet clean; add remaining 6 tablespoons butter, and melt. Add bell pepper, garlic, and onion to skillet, and sauté 5 minutes or until tender. Add tomatoes and olives, and cook 1 minute.

- Increase heat to high; add oregano and vinegar, and cook 30 seconds.

- Pour hot vegetable mixture over veal, and garnish, if desired.

Serves 4.

Medallions of Venison

1¼ cups soy sauce

½ cup red wine

1 tablespoon grated fresh or
   1 teaspoon ground ginger

½ cup apple or cranberry-
   apple juice

1 teaspoon garlic pepper

1 venison tenderloin

1 tablespoon minced onion

1 pound button mushrooms,
   sliced

1 pound wild mushrooms,
   sliced

1 tablespoon olive oil

1 package Knorr hunter
   sauce mix

- Combine first 6 ingredients in a shallow dish; chill 30 minutes.

- Sauté onion and mushrooms in hot oil in a skillet until tender. Remove from skillet.

- In a separate pan, prepare hunter sauce according to package directions; add onion and mushrooms.

- Remove venison from marinade, discarding marinade.

- Cook venison in skillet over high heat 5 minutes on each side or until lightly browned. Reduce heat to medium-low; cover and cook 10 minutes (rare to medium rare) or to desired degree of doneness. Do not overcook.

- Slice tenderloin thinly, and serve with hunter sauce.

Serves 4.

Venison is best served rare to medium rare. You may also use blackstrap molasses in this recipe.

Marinade for Game

1 cup olive oil
4 garlic cloves, minced
½ cup oyster sauce
¼ cup balsamic vinegar
2 teaspoons dried thyme
1 tablespoon coarsely ground
   pepper
1 teaspoon salt.

- Combine all ingredients. Chill overnight.

This marinade is fabulous on beef and wild game. The oyster sauce makes it.

Gourmet Lasagna

7 tablespoons butter, divided

¼ pound country ham, minced

1 cup chopped onion

¼ cup minced carrot

½ cup minced celery

1 pound ground beef and/or pork

2 tablespoons olive oil

½ cup red or white wine

½ pound chicken livers

2 cups beef stock or 1 (10½-ounce) can condensed beef broth, undiluted

2 tablespoons tomato paste

1 package lasagna noodles, cooked

3 tablespoons butter or margarine

6 tablespoons all-purpose flour

3 cups half-and-half

½ pound grated Parmesan or Romano cheese

- Melt 2 tablespoons butter in a skillet over medium heat; add ham and next 3 ingredients, and cook 10 minutes. Transfer mixture to a large Dutch oven.

- Brown ground meat in hot oil in skillet; transfer to ham mixture.

- Add wine to skillet, and cook, stirring to loosen browned particles. Transfer wine mixture to Dutch oven.

- Melt 2 tablespoons butter in a small skillet over medium heat; add chicken livers, and cook just until firm.

- Drain livers, and mince.

- Add beef stock and tomato paste to ham mixture, and bring to a simmer. Cook 25 minutes.

- Add liver mixture to ham mixture, and cook 10 minutes or until mixture has thickened.

- Melt remaining 3 tablespoons butter in a skillet over medium heat; add flour, stirring until smooth. Reduce heat, and simmer, stirring often, until lightly browned and slightly thickened. Add half-and-half, and cook, stirring occasionally, until slightly thickened.

- Layer one-third of meat sauce, one-third of béchamel sauce, and half of noodles in a 13- x 9-inch baking dish.

- Repeat layers once. Top with remaining meat sauce and béchamel sauce. Sprinkle with cheese.

- Bake at 350° for 30 minutes.

- Let stand at room temperature 15 to 30 minutes before serving.

Serves 6.

The chicken livers are essential for the outstanding flavor! You may also want to sprinkle freshly grated Parmesan cheese on each layer.

Veal Cutlet with Herbs

1 veal cutlet

Salt

Pepper

2 tablespoons butter

3 tablespoons white wine

1 sprig fresh tarragon

½ teaspoon chopped fresh chervil

½ shallot

1 teaspoon chopped fresh parsley

1 teaspoon chopped fresh chives

- Season veal with salt and pepper.

- Melt butter in a cast-iron skillet; add veal, and cook 1½ minutes on each side.

- Remove from skillet; keep warm.

- Add wine to skillet, and cook, stirring to loosen browned particles. Stir in tarragon and next 4 ingredients; remove from heat.

- Pour sauce over veal, and serve immediately.

1 serving.

Sassy Meat Loaf

⅔ cup seasoned breadcrumbs

1 cup milk

1½ pounds ground chuck

2 large eggs, lightly beaten

¼ cup grated onion

1 teaspoon salt

⅛ teaspoon pepper

½ teaspoon dried sage

Piquante Sauce

4 to 5 bay leaves

- Preheat oven to 350°.

- Combine breadcrumbs and milk; let stand 10 minutes.

- Combine ground chuck and next 5 ingredients; add to breadcrumb mixture, stirring well.

- Press mixture into a 9- x 5-inch loafpan lightly coated with vegetable cooking spray. Top with Piquante Sauce. Stick bay leaves in top.

- Bake at 350° for 1 hour.

Serves 6.

Piquante Sauce

3 tablespoons light brown sugar

¼ cup ketchup

¼ teaspoon ground nutmeg

1 teaspoon dry mustard

- Combine all ingredients.

For individual servings, bake in large muffin cups. Put half of a bay leaf in the top of each cup. Bake at 350° for 30 minutes.

Spinach and Pasta Lasagna

1 pound spinach pasta,
  cooked al dente

Meat Sauce

¾ cup grated Parmesan
  cheese

Cream Sauce

- Place a layer of pasta in a buttered 13- x 9-inch baking dish. Top with one-third of Meat Sauce, and sprinkle with 2 tablespoons Parmesan cheese.

- Top with another layer of pasta, one-third of Cream Sauce, and 2 tablespoons Parmesan cheese.

- Repeat these layers twice, ending with Cream Sauce and Parmesan cheese.

- Bake at 350° for 20 to 30 minutes or until thoroughly heated.

- Let stand at room temperature 15 minutes before serving.

Meat Sauce

¼ cup butter

2 onions, minced

½ cup minced celery

2 small carrots, minced

2 teaspoons salt

½ teaspoon pepper

1 teaspoon ground oregano

1 pound ground round or
  chuck, browned and
  drained

1 pound ground sausage,
  browned and drained

½ cup dry white wine

6 tablespoons tomato sauce

- Melt butter in a skillet over medium heat; add onion, celery, and carrot, and sauté 10 minutes. Sprinkle with salt, pepper, and oregano.

- Add meat, wine, and tomato sauce. Reduce heat to low, and simmer, stirring often, 15 minutes.

Spinach and Pasta Lasagna (continued)

Cream Sauce

½ cup butter

½ cup all-purpose flour

1 teaspoon salt

¼ teaspoon ground white pepper

1 quart milk, heated

1 cup heavy cream

1 cup (4 ounces) shredded Swiss cheese

- Melt butter in a skillet over medium heat; add flour, salt, and pepper, stirring well. Cook 2 to 3 minutes.
- Add hot milk; cook, stirring often, until smooth and thickened. Reduce heat to low, and stir in cream.
- Add Swiss cheese, stirring until melted.

Serves 10.

Reuben Pie

1 tablespoon caraway seeds

1 unbaked 9-inch deep-dish pastry shell

½ pound corned beef, shredded

1 tablespoon Dijon mustard

¼ cup Thousand Island dressing

¾ cup sauerkraut, well drained

1½ cups (6 ounces) shredded Swiss cheese

3 large eggs, lightly beaten

1 cup half-and-half

1 tablespoon grated onion

¼ teaspoon dry mustard

- Preheat oven to 425°.
- Press caraway seeds into pastry shell; prick crust with a fork a few times.
- Bake at 425° for 8 minutes.
- Remove from oven; reduce oven temperature to 350°.
- Spread corned beef in bottom of prepared pastry shell.
- Combine mustard and dressing, and spread over corned beef. Top with sauerkraut and cheese.
- Whisk together eggs and next 3 ingredients. Pour over pie.
- Bake 40 to 50 minutes or until done.
- Let stand at room temperature 5 minutes before cutting.

Serves 6.

Real Italian Spaghetti Meat Sauce

1 stick butter, divided

2 pounds ground chuck

8 medium onions, chopped

1½ medium-size green bell peppers, chopped

1½ large cans tomatoes

1 teaspoon dried Italian seasoning

2 tablespoons Worcestershire sauce

1 garlic clove, chopped

¼ cup sugar

1 teaspoon coarsely ground black pepper

4 (6-ounce) cans tomato paste

4 tablespoons chopped fresh parsley

½ cup vegetable oil

1 teaspoon dried oregano

3 bay leaves

2½ teaspoons salt

• Melt half of the butter in a large skillet; add ground chuck, and brown.

• Melt remaining half of butter in a separate skillet; add onion and bell pepper, and sauté until browned.

• Combine tomatoes and rest of ingredients in a large saucepan; stir in ground chuck, onion, and bell pepper. Simmer 2 hours, stirring occasionally, or until desired degree of thickness is reached, adding water if needed.

• Remove and discard bay leaves.

Serves 8.

> *Setting a table is so much more than just laying down knives and forks. It is creating a setting for food and conversation, setting a mood and an aura that lingers long after what was served and who said what is forgotten.*
>
> —Peri Wolfman

Stayabed Stew

2 pounds stew beef, cubed

1 small can tiny peas

1 cup sliced carrot

2 onions, chopped

1 (10¾-ounce) can cream of tomato, celery, or mushroom soup, undiluted

½ soup can water

1 large potato, sliced

1 teaspoon salt

Pepper

- Preheat oven to 275°,

- Combine all ingredients in a 2-quart baking dish.

- Bake, covered, at 275°.

- Go back to bed. It will cook happily all by itself and will be done in 5 hours.

Serves 6 to 8.

Marinated Flank Steak

1 (1½-pound) lean flank steak, trimmed

¾ cup rosé wine

1 teaspoon coarsely ground pepper

½ teaspoon salt

¼ teaspoon dried rosemary, crushed

1 medium onion, sliced

1 garlic clove, crushed

- Combine all ingredients in a large heavy-duty zip-top plastic bag; seal and chill 8 hours, turning occasionally.

- Remove steak from marinade, discarding marinade. Place steak on a rack lightly coated with vegetable cooking spray in a broiler pan.

- Broil 7 minutes on each side. Steak may also be grilled to desired doneness.

- To serve, cut diagonally across the grain.

Serves 4.

Beef Sauté Chasseur with Cumin Seed

2 cups all-purpose flour

1 tablespoon ground thyme

1 teaspoon salt

½ teaspoon pepper

3 pounds stew beef or porterhouse steak, cut into 1-inch cubes

¼ cup olive oil

6 tablespoons butter or margarine, divided

3 garlic cloves, crushed

1 onion, chopped

1 to 1½ cups beef stock

1 to 2 tablespoons cumin seed

1 teaspoon chili powder

1 bay leaf

½ to ¾ pound button mushrooms

1 cup red or dry white wine

2 tablespoons tomato paste

- Combine first 4 ingredients; dredge beef cubes in flour mixture, coating well. Reserve excess flour mixture.

- Heat oil and 4 tablespoons butter in a large ovenproof skillet; add beef, a few pieces at a time, and cook until browned. Transfer beef to a plate.

- Drain and discard excess oil; add garlic and onion to skillet, and sauté until tender. Add 2 tablespoons reserved flour mixture, and cook, stirring often, until browned. Add stock, stirring to blend, and bring to a boil.

- Return beef to skillet, and add cumin, chili powder, and bay leaf. Cover, reduce heat, and simmer 45 minutes or until tender.

- Melt remaining 2 tablespoons butter in a small skillet; add mushrooms, and sauté 2 minutes. Add wine, and cook until reduced by half. Stir in tomato paste.

- Remove and discard bay leaf from beef mixture; add mushroom sauce.

- Bake at 350° until thoroughly heated.

Serves 6.

Adjust the spices to taste. Recipe can be prepared ahead to the point of cooking beef mixture 45 minutes; do not prepare mushroom sauce. Cover and chill overnight, if desired. Proceed as directed. Recipe can also be refrigerated overnight once fully prepared. The taste develops further over time.

Cold Steak Parisienne

1 (1½-pound) T-bone steak

¼ pound fresh mushrooms, sliced

5 tablespoons olive oil, divided

½ cup dry red wine

¼ cup red wine vinegar

1 teaspoon salt or garlic salt

½ teaspoon lemon pepper

½ teaspoon dried thyme, crushed

¼ teaspoon dried basil, crushed

¼ teaspoon dried marjoram, crushed

6 cherry tomatoes

6 artichoke hearts, cooked

- Broil steak to rare. Cool and chill. Cut into ½-inch slices, and place in a shallow dish.

- Sauté mushrooms in 2 tablespoons hot oil in a skillet until barely tender. Cool and add to sliced steak.

- Whisk together remaining 3 tablespoons oil, wine, and next 6 ingredients.

- Pour dressing over steak mixture. Chill 3 to 4 hours.

- Add tomatoes and artichoke hearts before ready to serve.

- Drain steak mixture, reserving marinade.

- Transfer to a serving platter; arrange tomatoes and artichoke hearts around steak and mushrooms, and drizzle with reserved marinade.

Serves 2.

Horseradish Sauce

2 cups sour cream
1 tablespoon prepared
   horseradish
2 teaspoons lemon juice
Salt
¼ to ½ teaspoon lemon
   pepper
1 tablespoon chopped fresh
   chives or 1 teaspoon
   chopped fresh dill
Paprika

- *Combine first 6 ingredients in a bowl; sprinkle with paprika. Chill until ready to serve.*

Serves 12.

Elegant Beef Tenderloin 12-29-02

1 (5-pound) beef tenderloin, trimmed

1¼ teaspoons garlic salt

1 cup Burgundy wine

¼ cup soy sauce

¾ cup butter or margarine

1 teaspoon lemon pepper

very tender
& good.

- Preheat oven to 425°.

- Place tenderloin in a lightly greased shallow roasting pan; sprinkle with garlic salt.

- Bake at 425° for 10 minutes.

- Cook wine and next 3 ingredients in a small saucepan until thoroughly heated. Pour sauce over tenderloin.

- Bake 30 *or less if thin piece of beef* to 40 more minutes or until a meat thermometer inserted into thickest portion registers 140° (rare) or until desired degree of doneness, basting occasionally with pan drippings.

Serves 10.

Meat thermometer will read 150° for medium rare or 160° for medium.

Filet Mignon in White Wine Sauce

2 (8-ounce) beef fillets

White Wine Sauce

Garnishes: chopped fresh parsley, thin scallion slices (cut on the bias)

White Wine Sauce

½ cup dry white wine

1 shallot, minced

1 tablespoon tomato paste

½ cup beef consommé

2 tablespoons unsalted butter, cut up

Salt

Freshly ground pepper

- Broil fillets, turning to brown on all sides.

- Spoon White Wine Sauce over fillets. Garnish, if desired.

- Cook first 4 ingredients in a saucepan over medium heat until reduced by half.

- Remove from heat, and gradually add butter, stirring well. Season with salt and pepper.

Serves 2.

Once all four sides of the fillet have been browned the meat will be rare. When preparing the White Wine Sauce, the sauce should not boil once the butter has been added.

Filet Mignons with Green Peppercorn Sauce

8 filet mignons of beef

Green Peppercorn Sauce

- Cook fillets in a heavy skillet over high heat until desired degree of doneness.

- Top each fillet with a generous spoonful of Green Peppercorn Sauce.

Green Peppercorn Sauce

1 tablespoon butter

2 tablespoons minced shallot

¼ pound fresh mushrooms, minced

2 tablespoons minced fresh parsley

1 teaspoon whole green peppercorns, rinsed and drained

2 to 3 drops hot sauce

2 tablespoons brandy

1 cup whipping cream

Salt

- Melt butter in a small saucepan; add shallot, and sauté until tender. Add mushrooms, and sauté, stirring often, 5 minutes. Add parsley, peppercorns, and hot sauce, stirring well.

- Warm brandy, and ignite it.

- Pour flaming brandy into mushroom mixture, and stir until flames subside.

- Add whipping cream, and bring to a boil. Boil, stirring constantly, until thickened. Season with salt.

Yield: ¾ cup.

Serves 8.

Fillets can also be grilled, covered with lid, over medium-high heat (350° to 400°) until desired degree of doneness.

Food sustains life, and every occasion of eating and drinking is an act of communion with God who is the giver of life in all its dimensions.
—Edward Hayes, Monk

Tenderloin Pepper Steaks

4 (6- to 8-ounce) tenderloin
steaks

Salt

2 tablespoons coarsely
crushed black
peppercorns

Half a recipe of Herb Butter

- Sprinkle steak lightly with salt; rub ½ table-spoon pepper into each steak, pressing firmly into meat.

- Grill, covered with grill lid, 4 to 6 inches above medium heat (300° to 350°) 8 to 10 minutes or until desired degree of doneness, turning every 1 to 2 minutes.

- To serve, top each steak with a slice of Herb Butter.

Herb Butter

½ cup unsalted butter, at
room temperature

2 tablespoons chopped
fresh or 2 teaspoons
dried tarragon

2 tablespoons chopped
fresh parsley

½ teaspoon salt

½ teaspoon freshly ground
pepper

- Beat butter at medium speed with a handheld mixer until creamy; add tarragon and next 3 ingredients, beating well.

- Form butter into a 4- x 1-inch log. Wrap in plastic wrap, and chill until firm.

- Cut into 8 slices, and reserve half for another use.

Serves 4.

When the Herb Butter is placed on the hot meat, it will make an almost-instant bit of sauce.

Busy families need to spend time together to stay in touch with one another and to strengthen the bonds of the family.

Roast Fillet of Beef with Stilton Sauce

3 garlic cloves, minced

½ stick unsalted butter

1 teaspoon pepper

1 teaspoon salt

1 (4½- to 5-pound) fillet of beef, trimmed and tied with string

Stilton Sauce

- Preheat oven to 500°.

- Combine first 4 ingredients, mashing to make a paste. Rub paste on beef.

- Bake beef in a buttered roasting pan at 500° for 22 minutes. Remove from oven, and cover tightly with aluminum foil.

- Let stand in a warm place (85°) 20 minutes.

- Remove and discard string; cut meat into ½-inch slices.

- Serve with Stilton Sauce.

Serves 6.

Stilton Sauce

1½ cups dry white wine

3 cups heavy cream

½ pound Stilton cheese, crumbled

½ teaspoon ground black pepper

- Cook wine in a heavy saucepan over high heat 15 minutes or until reduced to ¼ cup. Add cream, and cook until reduced to 2 cups.

- Add cheese and pepper. Reduce heat, and simmer, stirring constantly, until cheese is melted and sauce thickens.

The beef will be rare in the thickest part and medium in the thinnest part.

Texas Beef Barbecue

1 cup beef broth

3 cups ketchup

½ cup cider vinegar

¼ cup Worcestershire sauce

¼ cup firmly packed light
brown sugar

2 teaspoons salt

1 teaspoon liquid smoke

1 (6-pound) chuck roast

- Bring first 6 ingredients to a simmer in a 2-quart saucepan. Cover, reduce heat, and simmer 30 minutes or until slightly thickened. Stir in liquid smoke, and remove from heat.

- Place roast in a large roasting pan; add sauce, and let stand at room temperature 2 hours or chill overnight, turning once.

- Remove roast from marinade, reserving marinade; wipe off extra sauce.

- Bake roast, covered tightly, in a separate roasting pan at 325° for 3 hours and 30 minutes or until tender, turning after 2 hours.

- Uncover and cook 30 more minutes or until browned, basting often with reserved sauce.

- Remove roast from pan, and let stand at room temperature 15 minutes.

- Bring remaining sauce to a boil; boil 7 minutes.

- Slice roast thinly, and serve with sauce.

Serves 12.

If grilling, omit liquid smoke. Use wet hickory chips, and smoke over medium-low heat for several hours or until done.

Shrimp Pasta Supreme

6 tablespoons butter, divided

4 tablespoons all-purpose flour

1 cup chicken broth

1 cup heavy cream

¼ cup (1 ounce) shredded Swiss cheese

3 tablespoons sherry

Ground white pepper

¼ pound fresh mushrooms, quartered

1½ pounds peeled medium-size cooked shrimp

8 ounces uncooked vermicelli, cooked

⅓ cup grated Parmesan cheese

½ cup toasted slivered almonds

• Melt 4 tablespoons butter in a large saucepan; add flour, stirring until smooth. Gradually stir in broth and cream. Cook over low heat, stirring constantly, until thickened.

• Stir in Swiss cheese, sherry, and pepper; cook, stirring constantly, until cheese melts.

• Melt remaining 2 tablespoons butter in a small skillet; add mushrooms, and sauté until tender. Add to cheese sauce.

• Remove from heat, and stir in shrimp and hot cooked pasta.

• Spoon mixture into an 11- x 7-inch baking dish. Sprinkle with Parmesan cheese and almonds.

• Broil 6 minutes or until lightly browned.

Serves 6.

Broccoli and Shrimp Mornay

1 pound broccoli

¼ cup butter

5 tablespoons all-purpose flour

2 cups milk

1 cup (4 ounces) shredded Swiss or mozzarella cheese

2 tablespoons vermouth

Salt

Pepper

⅛ teaspoon ground nutmeg

1 pound peeled medium-size cooked shrimp – *barely cooked*

Grated Parmesan cheese

⅛ teaspoon paprika

• Preheat oven to 400°.

• Arrange broccoli in a steamer basket over boiling water. Cover and steam 15 to 20 minutes or until tender.

• Melt butter in a skillet over medium heat; add flour, stirring until smooth.

• Heat milk in a separate skillet over medium heat; add butter mixture, and cook, stirring often, until thickened and smooth. Add Swiss cheese, and cook, stirring often, until melted. Stir in vermouth and next 3 ingredients. *or make cream sauce my way*

• Arrange broccoli and shrimp in an 11- x 7-inch baking dish. Top with cheese sauce. Sprinkle with Parmesan cheese and paprika.

• Bake at 400° for 10 to 20 minutes.

Serves 6.

Stuffed Salmon

1 pound fresh spinach

1 teaspoon olive oil

1 cup cream cheese

½ cup freshly grated Parmesan cheese

8 salmon tails, split and skinned

Salt

Pepper

• Preheat oven to 350°.

• Sauté spinach in hot oil in a skillet until wilted. Stir in cheeses.

• Spoon mixture evenly into salmon tails. Season with salt and pepper.

• Bake in a lightly greased 13- x 9-inch baking dish at 350° for 10 to 15 minutes or until done (do not overcook).

Serves 8.

Curried Shrimp Over Green Rice

1 cup uncooked rice

2 large eggs, well beaten

1 cup milk

¼ cup butter

¼ cup (1 ounce) shredded sharp Cheddar cheese

½ tablespoon grated onion

⅓ cup minced fresh parsley

⅔ cup minced fresh spinach

1 teaspoon Worcestershire sauce

1¼ teaspoons salt

6 tablespoons butter

6 tablespoons all-purpose flour

1 teaspoon salt

½ teaspoon ground white pepper

2 teaspoons curry powder

3 cups milk

Juice of 2 lemons

1½ pounds unpeeled medium-size fresh shrimp, peeled and deveined

• Preheat oven to 325°.

• Prepare rice according to package directions in a large saucepan. Stir in eggs and next 8 ingredients; pour into a greased and floured 8-inch baking dish.

• Bake at 325° for 45 minutes.

• Melt 6 tablespoons butter in a heavy saucepan over low heat; add flour and next 3 ingredients, stirring until smooth. Cook, stirring constantly, until bubbly.

• Stir in milk; bring to a boil, stirring constantly. Cook until thickened. Stir in lemon juice and shrimp just before serving. Cook until shrimp turn pink.

• Serve over rice mixture.

Serves 6.

Both the shrimp and the rice are absolutely wonderful on their own, and the combination is terrific. The rice can be prepared ahead.

Louisiana Baked Shrimp

¾ pound uncooked medium-size fresh shrimp, peeled and deveined

1 teaspoon chili powder

⅛ teaspoon ground red pepper

2 teaspoons Worcestershire sauce

¼ teaspoon salt

3 tablespoons unsalted butter

1 teaspoon freshly ground black pepper

1 teaspoon minced garlic

2 teaspoons red wine

• Preheat oven to 400°.

• Arrange shrimp in a single layer in a baking pan.

• Bring chili powder and next 7 ingredients to a boil in a small saucepan; pour over shrimp.

• Bake at 400° for 8 to 10 minutes.

Serves 2.

Serve with crusty French bread and plenty of napkins.

Frogmore Stew

1 large onion, chopped

1 large bell pepper, chopped

3 celery ribs, chopped

2 tablespoons Old Bay seasoning

1 lemon, quartered

Salt

Pepper

6 (6-inch) Polish sausage links, cut into 1½-inch pieces

6 ears of corn, halved

3 pounds uncooked, unpeeled medium-size fresh shrimp

• Bring enough water to cover all ingredients to a boil in a large Dutch oven; add first 7 ingredients. Add sausage, and boil 10 minutes.

• Add corn, and boil 5 to 10 minutes. Add shrimp, and boil 2 minutes or until shrimp turn pink.

• Remove from heat; cover and let stand at room temperature 4 to 5 minutes.

• Drain and serve immediately.

Serves 6.

This stew makes a great meal for a crowd. Recipe may be doubled—use ½ pound shrimp, 1 ear of corn, and 1 sausage link per person. Asparagus may be added after corn, if desired. McCormick Crab and Shrimp Boil may be substituted for Old Bay seasoning, if desired.

Seafood Paella

32 unpeeled medium-size
    fresh shrimp

1 bay leaf

1 medium onion, grated

2 garlic cloves, pressed

¼ pound fresh button
    mushrooms

¼ pound fresh wild
    mushrooms

¼ cup olive oil

2 (5-ounce) packages
    saffron rice mix

2⅓ cups chicken broth

8 (4 to 6 ounce) rock
    lobster tails

40 littleneck clams in shells

40 sea scallops

½ cup frozen peas

40 asparagus spears

Garnish: fresh parsley
    sprigs

- Boil shrimp and bay leaf in water to cover until shrimp turn pink. Drain, reserving 1 cup cooking liquid. Remove and discard bay leaf.

- Sauté onion and next 3 ingredients in hot oil in a large heavy skillet or a paella pan until tender.

- Transfer mixture to a plate. Add reserved 1 cup cooking liquid, rice mix, and broth to skillet; bring to a boil. Add lobster, underside down.

- Cover, reduce heat, and simmer 10 minutes. Add clams; cover and simmer 10 minutes.

- Add mushroom mixture, scallops, peas, and asparagus to rice mixture; turn lobster tails. Cover and simmer 8 minutes.

- Add shrimp, and simmer 2 minutes or until all liquid is absorbed. (Make sure clam shells are open and lobster shells are pink.)

- Garnish, if desired.

Serves 8.

If you prefer "turf" paella, use chunks of beef, pork, chicken, and lamb. When preparing, you may need to place the pan on two stove eyes because a traditional paella pan is too large for one.

Shrimp, Sausage, and Grits

1½ pounds Italian sausage

2 tablespoons unsalted butter

1½ pounds unpeeled medium-size fresh shrimp, peeled and deveined

Tasso Gravy

¼ cup whipping cream

Creamy Grits

¼ cup chopped fresh parsley

- Preheat oven to 350°.

- Prick sausage several times with a fork.

- Bake on a rack in a broiler pan at 350° for 10 minutes on each side. Remove from oven.

- Melt butter in a large skillet; add shrimp, and sauté 3 to 5 minutes or until pink. Add sausage and 2½ cups Tasso Gravy to skillet. Cook over medium heat 1 to 2 minutes.

- Stir in whipping cream, and cook until thoroughly heated. Thin with water or chicken broth, if necessary.

- Spoon Creamy Grits evenly into individual shallow bowls. Spoon shrimp-sausage mixture evenly over grits.

- Sprinkle with parsley, and serve with remaining Tasso Gravy.

Tasso Gravy

¼ cup butter or margarine

½ cup all-purpose flour

3 (10½-ounce) cans condensed chicken broth, undiluted

3 ounces tasso, chopped

- Melt butter in a heavy saucepan over low heat; add flour, stirring until smooth. Cook over low heat, stirring constantly, 3 to 5 minutes or until lightly browned.

- Gradually whisk in broth, and cook, whisking constantly, until thickened. Bring to a boil.

- Reduce heat, and simmer, stirring occasionally, 10 to 15 minutes.

- Stir in tasso.

3¾ cups.

Shrimp, Sausage, and Grits continued

Creamy Grits

6 (10½-ounce) cans
condensed chicken
broth, undiluted

2½ cups uncooked regular
grits

1 cup whipping cream

½ teaspoon ground white
pepper

- Bring broth to a boil in a large heavy Dutch oven; add grits, stirring constantly.
- Bring mixture to a boil. Cover, reduce heat, and simmer, stirring frequently, 25 minutes or until grits are soft.
- Stir in whipping cream and white pepper. Cook over low heat, stirring frequently, 20 minutes.

10 cups.

Serves 8.

Country ham or low-fat sausage may be substituted for tasso, if desired.

Tarragon Shrimp

1 teaspoon chopped fresh
tarragon

¾ cup mayonnaise

Ground red pepper

1 (14-ounce) can artichoke
hearts, drained and
chopped

¼ cup grated Parmesan
cheese

Salt

2 pounds unpeeled extra-
large fresh shrimp

- Combine first 6 ingredients; cover and chill overnight.
- Boil shrimp in water to cover until shrimp turn pink. Peel shrimp, leaving tails intact. Chill.
- Bake tarragon mixture in a baking dish at 400° for 10 minutes or until warm.
- Place a dollop of tarragon mixture on each shrimp stomach (with tail up in the air).

Serves 4.

This dish makes a lovely display. If extra large shrimp are not available, use medium-size shrimp. Place the tarragon mixture in a baking dish and add whole or chopped shrimp. Bake at 400° until bubbly and thoroughly heated. Serve with crackers or fresh vegetables. Add 2 teaspoons sherry and 1 cup sautéed sliced mushrooms or chopped purple onion, if desired.

Scallops Provençal

½ teaspoon sweet red pepper flakes

1½ teaspoons paprika

1 teaspoon dried basil

¾ teaspoon ground white pepper

¾ teaspoon dry mustard

½ teaspoon garlic powder

½ teaspoon dried thyme

½ teaspoon dried oregano

½ teaspoon ground black pepper

½ teaspoon ground savory

3 tablespoons unsalted butter, divided

¼ cup olive oil, divided

1 cup chopped onion

1 teaspoon minced garlic

1 cup chicken stock

1½ cans crushed Italian plum tomatoes

4 tablespoons minced garlic

⅔ cup chopped shallots

1½ pounds sea scallops

Hot cooked rice or linguine

- Combine first 10 ingredients.

- Heat 1 tablespoon butter and 2 tablespoons oil in a large heavy skillet over medium heat; add onion and 1 teaspoon garlic, and sauté 2 to 3 minutes. Add 3 tablespoons spice mixture to skillet, reserving remaining spice mixture for another use.

- Stir in chicken stock and tomatoes. Cover, reduce heat, and simmer 8 to 10 minutes.

- Heat remaining 2 tablespoons butter and 2 tablespoons oil in a medium-size heavy skillet over medium heat; add 4 tablespoons garlic and shallots, and sauté 2 to 3 minutes. Add scallops, and cook, stirring constantly, 3 minutes or until scallops are opaque (do not overcook).

- Add scallop mixture to tomato sauce, stirring gently.

- Season to taste. Serve over hot cooked rice or linguine.

Serves 4.

Every man should eat and drink, and enjoy the good of all his labour; it is the gift of God.
—Ecclesiastes 3:13

Skewered Scallops

1 pound sea scallops, rinsed in cold water and patted dry

½ cup vegetable oil

¼ cup vinegar

1 teaspoon sugar

1 teaspoon salt

¼ cup chopped fresh or ½ teaspoon dried basil

¼ teaspoon paprika

⅛ teaspoon pepper

2 tablespoons chili sauce

1 teaspoon prepared mustard

1 garlic clove, minced

2 large limes, each cut into 6 wedges

- Combine first 11 ingredients in a bowl; cover and chill at least 3 hours.

- Remove scallops from marinade, reserving marinade. Alternate lime wedges and scallops on skewers.

- Grill, covered with grill lid, over medium-high heat (350° to 400°) 10 minutes, turning often and basting with marinade.

- Serve immediately.

Serves 2.

Salmon Steaks with Sauce Choron

2 (1¼-inch-thick) center-cut salmon steaks

Juice of 1½ lemons, divided

Salt

Pepper

¼ cup white wine vinegar

2½ tablespoons minced shallots or onion

2 tablespoons minced fresh tarragon, divided

2 egg yolks

2 tablespoons water

1 stick unsalted butter, cut up

1 small tomato, peeled, seeded, and finely chopped

1 tablespoon minced fresh parsley

• Place salmon in a broiler pan; squeeze juice of ½ a lemon over fish. Season with salt and pepper.

• Combine vinegar, shallots, and 1 tablespoon tarragon in the top of a double boiler.

• Bring water to a boil over medium heat; cook until liquid evaporates but shallots and tarragon are still moist. Remove from heat, and let cool.

• Add egg yolks and 2 tablespoons water to a saucepan, and cook, whisking constantly, over simmering water. Whisk in juice of ½ a lemon, butter, and chopped tomato.

• Cook over low heat, whisking constantly, 5 minutes or until thickened. Season with salt and pepper.

• Stir in remaining 1 tablespoon tarragon and parsley. Keep sauce warm.

• Broil fish 4 inches from heat 5 minutes. Turn and squeeze remaining ½ of lemon over fish.

• Broil 5 more minutes or until done.

• Spoon sauce onto a heated serving plate, and top with salmon.

• Serve immediately.

Serves 2.

Think about it: There's a <u>chance</u> that your teenager will talk with you—if the family is together at the table.

"Oven-Smoked" Salmon

1¼ pounds salmon fillets

Olive oil (optional)

Lemon pepper

Old Bay seasoning

Dried salad herbs

Liquid Smoke

- Preheat oven to 425°.

- Wash and dry fillets; place, skin side down, on paper towels. Brush with oil, if desired, and sprinkle with seasonings.

- Fill a baking pan one-third to one-half full with water, and add 5 to 10 drops Liquid Smoke.

- Place fillets, skin side down, on a rack over the pan.

- Bake at 425° for 25 minutes.

Serves 2.

Serve this wonderful fish with shredded cucumbers and sour cream. The moist cooking process guarantees the fish will be succulent and not overcooked. Be careful removing the pan from the oven so you don't spill the hot water. Be sure not to use a broiling pan. The salmon cooks better on a rack over the water.

Grilled Trout with Caper Sauce

3 tablespoons butter

3 tablespoons all-purpose flour

¾ cup hot water

¾ cup hot beer

½ teaspoon salt

½ cup capers

2 tablespoons chopped fresh parsley

2 tablespoons lime juice

6 (1-pound) pieces rainbow or brook trout, split

- Melt butter in a saucepan over medium heat; add flour, stirring until smooth. Gradually whisk in ¾ cup hot water and beer; cook, whisking constantly, until thickened and smooth.

- Stir in salt and next 3 ingredients; keep warm.

- Grill fish, covered with grill lid, over medium heat (300° to 350°) 10 to 12 minutes or until flaky.

- Serve immediately with sauce.

Serves 6.

Salmon in Pastry

1 (17¼-ounce) package puff
   pastry sheets

8 (1-inch-thick) salmon
   fillets (with skin), cut
   into 2-inch squares

2 large eggs, lightly beaten

Béarnaise Sauce

Lemons

- Preheat oven to 350°.

- Roll out pastry sheets to ⅛-inch thickness. Cut each sheet into 4 squares.

- Place 1 salmon fillet, skin side up, on each pastry square. Fold pastry around fillets; brush edges with egg, and seal.

- Place, seam side down, on a baking sheet, and brush with egg.

- Bake at 350° for 30 minutes or until golden brown.

- Place two portions on each serving plate, and top with Béarnaise Sauce.

- Serve immediately with lemons on the side.

Béarnaise Sauce

4 egg yolks

Juice of 1 lemon

2 cups butter, melted

Salt

Pepper

4 tablespoons capers

¼ cup chopped fresh
   parsley

1 tablespoon dried dillweed

1 tablespoon tarragon
   vinegar

- Combine egg yolks and lemon juice in the top of a double boiler, beating with a wooden spoon. Cook over low heat (do not boil water).

- Gradually add butter, stirring constantly with a wooden spoon. Add salt and next 5 ingredients, stirring well.

Serves 4.

Poached Salmon with Dilled Sour Cream

1½ pounds fresh or frozen salmon fillets, thawed and skinned

⅛ teaspoon coarsely ground white pepper

⅔ cup dry white wine

⅓ cup water

1 teaspoon coriander seeds

3 star anise or ½ teaspoon anise seeds

½ lemon, cut into thick slices

1 large cucumber, peeled

1 head Bibb or Boston lettuce

Dilled Sour Cream

Garnish: fresh dill sprigs, cucumber slices

- Cut fish into 4 portions, and measure thickness. Sprinkle with white pepper.

- Bring wine and next 4 ingredients to a boil in a large skillet.

- Reduce heat, and add fish. Cover and simmer 4 to 6 minutes per ½-inch thickness or until fish flakes when tested with a fork.

- Remove fish using a slotted spatula; discard pan juices. Cover and chill several hours or overnight.

- Peel cucumber lengthwise into wide, paper-thin slices using a vegetable peeler. Wrap fish in cucumber slices, and serve on lettuce-lined plates.

- Spoon Dilled Sour Cream over each serving. Garnish, if desired.

Dilled Sour Cream

½ cup light sour cream

1 tablespoon chopped fresh dill

1 tablespoon lime juice

Salt

Pepper

- Combine all ingredients in a small bowl. Chill.

Serves 4.

Easier to fix than it looks, this elegant dish can be made the evening before and kept chilled.

Fine Fish

Once upon a time, fixing dinner for friends meant health concerns were ignored. Today, entertaining virtually demands taking your guests' health and nutrition into consideration. Fish fills the light dining bill easily. As the nouveau party dish, it's quick to prepare, low in saturated fat, and tastefully satisfying.

Roasted Fish Fillets on a Bed of Spinach

4 (6-ounce) skinned
flounder or snapper
fillets

1½ tablespoons fresh lemon
juice

4 to 5 tablespoons Dijon
mustard

8 tablespoons minced fresh
or 2 tablespoons dried
dillweed

2 (10-ounce) packages fresh
spinach, trimmed,
washed, and patted dry

1 to 2 garlic cloves, minced

1½ teaspoons olive oil

1 lemon, quartered
lengthwise

- Preheat oven to 450°.

- Arrange fish in a 13- x 9-inch baking dish
coated with vegetable cooking spray. Sprinkle
with lemon juice. Spread 1 tablespoon mustard
over each fillet. Sprinkle with 7 tablespoons
fresh (1½ tablespoons dried) dill.

- Bake at 450° for 10 minutes or until done.

- Sauté spinach and garlic in hot oil in a large
nonstick skillet 3 minutes or until spinach is
wilted.

- Transfer mixture to a serving platter using tongs
and discarding pan juices.

- Serve fish on bed of spinach. Top with remaining dill and lemon quarters.

Serves 4.

Red Clam Sauce

1 (6½-ounce) can minced clams

2 to 3 garlic cloves, minced

¼ cup olive oil

½ cup red wine

1 (16-ounce) can stewed tomatoes

Salt

Pepper

- Drain clams, reserving clam juice.

- Sauté garlic in hot oil in a skillet for 1 minute. Add reserved clam juice and wine; reduce heat, and simmer 5 minutes.

- Add clams, tomatoes, salt, and pepper. Simmer 15 to 20 minutes.

Serves 2.

Serve this savory sauce over angel hair or vermicelli pasta.

Lemon-Soy Swordfish

⅓ cup soy sauce

1 teaspoon grated lemon rind

¼ cup fresh lemon juice

1 garlic clove, crushed

2 teaspoons Dijon mustard

½ cup olive oil

8 small swordfish steaks

Garnish: lemon wedges, fresh parsley sprigs

- Whisk together first 6 ingredients.

- Place fish in a 13- x 9-inch baking dish, and top with soy sauce mixture, pricking fish with a fork. Cover and chill, turning occasionally, 1 to 3 hours.

- Broil fish in marinade 5 to 6 minutes on each side or until done. Garnish, if desired.

Serves 8.

Four large swordfish steaks, halved, may also be used in this recipe. Fish may also be grilled. Remove from marinade, reserving marinade. Grill, covered with grill lid, over medium-high heat (350° to 400°) 4 to 5 minutes on each side or until done, basting with reserved marinade. Grilling the fish brings out a better flavor. Tuna may be substituted for swordfish.

Cook all fish 10 minutes per inch of thickness, measured at its thickest point. Your fish will be moist and not overcooked.

Holiday Hot Panned Oysters

¼ pound butter

1 quart fresh Select oysters, drained

¼ cup finely chopped celery

3 ounces Worcestershire sauce

20 dashes of hot sauce

Salt

Pepper

¼ pound saltine crackers, crumbled

Paprika

- Preheat oven to 250°.

- Melt butter in a shallow ovenproof baking dish in a 250° oven; layer half each of oysters and next 6 ingredients.

- Repeat layers, and sprinkle with paprika.

- Bake at 250° for 1 hour.

Serves 6.

Do not stir this dish while baking.

Oysters and Spinach

1 (10-ounce) package frozen chopped spinach

2 tablespoons corn oil margarine

1 small onion, chopped

2¼ tablespoons all-purpose flour

⅓ cup oyster liquor

⅔ cup half-and-half or milk

¼ teaspoon ground nutmeg

1 pint fresh oysters

½ cup fine, dry breadcrumbs

Butter or margarine, cut up

- Preheat oven to 400°.

- Cook spinach according to package directions; drain.

- Melt margarine in a skillet over medium heat; add onion, and sauté until tender. Sprinkle with flour. Add oyster liquor and half-and-half; cook, stirring, until bubbly.

- Stir in nutmeg, and gently fold in oysters. Reduce heat, and simmer until oyster edges curl.

- Place spinach in the bottom of a 1½-quart baking dish lightly coated with vegetable cooking spray; top with oyster mixture. Sprinkle with breadcrumbs, and dot with butter.

- Bake at 400° for 15 minutes.

- Turn oven off, and leave in oven for 10 to 15 minutes.

Serves 2.

Carolina Crab Cakes with Basil Tartar Sauce

1 large egg, lightly beaten

1 egg yolk, lightly beaten

4½ teaspoons half-and-half

1 teaspoon lemon juice

½ teaspoon ground red pepper

½ teaspoon dry mustard

¼ teaspoon Worcestershire sauce

¼ teaspoon ground black pepper

2 tablespoons chopped green onions

2 tablespoons chopped fresh parsley

1 pound fresh crabmeat

2 tablespoons round buttery cracker crumbs

¼ to ½ cup round buttery cracker crumbs

2 tablespoons butter, melted

Basil Tartar Sauce

- Preheat oven to 475°.

- Combine first 10 ingredients.

- Drain and flake crabmeat, removing any bits of shell. Add crabmeat and 2 tablespoons cracker crumbs to egg mixture, stirring well. (Mixture will be crumbly.)

- Divide mixture into 8 portions, and shape into patties.

- Sprinkle both sides of patties with ¼ cup cracker crumbs, and place on a greased baking sheet. Drizzle with melted butter; cover and chill until ready to cook.

- Bake on the highest oven rack at 475° for 10 minutes or until lightly browned.

- Serve with Basil Tartar Sauce.

Could serve in hot rolls w/ tom. & lettuce

Basil Tartar Sauce

½ cup firmly packed fresh basil leaves

½ cup mayonnaise

1 tablespoon sour cream

1 teaspoon lemon juice

½ teaspoon minced garlic

⅛ teaspoon salt

Ground red pepper

Dash of hot sauce

- Rinse basil in hot water, and pat dry.

- Process basil and remaining ingredients in a food processor or blender until well blended. Chill.

Serves 8.

Fried Soft-shell Crabs

2 large eggs

1 teaspoon freshly ground
black pepper, divided

4 large soft-shell crabs,
cleaned

½ cup cornmeal

½ cup all-purpose flour

½ teaspoon baking powder

½ teaspoon salt

1 tablespoon garlic powder

1 teaspoon Old Bay
seasoning

½ teaspoon freshly ground
red pepper

Canola oil

- Whisk together eggs and ½ teaspoon black
pepper in a bowl; add crabs, turning to coat. Let
stand at room temperature 10 minutes.

- Combine cornmeal, remaining ½ teaspoon
black pepper, flour, and next 5 ingredients in a
zip-top plastic bag.

- Remove crabs from egg mixture, discarding egg
mixture. Add crabs to flour mixture; seal and
shake to coat.

- Let stand at room temperature 5 minutes.

- Sauté crabs in hot oil 1 layer deep in a large
skillet over medium heat, 2 minutes on each
side, or until golden and firm. Drain on paper
towels.

Serves 2 to 4.

BACK TO THE TABLE
Vegetables & Side Dishes

Sloan Bridger

Eat your vegetables

"You're going to sit there at that table until you eat ALL your vegetables!"

At best, this is the signal of major childhood confrontation. At worst, it is a moment of truth.

These few simple words have led countless otherwise sane, rational, caring, health-conscious adults to shun cauliflower, artichokes, asparagus, green beans, limas, squash, and stewed tomatoes because they were, at least once, forced, almost at gun point, to eat them. Unyielding offenders were condemned to the purgatory of sitting at the table, alone, staring at a stone-cold vegetable while friends and siblings played just outside.

Sometimes, indignity would be heaped on outrage when mom would stroll by and inquire, "Would you like me to heat those up for you? They're ever so much better that way." Bowed by unrelenting pressure, we would eventually succumb. NO WONDER vegetables get a bum rap.

Now, vegetables very seldom play a starring role at dinnertime. That's usually reserved for the chicken marsala. Or a brilliant soufflé. Or a parfait to die for. When was the last time you raced to La Cirque to order haricots verts or choufleur au chasseur or tomates et fromage vinaigrettes? Or to some country diner for their collards? Or to a chic neighborhood bistro to wolf down a captivating petits pois aux onions?

But where would the star be without a supporting cast? Why do they place diamonds on black velvet? Why are there three rings in a circus? Why is there only one Himalaya at the county fair, surrounded by a host of tilt-a-whirls? Where would the bangers be without the mash? Or the franks without the beans? Or the burger without the fries?

Vegetables and other "sides" may not be the reason we remember a meal. But like parts of a symphony, they add immeasurably to the experience. Imagine a Sousa march played without a brass section. Or Wagner without a chorus. Or Vivaldi without strings.

From truffles to parsleyed red potatoes, we salute the unsung culinary heroes that can, and most times do, make the meal. The vegetables.

Oh, and remember, eat yours before they get cold.

Applesauce with Pears and Grand Marnier

2 tablespoons water

Juice of ½ lemon

6 McIntosh apples, peeled and chopped into 1-inch pieces

6 pears, peeled and chopped into 1-inch pieces

¾ cup firmly packed brown sugar

2 to 3 tablespoons Grand Marnier

• Cook first 4 ingredients, covered, in a large saucepan over medium heat, stirring often, for 20 minutes. Stir in brown sugar and Grand Marnier.

• Cover and cook, stirring often, for 10 more minutes.

Serves 8.

Baked Apple and Cranberry Crisp

2 cups fresh cranberries

3 cups apples, peeled and diced

1 cup granulated sugar

1¾ cups uncooked quick-cooking oats

½ cup firmly packed brown sugar

½ cup butter, melted

¾ cup pecans

• Preheat oven to 350°.

• Combine first 3 ingredients, and spoon into a greased 13- x 9-inch baking dish.

• Combine oats and next 3 ingredients; sprinkle over apple mixture.

• Bake at 350° for 1 hour.

Serves 10.

This is a wonderful addition to the Thanksgiving or Christmas table. It also goes well with Eastern North Carolina Barbecue at a picnic.

Curried Bananas

1 tablespoon unsalted
  butter

1 tablespoon curry powder

3 bananas, cut in half
  lengthwise and then
  crosswise

- Melt butter in a saucepan over medium heat;
  add curry powder, and cook, stirring constantly,
  1 to 2 minutes or until blended.

- Add banana, and cook, stirring to coat, until hot
  but not mushy.

Serves 6.

Parsnip and Pear Puree

2 cups coarsely chopped
  parsnips (about 3 large)

2 tablespoons butter

2 Anjou pears, peeled

1 tablespoon cognac

½ cup sour cream

½ teaspoon ground allspice

Salt

Freshly ground pepper

- Bring chopped parsnips and water to cover to a
  boil in a saucepan. Cover, reduce heat, and
  simmer 15 minutes or until tender. Drain.

- Melt butter in a small skillet over medium heat;
  add pears, and sauté 5 minutes. Stir in cognac;
  cook, stirring often, for 10 minutes.

- Process parsnips and pears in a food processor
  until smooth.

- Add sour cream and next 3 ingredients; process
  until blended.

- Serve warm.

Serves 6.

*A house is no home unless
it contains food and fire
for the mind as well as for
the body.*
  —*Margaret Fuller*

Scalloped Pineapple

1 can crushed pineapple

½ cup all-purpose flour

½ cup sugar

2 cups (8 ounces) shredded mild Cheddar cheese

⅓ cup butter, cut up

- Preheat oven to 325°.

- Drain pineapple, reserving juice.

- Combine reserved juice, flour, and sugar in the top of a double boiler, stirring well; bring water to a simmer. Cook over low heat, stirring until thickened.

- Place pineapple and Cheddar cheese in a buttered 11- x 7-inch baking dish. Add sugar mixture, stirring to blend. Dot with butter.

- Bake at 325° for 30 minutes.

Serves 8.

Potatoes Grand-mere

5 pounds potatoes, unpeeled and sliced

6 cups whipping cream

6 tablespoons Dijon mustard

6 garlic cloves, minced

6 tablespoons butter

Salt

Pepper

¾ cup grated Parmesan cheese

- Preheat oven to 350°.

- Layer potato slices in a greased 9-quart baking dish.

- Bring cream and next 5 ingredients to a boil in a saucepan; pour over potatoes.

- Bake at 350° for 1 hour.

- Sprinkle cheese over mixture.

- Bake at 350° for 30 minutes longer or until tender.

Serves 10.

For a reduced-fat version, substitute half-and-half for cream and use less butter.

Potatoes and Tomatoes

2¾ pounds Yukon Gold
  potatoes, peeled and
  thinly sliced

Salt

Pepper

2½ pounds tomatoes, sliced

2 pounds onion, sliced

1½ tablespoons chopped
  fresh thyme or rosemary

5 garlic cloves, minced

1¼ cups dry white wine

¼ cup olive oil

• Preheat oven to 400°.

• Place half of potatoes in a buttered large shallow
  baking dish. Season with salt and pepper.

• Layer half each of tomato and onion over
  potato. Sprinkle with half each of thyme and
  garlic. Season with salt and pepper.

• Repeat layers once.

• Pour wine and oil over mixture.

• Bake at 400° for 1 hour and 30 minutes or until
  potatoes are tender and wine has almost
  evaporated.

• Serve hot or at room temperature.

Serves 10.

This dish is great chilled or at room
temperature the next day.

Parmesan and Garlic Potatoes

4 large potatoes, peeled and
  cubed

2 celery ribs, diced

1 small onion, chopped

½ stick butter, melted

3 tablespoons chopped
  fresh parsley

½ teaspoon salt

½ teaspoon pepper

½ teaspoon garlic powder

⅓ cup grated Parmesan
  cheese

• Preheat oven to 350°.

• Combine all ingredients, tossing well.

• Spoon into a greased 13- x 9-inch baking dish.

• Bake at 350° for 1 hour and 30 minutes.

Serves 4 to 6.

Hot Potato Spinach

3 pounds new potatoes, quartered

2 tablespoons olive oil

1 teaspoon fines herbes

2 tablespoons chopped fresh rosemary

½ teaspoon garlic salt

1 teaspoon freshly ground pepper, divided

1 (16-ounce) package bacon, cut into 1-inch pieces

¼ cup vegetable oil

¼ cup red wine vinegar

2 tablespoons sugar

½ teaspoon salt

2 garlic cloves, pressed

2 (10-ounce) packages fresh spinach

6 ounces freshly grated Parmesan cheese

- Preheat oven to 400°.

- Combine first 5 ingredients and ½ teaspoon pepper, tossing gently. Spread in a lightly greased 15- x 10-inch jellyroll pan.

- Bake at 400° for 30 to 40 minutes or until potato quarters are tender or lightly browned.

- Remove from oven, and keep warm.

- Fry bacon, in batches, in a large skillet until crisp.

- Remove bacon from skillet, reserving ¼ cup bacon drippings. Whisk into these drippings oil, next 4 ingredients, and remaining ½ teaspoon pepper.

- Cook over medium heat, whisking constantly, 3 to 4 minutes or until thoroughly heated.

- Combine spinach and Parmesan cheese; add warm dressing, tossing to coat.

- Top with potatoes and bacon. Serve immediately.

Serves 8.

Fines Herbes

A mixture of very finely chopped herbs. These herbs usually consist of chervil, chives, parsley and tarragon.

Potatoes with Gruyère Cheese

2 pounds Idaho potatoes,
   peeled and cut into
   ¼-inch-thick slices

¾ pound Gruyère cheese,
   cubed

2 cups milk

Salt

Pepper

Ground nutmeg

2 large eggs

- Preheat oven to 350°.

- Layer potato slices and cheese in a well-buttered baking dish.

- Whisk together milk and next 4 ingredients; pour over potato-cheese mixture.

- Bake at 350° for 40 minutes or until potatoes are tender.

Serves 6.

Basque Potatoes

3 pounds baking potatoes,
   peeled and quartered

6 tomatoes, quartered

5 garlic cloves, divided and
   minced

8 bacon slices, cooked and
   crumbled (optional)

2 teaspoons chopped fresh
   or ¾ teaspoon dried
   thyme

2 cups sliced mushrooms

1½ cups kalamata olives,
   pitted and sliced

Salt

Pepper

½ cup dry sherry

½ cup butter, melted

- Preheat oven to 350°.

- Layer potato and tomato alternately in a large shallow baking dish. Sprinkle with 3 minced garlic cloves, bacon, and next 5 ingredients. Pour sherry over mixture.

- Bake, covered, at 350° for 30 minutes.

- Combine remaining 2 minced garlic cloves and butter. Pour over mixture.

- Bake, uncovered, 45 to 50 more minutes or until tender.

Serves 8 to 10.

Bacon can be omitted without loss of flavor.

Cheese and Chile Potatoes

4 large baking potatoes,
scrubbed and dried

Salt

Freshly ground pepper

4 tablespoons chopped
pitted ripe olives

1 (4-ounce) can diced green
chiles

6 to 8 tablespoons heavy
cream

1/2 cup (4 ounces) shredded
sharp Cheddar cheese

Shredded sharp Cheddar
cheese

Toppings: sour cream,
pitted ripe olives

• Preheat oven to 375°.

• Cut a small deep slit in the top of each potato.

• Bake at 375° for 1 hour or until tender. Remove
from oven, and let cool.

• Cut off tops, and spoon pulp into a bowl.

• Season the potato shells with salt and pepper.

• Mash pulp, and stir in olives, chiles, and cream.
Season with salt and pepper; stir in 1/2 cup
Cheddar cheese.

• Spoon pulp mixture evenly into shells, mound-
ing slightly. Sprinkle with additional Cheddar
cheese.

• Bake at 400° until thoroughly heated and cheese
is melted.

• Serve immediately with desired toppings.

Serves 4.

Can be served with salsa on the side.

Creamy Mashed Potatoes

3 pounds red new potatoes, peeled if desired
1/2 stick butter
1/2 cup sour cream
2 ounces cream cheese
2 teaspoons salt
2 teaspoons pepper
Boil potatoes until tender. Drain. Mash with potato
masher. Beat with handheld mixer until smooth.
Add next three ingredients. Beat at medium speed
3-5 minutes. Add salt and pepper and beat an
additional minute.
Serves 6.

Duchess Sweet Potatoes

1 pound sweet potatoes,
    peeled and quartered

½ pound baking potatoes,
    peeled and quartered

2 tablespoons butter

1 large egg

1 egg yolk

Melted butter

- Preheat oven to 350°.

- Boil potatoes in water to cover 30 to 40 minutes or until tender.

- Put through a food mill into a large bowl. Add butter, egg, and yolk, beating at medium speed with a handheld mixer until smooth.

- Spoon mixture into a pastry bag fitted with a decorative tip. If mixture is too thick, thin carefully with heavy cream.

- Pipe rosettes onto a buttered baking sheet; drizzle with melted butter.

- Bake at 350° for 15 minutes. Broil 6 inches from heat several minutes or until lightly browned (do not let burn).

Serves 4.

This recipe may be prepared ahead to the point of drizzling rosettes with melted butter. Do not bake. Chill until ready to serve. Bake at 350° for 30 minutes. Broil as directed above.

Recycling

Contrary to popular belief, french fries which end up in the center console of a Volvo wagon do not reproduce. Neither do chocolate chip cookies, M&Ms, Goobers or Cheetos. Just thought you'd like to know.

Praline Sweet Potatoes

⅔ cup firmly packed brown sugar, divided

¼ cup butter or margarine

½ cup chopped pecans

½ teaspoon ground cinnamon

2 tablespoons butter or margarine, melted

⅓ cup fresh orange juice

2 to 3 tablespoons brandy

1 teaspoon salt

Pepper

1 teaspoon grated orange rind

½ teaspoon ground ginger

¼ teaspoon ground allspice

4 cups cooked sliced sweet potato

- Combine ⅓ cup brown sugar, ¼ cup melted butter, pecans, and cinnamon, mixing thoroughly.

- Combine remaining ⅓ cup brown sugar, 2 tablespoons melted butter, and next 7 ingredients, stirring well.

- Place sweet potato in a 13- x 9-inch baking dish; pour orange juice mixture over top. Sprinkle with pecan mixture.

- Bake at 350° for 30 minutes.

Serves 8.

Bourbon Sweet Potatoes

2 quarts cooked sweet potatoes

1 stick butter or margarine

1 cup firmly packed brown sugar

1 teaspoon apple pie spice

¼ cup bourbon

¼ cup evaporated milk

Marshmallows (optional)

- Preheat oven to 350°.

- Beat sweet potatoes and butter at medium speed with an electric mixer until smooth.

- Cook potato mixture, brown sugar, and next 3 ingredients in a heavy pan over medium heat until thoroughly heated.

- Beat at medium speed with a handheld mixer until smooth.

- Bake mixture in a 13- x 9-inch baking dish at 350° until thoroughly heated.

- Top with marshmallows, if desired, and bake until melted.

Serves 12.

Brown Rice with Pecans

½ cup butter

1 (8-ounce) package fresh
  mushrooms, sliced

2 green onions, thinly sliced

1 garlic clove, minced

1 cup uncooked brown rice

¼ teaspoon dried marjoram

⅛ teaspoon pepper

3 cups chicken stock

¾ cup chopped pecans

Garnish: thinly sliced green
  onions

• Preheat oven to 400°.

• Melt butter in an ovenproof skillet over medium
  heat; add mushrooms, green onions, and garlic,
  and sauté 5 minutes. Stir in rice, and sauté 2 to
  3 minutes.

• Stir in marjoram, pepper, and chicken stock.
  Bring to a boil.

• Bake, covered, at 400° for 1 hour or until water
  is absorbed.

• Remove from oven, and stir in pecans. Garnish,
  if desired.

Serves 4.

Curried Rice

2½ tablespoons butter,
  divided

3 tablespoons minced onion

1 cup uncooked rice

1 tablespoon curry powder

1½ cups chicken broth

½ bay leaf

• Preheat oven to 400°.

• Melt 1 tablespoon butter in a heavy ovenproof
  saucepan; add onion, and sauté until tender.

• Add rice; reduce heat, and cook, stirring
  constantly, until coated with butter. Sprinkle
  with curry powder, stirring well.

• Add broth, stirring to remove rice lumps. Add
  bay leaf.

• Bake, covered, at 400° for 17 minutes. Remove
  and discard bay leaf.

• Stir in remaining butter, using a fork.

• Keep covered until ready to serve.

Serves 4.

Fried Rice

½ pound bacon

1 celery stalk, chopped

1 small onion, chopped

1 can bean sprouts, drained
(optional)

1 can water chestnuts,
drained and chopped
(optional)

1 large egg

1 cup uncooked rice, cooked

Soy sauce

- Fry bacon in a skillet until crisp.

- Remove bacon from skillet, reserving a small
amount of bacon drippings in skillet. Chop
bacon.

- Sauté celery and onion in bacon drippings until
tender. Return bacon to skillet. Stir in sprouts
and water chestnuts, if desired.

- Scramble egg, and add to vegetable mixture.

- Stir in cooked rice and soy sauce, mixing well.

Serves 4.

Herb Wild Rice

¼ cup butter or margarine

1 (8-ounce) package fresh
mushrooms, minced

¼ cup minced onion

½ cup minced celery

¼ cup minced prosciutto

½ cup uncooked wild rice,
rinsed

½ teaspoon dried marjoram

½ teaspoon dried sage,
crushed

½ teaspoon dried thyme

½ teaspoon dried rosemary

⅛ teaspoon pepper

1 (14-ounce) can chicken
broth

¼ cup uncooked white rice

- Melt butter in a heavy saucepan over medium
heat; add mushrooms, onion, and celery, and
sauté until liquid is evaporated about 8 minutes.

- Add prosciutto, and cook 1 minute. Add wild
rice and next 4 ingredients, and cook 1 minute.

- Stir in pepper and broth, and bring to a boil.

- Reduce heat, and simmer for 30 minutes. Add
white rice, and simmer 20 minutes more or
until liquid is absorbed.

Serves 6.

Lemon Rice with Almonds

1 tablespoon butter

⅓ cup minced onion

1 cup uncooked rice

1¾ cups chicken broth

¼ cup lemon juice

Grated rind of 1 lemon

¼ cup slivered almonds, lightly toasted

- Melt butter in a skillet over medium heat; add onion, and sauté until tender. Add rice, stirring to coat.

- Add broth, lemon juice, and rind; bring to a boil.

- Cover, reduce heat, and simmer 20 minutes.

- Stir in almonds.

Serves 4.

This recipe is so simple yet so flavorful. It proves that recipes don't have to be complicated to be good!

Hoppin' John

6 to 8 bacon slices, diced

1 medium onion, chopped

1 cup sliced celery

¼ teaspoon dried thyme, crushed

2 (15½-ounce) cans black-eyed peas

3 cups water

1 cup uncooked white rice

2 tablespoons chopped fresh parsley

1 teaspoon salt

¼ teaspoon dried crushed red pepper

- Cook first 4 ingredients in a saucepan over medium heat until onion is tender. Stir in peas and all remaining ingredients.

- Bring to a boil. Cover, reduce heat, and simmer 20 minutes or until rice is tender.

Serves 6.

Nutted Orange Rice

4 tablespoons butter

1 small onion, chopped

1 teaspoon salt

1 cup uncooked rice

1¾ cups chicken stock

¼ cup fresh orange juice

Grated rind from 1 orange

½ cup golden raisins

½ cup chopped walnuts or pecans

1 orange

¼ teaspoon dried thyme (optional)

¼ teaspoon ground cinnamon (optional)

- Melt butter in a saucepan over medium heat; add onion, and sauté until tender. Stir in salt.

- Stir in rice and next 3 ingredients, and cook 20 minutes or until rice is tender.

- Cut orange in half, reserving outer shells for serving rice; section orange.

- Combine rice mixture, orange sections, raisins, nuts, and, if desired, thyme and cinnamon, tossing well.

- Serve in reserved orange shells.

Serves 2.

Rune of Hospitality

I saw a stranger yestreen;
I put food in the eating place,
drink in the drinking place,
music in the listening place;
and in the blessed name of the Triune
he blessed myself and my house,
my cattle and my dear ones.
And the lark said in her song,
often, often, often
goes the Christ in the stranger's guise;
often, often, often
goes the Christ in the stranger's guise.
—an old Gaelic rune

Spicy Caribbean Black Beans with Rice

1 large onion, chopped

2 tablespoons olive oil

2 garlic cloves, chopped

1½ teaspoons chili powder

2 (15-ounce) cans black beans, well drained

3 cups water, divided

1 bay leaf

1 tablespoon red wine vinegar

½ teaspoon hot sauce

Sugar, 1 pinch

Salt to taste

Pepper to taste

1 cup uncooked long-grain rice

½ teaspoon ground turmeric

¾ cup chopped red onion

2 jalapeño peppers, seeded and minced

½ (7-ounce) jar roasted sweet red peppers, drained and thinly sliced

• Sauté onion in hot oil in a large heavy saucepan 5 minutes or until tender. Add garlic and chili powder, and cook, stirring constantly, 1 minute.

• Stir in beans, 1 cup water, and bay leaf. Reduce heat, and simmer 20 minutes or until reduced to soup consistency. Remove and discard bay leaf.

• Stir in vinegar and next 4 ingredients.

• Bring remaining 2 cups water to a boil in a heavy medium saucepan; stir in rice, turmeric, and salt. Cover, reduce heat, and simmer 20 minutes or until liquid is absorbed.

• Combine red onion and jalapeño in a small bowl.

• Spoon rice in the center of a serving platter. Spoon beans around rice. Arrange roasted pepper slices over beans.

• Serve with red onion relish.

Serves 6.

> *As we head into the 21st century, our lives have become fragmented and hectic. That's all the more reason why the special times we share at the dinner table should be sacred and protected.*

Onion and Leek Tart

4 tablespoons unsalted butter

4 tablespoons olive oil

6 large onions, thinly sliced

6 leeks, sliced to dark green part and rinsed

3 garlic cloves, minced

Salt

Pepper

1 cup heavy cream

1 cup milk

4 large eggs

1 to 2 (15-ounce) packages refrigerated piecrusts

1 tablespoon herbes de Provence or mixture of dried basil, thyme, and oregano

1 cup freshly grated Gruyère or Parmesan cheese

- Preheat oven to 350°.

- Melt butter and oil in a large Dutch oven over medium heat; add onion, and sauté 10 minutes. Add leeks and garlic, and sauté until crisp-tender.

- Season with salt and pepper. Remove from heat.

- Combine cream and milk in large bowl; whisk in eggs, and season with salt and pepper.

- Fit piecrusts into 2 to 4 tart pans, depending on pan size, according to package directions. Trim edges, and crimp. Prick bottom with a fork.

- Bake at 350° for 10 minutes.

- Spoon leek mixture evenly into prepared tart pans; add enough milk mixture to moisten (do not overdo). Sprinkle with cheese and herbes de Provence.

- Bake at 400° for 30 to 40 minutes or until lightly browned and set. Remove from oven.

- Release from tart pan, and slide tarts onto serving plates.

- Slice into wedges. Serve warm.

To clean a leek:

- *Trim the root end and the dark green leaves. The remaining leaves should be white or light green in color.*

- *Halve the stalk lengthwise.*

- *Rinse well under cold water, making sure all sand is removed from between the leaves.*

- *Pat dry.*

Serves 10.

The onions really cook down, so don't scrimp. Sautéed sliced portobello mushrooms and sliced red bell pepper are both nice additions. Add sautéed wild mushrooms to tart before pouring on cream mixture. This tart is a great made-ahead side dish for company when grilling meat. It freezes well. Do not cook before freezing, and let thaw completely before baking.

Vidalia Onion Pie

1 stick butter

4 medium Vidalia onions, thinly sliced

3 large eggs

¼ teaspoon salt

½ teaspoon pepper

Dash of hot sauce

1 cup sour cream

Shredded Swiss cheese

Grated Parmesan cheese

1 unbaked 9-inch pastry shell

- Preheat oven to 450°.

- Melt butter in a skillet over medium heat; add onion, and sauté until tender. Remove from heat.

- Whisk together eggs and next 4 ingredients; add onion, stirring well.

- Spoon mixture into pastry shell, and top with cheeses.

- Bake at 450° for 10 minutes.

- Reduce oven temperature to 325°, and bake 20 minutes.

Serves 6.

Storing Vidalias

True Vidalia onion afficionados learned a while back that the secret to keeping these delectable vegetables fresh and tasty is as close as your lingerie drawer. Tie onions one at a time in the legs of an old pair of panty hose, separated by knots. Hang the hose from a joist in the basement or, if you're not proud, out on the back porch. Looks kinky, but it works.

Western Tomato Pie

1 unbaked 9-inch deep-dish pastry shell

¼ cup all-purpose flour

½ teaspoon salt

⅛ teaspoon pepper

2 large tomatoes, cut into ½-inch-thick slices

3 to 5 tablespoons olive oil

½ cup pitted black olives, sliced

3 provolone cheese slices

2 large eggs

1 cup (4 ounces) shredded Cheddar cheese

1 cup heavy cream

1 cup minced green onions

- Bake pastry shell at 425° for 8 minutes. Remove from oven, and let cool.

- Combine flour, salt, and pepper.

- Dredge tomato slices in flour mixture, and sauté in hot oil in a skillet until lightly browned.

- Spread olives on bottom of prepared piecrust. Cover with cheese slices torn to fit. Top with tomato slices.

- Whisk together eggs, cheese, and cream, and pour over tomato.

- Bake at 375° for 40 minutes or until filling is set.

- Sprinkle green onions over top. Let stand at room temperature 5 minutes before serving.

Serves 6.

Whole milk can be substituted for cream, if desired.

Scalloped Tomatoes and Artichoke Hearts

1 stick butter

½ cup minced onion

2 tablespoons minced shallots

1 (32-ounce) can whole plum tomatoes, drained

1 (14-ounce) can artichoke hearts, drained, rinsed, and quartered

½ teaspoon dried basil

2 tablespoons sugar

Salt

Pepper

- Preheat oven to 325°.

- Melt butter in a large skillet over medium heat; add onion and shallots, and sauté until tender. Add tomatoes, artichokes, and basil.

- Cook, stirring gently, 2 to 3 minutes. Stir in sugar, salt, and pepper.

- Bake in a greased 13- x 9-inch baking dish at 325° for 10 to 15 minutes or until thoroughly heated.

Serves 6.

Basil-Tomato Tart

½ (15-ounce) package
   refrigerated piecrusts

1½ cups (6 ounces)
   shredded skim
   mozzarella cheese,
   divided

10 plum tomatoes, cut into
   wedges

1 cup loosely packed fresh
   basil

4 garlic cloves

½ cup mayonnaise

¼ cup Parmesan cheese

⅛ teaspoon ground white
   pepper

Garnish: fresh basil leaves

• Fit piecrust into a 9-inch pie plate according to package directions; fold edges under, and crimp. Prick bottom and sides of piecrust with a fork.

• Pre-bake according to package directions.

• Remove from oven, and sprinkle with ½ cup mozzarella cheese. Cool on a wire rack.

• Drain tomato wedges on paper towels, and arrange over melted mozzarella cheese.

• Process basil and garlic in a food processor until coarsely chopped. Sprinkle over tomatoes.

• Combine remaining 1 cup mozzarella cheese, mayonnaise, Parmesan cheese, and pepper; spoon over basil mixture, spreading evenly to cover.

• Bake at 375° for 35 to 40 minutes or until bubbly and golden.

• Garnish, if desired. Serve warm.

Artichokes, Tomatoes, Mushrooms au Gratin

Grated Parmesan cheese

3 large tomatoes, peeled and sliced

Pepper

¼ cup chopped fresh basil

2 teaspoons chopped fresh thyme

2 teaspoons chopped fresh oregano

1 (16-ounce) can artichoke hearts, drained and sliced

1 medium onion, thinly sliced

10 large fresh mushrooms, sliced

Tomato slices

Sliced mushrooms

2 to 3 tablespoons olive oil

3 tablespoons reduced-fat margarine, melted

1 tablespoon lemon juice

1 tablespoon wine vinegar

Toasted soft breadcrumbs

- Preheat oven to 375°.

- Sprinkle Parmesan cheese in a quiche or au gratin dish lightly coated with vegetable cooking spray. Layer 3 sliced tomatoes over cheese, and sprinkle with pepper and half each of the basil, thyme, and oregano.

- Layer artichoke hearts, onion, and 10 sliced mushrooms over tomato slices, sprinkling each layer with remaining herbs and pepper.

- Arrange additional tomato slices and sliced mushrooms in a fan on top of mixture.

- Combine oil and next 3 ingredients; pour over vegetable mixture. Sprinkle with additional cheese and toasted breadcrumbs.

- Bake at 375° for 20 to 30 minutes.

Serves 6.

> It's difficult to think anything but pleasant thoughts while eating a home-grown tomato.
> —Lewis Grizzard

Scalloped Corn and Tomatoes

¼ cup butter or margarine

1 cup thinly sliced onion

2 pounds tomatoes, peeled and chopped

2 teaspoons sugar

2 teaspoons salt

1 teaspoon dried marjoram

¼ teaspoon pepper

2 packages frozen white shoepeg corn, thawed

2 tablespoons butter or margarine, melted

2 cups soft breadcrumbs

2 teaspoons chopped fresh parsley

- Melt ¼ cup butter in a skillet over medium heat; add onion, and sauté 5 minutes or until tender. Stir in tomatoes and next 5 ingredients.

- Spoon mixture into a 2-quart baking dish.

- Combine 2 tablespoons melted butter, breadcrumbs, and parsley. Sprinkle over corn mixture.

- Bake at 350° until thoroughly heated and lightly browned.

Serves 8.

Green Corn Pudding

6 ears of young, tender corn with kernels scraped off cobs

1 tablespoon sugar

1 tablespoon cornstarch

1 teaspoon salt

2 tablespoons chopped pimiento

4 tablespoons butter, melted

1 cup milk

3 large eggs, separated

- Preheat oven to 350°.

- Combine all ingredients except eggs in a bowl.

- Beat egg yolks until light and pale; stir into corn mixture.

- Beat egg whites at high speed with an electric mixer until stiff peaks form; fold into corn mixture.

- Spoon pudding into a greased 1½-quart baking dish.

- Bake at 350° for 35 minutes.

Serves 6.

For Chicken and Corn Pudding, add 1 cup chopped poached chicken to pudding before adding eggs.

Corn Relish

2 cans white corn

1 cucumber, peeled

1 celery stalk, chopped

1 medium-size red onion, chopped

½ cup chopped green bell pepper

½ cup sour cream

3 tablespoons mayonnaise

2 teaspoons white wine vinegar

1 teaspoon Jane's Crazy Salt or seasoned salt

½ teaspoon dry mustard

½ teaspoon celery seed

½ teaspoon ground white or black pepper

• Combine all ingredients, and chill.

Serves 12.

Can be made days in advance, and chilled until ready to serve. For a festive variation, add chopped red, orange, and yellow bell pepper.

Sweet and Sour Red Cabbage

¼ cup vinegar, divided

1 teaspoon salt, divided

1 medium red cabbage, coarsely chopped

6 bacon slices, diced

¼ cup firmly packed brown sugar

2 tablespoons all-purpose flour

½ cup water

⅛ teaspoon pepper

1 onion, sliced

• Bring 2 tablespoons vinegar, ½ teaspoon salt, and enough water to cover cabbage to a boil in a Dutch oven. Add cabbage, and cook 20 to 30 minutes or until tender; drain.

• Fry bacon in a skillet until crisp; drain, reserving 1 tablespoon drippings. Stir remaining ½ teaspoon salt, brown sugar, and flour into bacon drippings.

• Add remaining 2 tablespoons vinegar, ½ cup water, pepper, and onion. Cook, stirring frequently, until mixture is thickened.

• Combine cabbage, sauce, and bacon, stirring well.

Serves 6.

Drunk Roasting Ears

4 fresh ears of corn

½ cup butter

½ teaspoon garlic powder

1 tablespoon
    Worcestershire sauce

Pepper

1 teaspoon sugar

¼ teaspoon hot sauce

Chili powder (optional)

12 ounces beer

- Prepare 4 aluminum foil boats slightly larger than ears of corn.

- Melt butter in a shallow pan; stir in garlic powder and next 4 ingredients.

- Roll corn in butter mixture, and place each ear in a foil boat. Sprinkle with chili powder, if desired.

- Place foil boats on grill, and fill each half full with beer. Cover with aluminum foil.

- Grill, covered with grill lid, over medium heat (300° to 350°) 1 hour and 30 minutes or until done, turning each ear in its boat after 45 minutes.

Serves 4.

Do not use light beer. Corn may also be baked. Place all ears in a roasting pan, and fill half full with beer. Bake, covered, at 350° for 1 hour and 30 minutes, turning corn after 45 minutes.

Squash and Tomato Medley

1 medium onion, chopped

1½ pounds yellow squash, sliced

2 medium fresh tomatoes, chopped

1 cup (4 ounces) shredded Cheddar cheese

½ teaspoon salt

⅛ teaspoon pepper

1¼ cups fine, dry breadcrumbs

1¼ cups butter, melted

- Preheat oven to 350°.

- Cook onion and squash in a small amount of water in a saucepan until tender; drain.

- Combine squash mixture, tomato, and next 3 ingredients; spoon into a greased 11- x 7-inch baking dish.

- Combine breadcrumbs and butter, and sprinkle over casserole.

- Bake at 350° for 30 minutes.

Serves 4.

If good-quality fresh tomatoes are not available, substitute 1 cup Del Monte FreshCut peeled, diced tomatoes.

Company Carrots

2 pounds peeled carrots

½ cup mayonnaise

1 tablespoon minced onion

1 tablespoon prepared
   horseradish

Salt

Pepper

¼ cup fine, dry
   breadcrumbs

2 tablespoons butter or
   margarine, cut up and
   softened

Paprika

Chopped fresh parsley

- Preheat oven to 350°.

- Boil carrots in salted water to cover until crisp-tender; drain, reserving ¼ cup cooking liquid.

- Cut carrots lengthwise, and arrange in a shallow baking dish.

- Combine reserved ¼ cup cooking liquid, mayonnaise, and next 4 ingredients; pour over carrot slices. Sprinkle with breadcrumbs; dot with butter, and sprinkle with paprika and parsley.

- Bake at 350° for 20 minutes.

Serves 6.

Peppers, Sweet and Sour

1 tablespoon butter

Olive oil

8 red, yellow, and/or green
   bell peppers, each cut
   into 4 pieces

¼ cup sugar

½ cup vinegar

Salt

Pepper

Garnish: fresh basil leaves

- Melt butter in a skillet lightly filmed with olive oil over medium heat; add bell pepper, tossing to coat. Stir in sugar, and cook until slightly caramelized.

- Stir in vinegar, salt, and pepper; cook, partially covered, 15 minutes.

- Garnish, if desired.

Serves 4.

Grilled Marinated Eggplant

⅓ cup lemon juice

3 garlic cloves

1½ cups olive oil

1 teaspoon salt

2 eggplants

- Process lemon juice and garlic in a blender; with blender running, add oil in a slow steady stream. Add salt, and process until blended.

- Cut eggplants crosswise into ¾-inch-thick slices, and score cut sides of slices ¼ inch deep.

- Combine eggplant and lemon marinade in a shallow baking dish. Cover and chill 4 hours or overnight.

- Drain eggplant, discarding marinade.

- Grill on a well-oiled rack 5 to 6 inches from coals, preferably covered with grill lid, over medium-high heat (350° to 400°) 5 minutes on each side or until tender.

Serves 4.

Parmesan and Eggplant Sticks

½ cup freshly grated Parmesan cheese

¼ cup fine, dry breadcrumbs

1 tablespoon chopped fresh parsley

¼ teaspoon salt

¼ teaspoon pepper

2 eggplants, cut into fingers

¼ cup all-purpose flour

2 large eggs, lightly beaten

2 tablespoons butter, divided

- Preheat oven to 375°.

- Combine first 5 ingredients in a shallow dish.

- Coat eggplant in flour, and dip in egg. Dredge in breadcrumb mixture.

- Melt 1 tablespoon butter in each of 2 baking pans.

- Arrange eggplant in pans, making sure fingers are not touching.

- Bake, uncovered, at 375° for 25 minutes or until done.

Serves 4.

Portobello Mushrooms Stuffed with Zucchini Gratin

4 scallions, thinly sliced

3 garlic cloves, minced

1 tablespoon olive oil, divided

1½ pounds zucchini, shredded and well drained on paper towels

3 tablespoons coarsely chopped fresh basil

Salt

Pepper

½ cup (2 ounces) shredded Monterey Jack cheese

6 large portobello mushrooms, with stems removed

2 tablespoons salt

Garnish: fresh chopped herbs

- Sauté scallions and garlic in 2 teaspoons hot oil in a large nonstick skillet until tender, adding water if necessary to keep from burning. Remove from heat.

- Stir in zucchini and basil. Season with salt and pepper. Add cheese, tossing well.

- Place mushrooms, top side up, in a broiling pan. Brush with remaining 1 teaspoon oil, and sprinkle with 2 tablespoons salt and pepper.

- Broil 2 inches from heat 4 minutes.

- Remove from heat, and turn over. Fill with zucchini mixture.

- Broil 6 more minutes or until cheese is melted.

- Garnish, if desired.

Serves 6.

The magic table

Grandma's dining room table was magic. No matter how many people showed up for dinner, the table was always full. And, to the best anyone can recollect, it never ran out of food and nobody left hungry. Think the story of the loaves and fishes sounds fishy? Talk to Grandma.

Mushroom Ratatouille

1 cup coarsely chopped onion

1 garlic clove, crushed

1 pound fresh mushrooms, trimmed

½ cup olive oil

1 (1½-pound) eggplant, cubed

3 medium zucchini, cut crosswise into ½-inch slices

2 medium-size green bell peppers, cut into 1-inch pieces

1 (28-ounce) can plum tomatoes, well drained

2 to 3 teaspoons dried basil

3 teaspoons salt

¼ teaspoon pepper

• Sauté first 3 ingredients in hot oil in a large heavy saucepan, stirring often, until tender. Stir in eggplant and all remaining ingredients.

• Bring to a boil. Cover, reduce heat, and simmer, stirring occasionally, 30 minutes or until eggplant is tender.

• Drain mixture, reserving liquid.

• Bring reserved liquid to a boil in saucepan; boil until reduced to a small amount.

• Pour over vegetables. Adjust seasonings to taste. Cover and chill. Bring to room temperature before serving.

Serves 8 to 10

This can be served as is, on toast points, or in individual pastry shells.

Hiding the peas

Every child in America has been faced with the dilemma of having to eat something they, well, didn't like. By no coincidence, these items were vegetables for the most part. But that's when the cubby-holes and crannies of the family table came in real handy. Along with the family pet—labs were always great for eating just about anything—pants cuffs, pockets and a curiously folded napkin. Hey, necessity IS the mother of invention.

Vegetable Pie

1 unbaked 9-inch deep-dish pastry shell

2 teaspoons Dijon mustard

⅓ cup butter or margarine

3½ cups thinly sliced zucchini

1 cup chopped fresh mushrooms

1 cup chopped onion

½ cup chopped fresh parsley

¼ teaspoon garlic powder

¼ teaspoon dried basil

¼ teaspoon dried oregano

½ teaspoon salt

½ teaspoon pepper

2 large eggs

2 cups (8 ounces) shredded mozzarella cheese

- Preheat oven to 375°.

- Bake pastry shell at 375° for 5 to 7 minutes or until set (do not brown).

- Brush piecrust with mustard.

- Melt butter in a skillet over medium heat; add zucchini, mushrooms, and onion, and sauté, stirring occasionally, 10 minutes or until tender. Stir in parsley and next 5 ingredients.

- Whisk together eggs and cheese; add to vegetable mixture, stirring well.

- Spoon mixture into prepared piecrust.

- Bake at 375° for 20 minutes.

- Let stand at room temperature 10 minutes before serving.

Serves 6.

Dillicious Green Beans

1¼ pounds fresh green beans, trimmed

6 tablespoons butter

2 tablespoons fresh lemon juice

1½ teaspoons dried dill weed

½ garlic clove, crushed

1 tablespoon chopped fresh parsley

10 cherry tomatoes, halved

½ cup sliced ripe olives

Salt

Pepper

- Boil green beans in salted water to cover until crisp-tender; drain.

- Melt butter in a saucepan over medium heat; add beans, lemon juice, and next 3 ingredients.

- Cook, tossing gently, over low heat until thoroughly heated. Add tomato halves and olives, tossing gently. Season with salt and pepper.

Serves 6.

Haricots Vert

1 pound young, thin green beans, trimmed and cut

1 egg yolk

½ cup Dijon mustard

½ cup red wine vinegar

2 cups olive oil

Salt

Pepper

Juice of ½ lemon

Garnish: chopped fresh parsley

- Boil green beans in salted water to cover for a few minutes; cool.

- Beat egg yolk at medium speed with a handheld mixer. Beat in mustard. Add vinegar and oil, beating until creamy.

- Season with salt and pepper. Add lemon juice to 1 cup dressing, reserving remaining dressing for another use.

- Toss beans with lemon dressing. Chill.

- Garnish, if desired.

Serves 4.

This recipe will disappoint you if mature green beans with well-developed seeds are used. Be sure to pick over the beans at your grocery to get young and tender ones.

Cherry Tomatoes and Green Beans

1 pound fresh green beans,
  cut diagonally into
  1-inch pieces

1 pint cherry tomatoes

1 teaspoon minced garlic

2 tablespoons vegetable oil

⅛ cup minced fresh Italian
  parsley

Salt

Pepper

- Boil beans in water to cover 4 minutes or until crisp-tender. Drain and rinse in cold water.

- Sauté tomatoes and garlic in hot oil in a skillet over medium-high heat until tomatoes begin to blister. Add beans, and cook until thoroughly heated.

- Add parsley, and cook, tossing, 10 seconds.

- Season with salt and pepper, and serve immediately.

Serves 6.

Green Beans with Mustard Vinaigrette

2 pounds fresh green beans,
  trimmed

1 small onion, minced

2 tablespoons Dijon
  mustard

2 tablespoons balsamic
  vinegar

½ cup olive oil

Salt

Pepper

2 teaspoons dried dill weed

- Boil green beans in water to cover 5 minutes or until crisp-tender; drain well.

- Cook onion and next 5 ingredients in a small saucepan, whisking constantly, just until thoroughly heated. Add hot green beans, tossing to coat. Add dill, tossing well.

- Serve immediately.

Serves 6.

This dish may be prepared several hours ahead. Reheat when ready to serve.

Green Bean and Yellow Bell Pepper Mélange

1½ pounds fresh green beans, trimmed

3 tablespoons unsalted butter

2 large yellow bell peppers, cut into strips

½ teaspoon dried thyme, crushed

Salt

Pepper

- Boil green beans in salted water to cover 3 to 7 minutes or until crisp-tender. Rinse with cold water; drain well.

- Melt butter in a skillet over medium heat; add bell pepper and thyme. Cook, stirring constantly, 1 minute.

- Add beans, salt, and pepper; cook, stirring constantly, until thoroughly heated.

Serves 8.

Green beans may be cooked a day ahead, wrapped in paper towels and plastic wrap, and chilled overnight.

Broccoli in Orange-Shallot Butter

3 pounds fresh broccoli, cut into bite-size flowerets

½ cup fresh orange juice

¼ cup shallots, minced

1¼ sticks unsalted butter

2 tablespoons thinly sliced orange rind

Salt

Pepper

- Boil broccoli in salted water to cover 5 minutes or until crisp-tender. Drain, and rinse in cold water; pat dry.

- Bring orange juice and shallots to a simmer in a large saucepan; cook until liquid is reduced to 2 tablespoons. Add butter and orange rind, and cook until butter is melted.

- Add broccoli, tossing to coat; cook until thoroughly heated.

- Season with salt and pepper. Serve immediately.

Serves 6.

Broccoli Dijon

1 pound fresh broccoli, cut up

2 tablespoons butter

1½ teaspoons Worcestershire sauce

1 teaspoon Dijon mustard

1 tablespoon red wine vinegar

2 tablespoons olive oil

Ground cayenne pepper

Salt

Freshly ground black pepper

• Arrange broccoli in a steamer basket over boiling water. Cover and steam 15 to 20 minutes or until tender.

• Bring butter and next 4 ingredients to a boil, stirring constantly, in a saucepan. Season with salt and black pepper.

• Pour sauce over hot broccoli, and serve immediately.

Serves 8.

Broccoli may be stir-fried in 1 tablespoon vegetable oil instead of steamed before adding sauce and serving.

Asparagus Vinaigrette

1 pound fresh asparagus

2 tablespoons tarragon vinegar

4 tablespoons cider vinegar

1 tablespoon chopped fresh parsley

1 tablespoon salt

2 tablespoons sliced green onions

2 tablespoons sugar

2 tablespoons vegetable oil

2 tablespoons Dijon mustard

• Arrange asparagus in a steamer basket over boiling water. Cover and steam 5 minutes or until crisp-tender.

• Drain and rinse with cold water. Drain again.

• Whisk together tarragon vinegar and next 7 ingredients; pour over asparagus. Chill overnight.

• Serve chilled.

Serves 6.

Asparagus Milan

1 pound fresh asparagus, trimmed

1 onion, thinly sliced

3 tablespoons chopped celery

1 large tomato, sliced

⅛ teaspoon salt

¼ teaspoon pepper

¼ teaspoon ground oregano

⅛ teaspoon ground thyme

½ cup fine, dry breadcrumbs

¼ cup grated Parmesan cheese

3 tablespoons butter, melted

- Preheat oven to 375°.

- Place asparagus in the bottom of a 13- x 9-inch baking dish. Top with onion, celery, and tomato.

- Sprinkle with salt and next 5 ingredients. Drizzle with butter.

- Bake, covered, at 375° for 45 minutes.

Serves 4.

Braised Leeks and Asparagus with Lemon

3 to 4 medium leeks

2 tablespoons butter

¼ cup chicken broth

½ to 1 pound fresh asparagus, trimmed and rinsed

1 teaspoon grated lemon rind

Salt

- Cut off and discard outer tough leaves of leeks; trim and cut leeks lengthwise into quarters or eighths. Soak in cold water to cover in a shallow dish 15 minutes.

- Drain and rinse to remove any grit. Keep in cold water until time to cook.

- Melt butter in a large saucepan over medium heat; add leeks, and sauté 5 minutes.

- Add broth, asparagus, lemon, and salt, and cook 5 more minutes.

Serves 6.

Chinese Asparagus

1 pound asparagus, cut
  diagonally into 1½-inch
  pieces

2 tablespoons light soy
  sauce

1½ teaspoons vinegar

1 teaspoon sesame oil

1 teaspoon sugar

Garlic powder

Ground ginger

- Arrange asparagus in a steamer basket over boiling water. Cover and steam 3 minutes or until crisp-tender.

- Rinse with cold water; drain and let cool.

- Whisk together soy sauce and next 5 ingredients; pour over asparagus, and chill, stirring occasionally, 20 minutes or more.

- Serve cold.

Serves 4.

This dish may be prepared several hours ahead; chill until ready to serve. It may also be served as an appetizer with wooden picks.

French Epicurean Peas

1 to 2 tablespoons butter,
  divided

1 cup sliced fresh
  mushrooms

2 (10-ounce) packages
  frozen green peas

4 bacon slices, chopped

1 tablespoon chopped onion

1 tablespoon all-purpose
  flour

½ cup half-and-half

Salt

- Melt 1 tablespoon butter in a skillet over medium heat; add mushrooms, and sauté until tender. Set aside.

- Cook peas according to package directions; drain, reserving cooking liquid.

- Fry bacon in a large skillet until crisp. Remove bacon from skillet, reserving drippings.

- Sauté onion in bacon drippings until tender. Add flour, stirring until smooth.

- Stir in reserved cooking liquid and half-and-half; cook over medium heat, stirring occasionally, until thickened. Stir in mushrooms, peas, bacon, and salt.

- Stir in remaining 1 tablespoon butter, if desired.

Serves 8.

Grilled Vegetables with Basil Mayonnaise

4 carrots

2 red onions, peeled

2 yellow squash

8 radishes

8 small ripe tomatoes

1 red bell pepper, quartered

1 yellow or green bell
   pepper, quartered

¼ pound small okra

2 heads Bibb lettuce, halved
   lengthwise

Olive oil

Basil Mayonnaise

- Boil carrots and onions in salted water to cover 5 minutes. Drain. Rinse with cold water, and pat dry.

- Boil squash in salted water to cover for 1 minute; add radishes, and cook 3 more minutes. Drain and pat dry.

- Cut onions and squash in half lengthwise.

- Brush carrots, onion, squash, radishes, tomatoes, and next 4 ingredients with oil.

- Grill in a grill basket, covered with grill lid, over medium heat (300° to 350°) 5 to 8 minutes or until tender.

- Serve vegetables with chilled Basil Mayonnaise.

Basil Mayonnaise

1 cup mayonnaise

2 teaspoons fresh lemon
   juice

⅔ cup fresh basil leaves,
   finely chopped

- Combine all ingredients.

- Cover and chill.

Serves 6.

BACK TO THE *Desserts* TABLE

Terry Fisher

An apple a day

"The best of all physicians is apple pie and cheese." Eugene Field

There are people in this world who live for sweet stuff. Whenever they sit down for a meal they invariably ask, "What's for dessert?" They always have a pocket full of Hershey's Kisses or Junior Mints.

These are people who will forever brandish the burden — or perhaps the blessing — of a "sweet tooth." They crave dark chocolate and whipped cream topped with a gooey red cherry and fudge sauce. They stash M&M's and Dove Bars behind the Healthy Choice, and dream of sundaes and lemon squares oozing buttery tanginess. They fantasize about cherry tarts and brownies and layer cakes so thick and creamy they can only be cut through with a blowtorch. They hide the Halloween candy in secret places and feast on bite-size Snickers and candy corn until Thanksgiving.

These are people who adore eclairs and wedding cake and crème brulée and fresh-baked apple cobbler, creamy pumpkin pie and warm peach turnovers or Grandma's apple pie with "just a dab, please" of vanilla ice cream to top it all off.

They're kids at heart. They have the playful soul of a puppy and not a mean bone anyplace. They're disgustingly thin and never seem to gain an ounce. They have fewer cavities than the average six year old and smile incessantly to remind the rest of the world how good life is. But most of all, they're delightfully happy, these sweet tooths, and who wouldn't be if you walked around with a sugar high most of the time?

Just think. A world where Willy Wonka is king and the concession stand selling candied apples at the State Fair is something like a shrine. And sugar rules.

These are truly the children of God, people who experience life in small, delicious bites and are exceedingly grateful for each one. Deep inside, they have a sense that the world is sweet, that people are good and sunsets are a special gift from heaven.

To these people desserts are as much a part of life as drawing a breath. This chapter is dedicated to them.

Caramel Delight Layer Cake

2 cups sugar

4 large eggs

1 cup vegetable oil

1 cup buttermilk

2½ cups unbleached all-
purpose flour

½ teaspoon salt

2¼ teaspoons baking
powder

1 teaspoon vanilla extract

Caramel Frosting

- Preheat oven to 350°.

- Beat sugar and eggs at medium speed with an electric mixer 30 seconds. Add oil and next 5 ingredients, and beat 1 minute.

- Pour batter into 2 greased and floured 9-inch round cakepans. Bake at 350° for 30 minutes or until cake pulls away from pan sides and a knife inserted in center comes out clean. Let cool in pans 5 minutes.

- Invert onto wire racks, and let cool completely, about 2 hours.

- Spread Caramel Frosting between layers and on top and sides of cake.

Caramel Frosting

3 cups firmly packed light
brown sugar

¾ cup butter

Salt

¾ cup half-and-half or
evaporated milk

1 teaspoon vanilla extract

- Cook first 4 ingredients in a saucepan over low heat, stirring until sugar is dissolved.

- Bring to a boil, stirring often; cook over medium heat, stirring constantly, until a candy thermometer registers 234° to 240° (soft ball stage). Remove from heat.

- Beat at medium speed with a handheld mixer until cool; beat in vanilla.

Serves 12 to 16.

> *Food is the most primitive form of comfort.*
> —*Sheilah Graham*

Perfect Pound Cake *Try*

3 cups all-purpose flour

¼ teaspoon baking soda

2¼ sticks butter, softened
(no substitutions)

3 cups sugar

6 large eggs

1½ to 1¾ cups sour cream

1½ teaspoons vanilla
extract

Powdered sugar

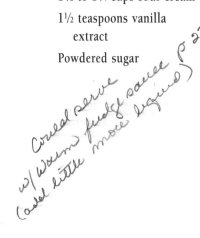

*Could serve
w/ warm fudge sauce
(added little more liquid) p 220*

- Preheat oven to 325°.

- Sift together flour and baking soda twice.

- Beat butter and sugar at low speed with an electric mixer until creamy. Add eggs, 1 at a time, beating at medium speed 1 minute after each addition.

- Gradually add flour mixture, beating well. Stir in sour cream and vanilla.

- Pour batter into a greased and floured 9-inch tube pan.

- Bake at 325° for 1 hour and 20 to 30 minutes. Remove from oven, and let cool completely.

- Invert onto a serving platter, and sprinkle with powdered sugar.

Serves 12 to 16.

Do not rush the mixing of this cake, and do not overbake. This is what makes it dense.

Five-Flavor Pound Cake

1 stick butter

2 sticks margarine

3 cups sugar

5 large eggs

3 cups all-purpose flour

½ teaspoon baking powder

½ teaspoon salt

1 cup milk

1 teaspoon vanilla extract

1 teaspoon coconut extract

1 teaspoon almond extract

1 teaspoon rum extract

1 teaspoon lemon extract

1 teaspoon butter extract

Five-Flavor Glaze

- Preheat oven to 325°.

- Beat butter and margarine at medium speed with an electric mixer until creamy; add sugar, beating well. Add eggs, 1 at a time, beating well after each addition.

- Sift together flour, baking powder, and salt.

- Add flour mixture to butter mixture alternately with milk, beginning and ending with flour mixture and beating well after each addition. Add extracts, beating well.

- Bake in a greased 9-inch tube pan at 325° for 1 hour and 30 minutes. Remove from oven, and let cool.

- Invert onto a serving platter, and drizzle with Five-Flavor Glaze.

Five-Flavor Glaze

1 cup sugar

½ cup water

1 teaspoon vanilla extract

1 teaspoon coconut extract

1 teaspoon almond extract

1 teaspoon rum extract

1 teaspoon lemon extract

1 teaspoon butter extract

- Cook all ingredients in a saucepan over low heat until sugar is dissolved.

Serves 12 to 16.

This cake freezes well, but be sure it is completely cool before freezing.

> *I loved my grandparents' home. Everything smelled older, worn but safe; the food aroma had baked itself into the furniture.*
> —Susan Strasberg

Bishop's Cake

2½ sticks butter, softened

2 cups sugar

5 large eggs, at room temperature

1 teaspoon almond extract

¾ cup milk

2½ cups unbleached all-purpose flour

1 teaspoon baking powder

½ teaspoon baking soda

⅓ cup cornstarch

1½ cups unsweetened grated fresh coconut

½ cup powdered sugar

- Preheat oven to 325°.

- Beat butter and sugar at medium speed with an electric mixer 5 minutes or until pale. Add eggs, 1 at a time, beating well after each addition. Add almond extract and milk, beating at low speed until well blended.

- Combine flour and next 4 ingredients in a separate bowl; add to butter mixture all at once, beating well.

- Spoon into a buttered and floured 9-cup Bundt or tube pan.

- Bake at 325° for 1 hour and 20 minutes or until a wooden pick inserted in center comes out clean. Remove from oven, and let cool 20 minutes.

- Loosen edges with a knife.

- Invert cake onto a serving plate. Let cool completely.

- Sprinkle with powdered sugar.

Serves 12 to 16.

Award-Winning Maple-Nut Chiffon Cake

2¼ cups cake flour, sifted

¾ cup granulated sugar

3 teaspoons baking powder

1 teaspoon salt

¾ cup firmly packed brown sugar

½ cup vegetable oil

5 egg yolks

¾ cup cold water

2 teaspoons maple flavoring

1 cup egg whites (about 8 eggs)

½ teaspoon cream of tartar

1 cup walnuts, finely chopped

Maple Frosting

- Preheat oven to 350°.

- Sift together first 4 ingredients; stir in brown sugar.

- Make a well in the center of dry ingredients; add oil and next 3 ingredients, and beat at medium speed with an electric mixer until smooth.

- Beat egg whites and cream of tartar in a separate large bowl at high speed with a handheld mixer until very stiff peaks form.

- Pour batter in a thin stream over entire surface of egg whites, gently cutting and folding (down, across bottom, up side, and over) just until blended. Fold in nuts.

- Bake in an ungreased 10-inch tube pan at 325° for 55 minutes.

- Increase oven temperature to 350°, and bake 10 to 15 minutes.

- Remove from oven, and invert cake onto a wire rack; let cool completely.

- Spread cake with Maple Frosting.

Maple Frosting

½ cup butter, softened

4 cups sifted powdered sugar

1½ teaspoons maple flavoring

3 tablespoons milk

- Beat first 3 ingredients at medium speed with an electric mixer until well blended. Add milk, and beat until smooth, adding additional milk if necessary to reach spreading consistency.

Serves 12 to 16.

Celebration Chocolate Cake

3 (1-ounce) unsweetened chocolate squares

1 stick unsalted butter (no substitutions)

1 cup boiling water

1 teaspoon bourbon

2 cups sugar

2 large eggs, separated

1 teaspoon baking soda

½ cup sour cream

2 cups less 2 tablespoons unbleached all-purpose flour, sifted

1 teaspoon baking powder

Chocolate Frosting

- Preheat oven to 350°.
- Place chocolate and butter in a bowl; add boiling water, and let stand until melted. Stir in bourbon and sugar. Add egg yolks, 1 at a time, whisking well after each addition.
- Combine baking soda and sour cream; whisk into chocolate mixture.
- Sift together flour and baking powder; add to chocolate mixture, stirring until well blended.
- Beat egg whites at high speed with a handheld mixer until stiff peaks form; stir one-fourth of egg whites into batter, and spoon remaining three-fourths on top of batter, gently folding in.
- Pour batter into a greased and floured 10-inch round cakepan.
- Bake at 350° for 40 to 50 minutes or until a knife inserted in center comes out clean. Remove from oven, and let cool in pan 10 minutes.
- Invert onto a wire rack, and let cool completely.
- Spread with warm Chocolate Frosting.

Chocolate Frosting

2 tablespoons unsalted butter

¾ cup semisweet chocolate morsels

6 tablespoons heavy cream

1¼ to 1½ cups sifted powdered sugar

1 teaspoon bourbon

- Cook all ingredients in a heavy saucepan over low heat, whisking often, until smooth. Remove from heat, and let cool slightly.
- Whisk in additional powdered sugar if necessary to reach spreading consistency.

Serves 12.

220

Chocoholic Sheet Cake

1 stick butter or margarine

1 cup sugar

4 large eggs

1 teaspoon baking powder

¼ teaspoon salt

1 teaspoon vanilla

1 cup all-purpose flour

1 (16-ounce) can chocolate syrup

Chocolate Icing

- Preheat oven to 350°.

- Beat butter and sugar at medium speed with an electric mixer until creamy. Add eggs, 1 at a time, beating well after each addition.

- Beat in baking powder, salt, and vanilla. Add flour alternately with syrup, beating well after each addition.

- Pour into a 13- x 9-inch pan. Bake at 350° for 25 to 30 minutes.

- While cake bakes, make Chocolate Icing. Pour over hot cake.

Chocolate Icing

1 stick butter or margarine

3 tablespoons cocoa

Instant coffee granules, 1 pinch

1 box powdered sugar

1 teaspoon vanilla extract

⅓ cup evaporated or sweet milk

- Melt butter in a saucepan over medium heat; stir in cocoa and next 3 ingredients.

- Stir in milk to desired spreading consistency.

Serves 12 to 16.

A child's response to his mom's request to finish his vegetables, "I can't, mom, the healthy side of my stomach is full, but the dessert side is empty.

Lo-fat

Mightylikea Chocolate Cheesecake

1¾ cups all-purpose flour

1½ teaspoons baking soda

1½ teaspoons baking powder

½ teaspoon salt

1½ cup sugar

¾ cup cocoa

4 egg whites

⅔ cup skim milk

⅓ cup amaretto or Kahlúa

½ cup applesauce

2 teaspoons vanilla extract

1 teaspoon almond or rum extract

¾ cup boiling water

¼ cup semisweet chocolate mini-morsels (optional)

½ cup raisins (optional)

- Preheat oven to 325°.
- Combine first 6 ingredients in a large bowl, and mix well; add egg whites and next 6 ingredients, and beat at high speed with an electric mixer 2 minutes.
- Pour batter into a 9-inch springform pan lightly coated with vegetable cooking spray. Sprinkle with chocolate mini-morsels, and, if desired, raisins (they will sink).
- Bake at 325° for 50 to 60 minutes or until completely set. Remove from oven, and let cool in pan 30 minutes or more.
- Loosen edges with a knife, and remove sides of pan to serve.
- Keep covered.

Serves 12 to 16.

This is a delicious trickster of a cake, with rich flavor that belies its low calorie and fat count. One serving has only 225 calories and 1.8 grams of fat.

Apple Dapple Cake

3 large eggs

1½ cups vegetable oil

2 cups granulated sugar

3 cups all-purpose flour

1 teaspoon baking soda

1 teaspoon salt

2 teaspoons vanilla extract

3 cups chopped apple

1½ cups chopped nuts

1 cup firmly packed brown sugar

¼ cup milk

1 stick margarine

- Preheat oven to 350°.
- Beat first 3 ingredients at medium speed with an electric mixer until smooth; add flour and next 5 ingredients, beating well.
- Pour into a greased 9-inch tube pan.
- Bake at 350° for 1 hour.
- Cook brown sugar, milk, and margarine in a saucepan over medium heat for 2½ minutes or until butter melts.
- Pour immediately over hot cake in pan.

Serves 12 to 16.

Awesome Apple Crisp *Try*

2½ pounds Granny Smith or Rome apples, peeled and sliced

⅓ cup sugar

1 teaspoon lemon juice

1 teaspoon ground cinnamon

¼ teaspoon ground nutmeg

Cinnamon Topping

- Preheat oven to 375°.
- Toss together first 5 ingredients; spoon mixture into a greased 3-quart rectangular baking dish.
- Sprinkle with Cinnamon Topping.
- Bake at 375° for 50 minutes. Serve warm.

Cinnamon Topping

½ teaspoon ground cinnamon

½ cup sugar

⅛ teaspoon salt

½ cup butter, softened

¾ cup all-purpose flour

¼ cup uncooked regular oats

1 cup toasted pecans, broken

- Combine all ingredients.

Serves 8.
Serve with vanilla ice cream.

Fat-Free Yummy Peach Cobbler w/ Butter Buds

1 package (½ cup) liquid Butter Buds

2 cups sugar, divided

4 cups sliced peaches

1 cup cake or self-rising flour

1 cup skim milk

- Preheat oven to 350°.
- Prepare Butter Buds according to package directions.
- Bring 1 cup sugar and peaches to a boil in a saucepan.
- Pour Butter Buds into a 13- x 9-inch baking dish.
- Combine remaining 1 cup sugar, flour, and milk; pour over Butter Buds. Do not stir.
- Pour peach mixture over flour mixture.
- Bake at 350° for 30 minutes.

Serves 8.

Strawberry-Rhubarb Crumble

1¾ cups unbleached all-purpose flour, divided

¾ cup firmly packed light brown sugar

½ cup unblanched almonds

½ cup uncooked regular oats

1 teaspoon ground allspice

¾ cup unsalted butter, chilled and cut up

3 pints fresh strawberries, halved

1¾ pounds fresh rhubarb, cut into ½-inch pieces

1½ cups granulated sugar

1 tablespoon vanilla extract

2 teaspoons ground allspice

Whipped cream

- Process 1 cup flour, brown sugar, and next 4 ingredients in a food processor 45 seconds or until crumbly. Cover and chill overnight, if desired.

- Combine remaining ¾ cup flour, strawberries, and next 4 ingredients in a large bowl; cover and let stand at room temperature, stirring occasionally, 30 minutes.

- Spoon strawberry mixture into a 13-x 9-inch baking dish. Sprinkle with brown sugar mixture.

- Bake at 375° for 40 minutes or until golden brown. Remove from oven, and let cool slightly.

- Serve in individual dishes, and pass whipped cream separately.

Serves 8.

Grandma's Perfect Pie Crust

2 cups all-purpose flour

⅛ teaspoon salt

¾ cup solid shortening

4 tablespoons ice water

- Combine flour and salt; cut in shortening using a pastry blender until crumbly. Add 4 tablespoons ice water, stirring with a fork.

- Divide dough into 2 portions, and chill 10 minutes.

- Roll dough out on a lightly floured surface.

1 pie crust.

Lemon Chess Pie

2 cups sugar

1 tablespoon all-purpose
flour

1 tablespoon cornmeal

4 large eggs

¼ cup butter

¼ cup milk

1 tablespoon grated lemon
rind

¼ cup fresh lemon juice

1 unbaked 9-inch pie shell

- Preheat oven to 350°.

- Combine first 3 ingredients in a large bowl,
tossing lightly. Add eggs and next 4 ingredients,
beating at medium speed with a handheld mixer
until smooth.

- Pour into pie shell, and bake at 375° for 35 to
45 minutes or until golden brown.

Serves 6 to 8.

Blender Lemon Pie *Try*

4 large eggs

2 cups sugar

1 lemon, quartered (rind,
seeds, and all)

1 stick butter, chilled and
cut into 8 pieces

1 prebaked 9-inch deep-dish
pie shell

- Preheat oven to 350°.

- Process eggs in a blender; add sugar and lemon,
blending thoroughly. Add chilled butter, and
process just until blended.

- Pour into prebaked pie shell.

- Bake at 350° for 30 minutes or until firm.

Serves 8.

*Help make your child's memories be filled
with special thoughts that family
togetherness can bring.*

Mountain High Lemon Meringue Pie

1¼ cups sugar

6 tablespoons cornstarch

2 cups water

⅓ cup lemon juice

3 egg yolks

1½ teaspoons lemon extract

2 teaspoons vinegar

3 tablespoons butter

1 baked 9-inch deep-dish
  pastry shell

Never-Fail Meringue

- Combine sugar and cornstarch in the top of a double boiler; stir in 2 cups water.

- Combine lemon juice and yolks in a bowl; stir into sugar mixture.

- Bring water to a boil in lower pan; cook, stirring constantly, 25 minutes or until thickened. Stir in lemon extract, vinegar, and butter.

- Pour into pastry shell. Cool.

- Cover with Never-Fail Meringue.

- Bake at 350° for 10 minutes or until lightly browned.

Never-Fail Meringue

1 tablespoon cornstarch

2 tablespoons cold water

½ cup boiling water

3 egg whites

6 tablespoons sugar

1 teaspoon vanilla

Salt, 1 pinch

- Stir together cornstarch and 2 tablespoons cold water in a saucepan; stir in ½ cup boiling water.

- Cook over medium heat, stirring constantly, until thickened and clear. Remove from heat, and let cool completely.

- Beat egg whites at high speed with an electric mixer until foamy. Gradually add sugar, beating until stiff peaks form.

- Beat in vanilla and salt. Gradually beat in cornstarch mixture.

Serves 8.

"Go, eat your bread in gladness and drink your wine in joy."

—Ecclesiastes 9:7

Lemon Curd Tartlets

3 cups sifted all-purpose
  flour
1½ teaspoons salt
1 cup shortening
6 tablespoons cold water
Lemon Curd
Garnish: whipped cream

- Preheat oven to 450°.

- Sift together flour and salt; cut in shortening using a pastry blender until crumbly. Sprinkle 6 tablespoons cold water over mixture, stirring until a smooth ball is formed.

- Roll dough out on a lightly floured surface to ⅛-inch thickness.

- Cut using a 2½-inch round cookie cutter.

- Fit dough rounds into miniature muffin cups; prick with a fork.

- Bake at 450° for 10 to 20 minutes or until lightly browned. Remove from oven, and let cool.

- Spoon Lemon Curd evenly into tartlet shells.

- Garnish, if desired.

Lemon Curd

Grated rinds of 2 lemons
½ cup fresh lemon juice
2 cups sugar
1 cup butter
4 large eggs, lightly beaten

- Combine first 3 ingredients in the top of a double boiler; add butter. Cook over boiling water, stirring constantly, until butter is melted.

- Stir in eggs; cook, stirring constantly, 15 minutes or until mixture is thickened.

- Remove from heat, and let cool completely.

4 dozen.

Fresh blueberries are a wonderful topping!

> *The busier and more involved our families become…the more important it is to break bread together.*

Caramel Pecan Pie

3 tablespoons butter

1 cup firmly packed brown sugar

5 tablespoons all-purpose flour

2 large eggs

1 cup whole milk

½ to ¾ cup pecans, chopped

1 teaspoon vanilla extract

1 pint whipping cream, chilled

2 to 4 tablespoons powdered sugar

1 baked 9-inch pastry shell

- Combine first 3 ingredients in the top of a double boiler; beat at medium speed with a handheld mixer until creamy.

- Beat eggs in a bowl at medium speed with a mixer until pale; beat in milk. Add egg mixture to butter mixture, beating well.

- Place over boiling water. Cook, stirring constantly, until mixture is thickened. If lumps form, use mixer or egg beater to smooth.

- Fill bottom of double boiler with cold water to cool mixture. Stir in vanilla and nuts.

- Pour mixture into pastry shell. Chill.

- Beat whipping cream in a chilled bowl at medium speed with chilled beaters; gradually add powdered sugar, beating until soft peaks form.

- Spread whipped cream over pie 2 hours before ready to serve; chill.

Serves 8.

Make this pie a day ahead to allow plenty of time to set. Do not top with whipped cream until 2 hours before serving.

Heart of the Family

Much more than eating takes place on top of the round pine kitchen table. The sports page is memorized, budgets are created, homework is completed, taxes are calculated, Easter eggs are dyed, gin rummy is played, problems are solved, cookies are cooled, milestones are celebrated, friends and family are gathered. The round pine kitchen table truly is the heart of the family.

Mystery Pecan Pie

1 (8-ounce) package cream
  cheese, softened
½ cup sugar, divided- ¼ & ¼
2 teaspoons vanilla extract,
  divided 1 t. + 1 t.
½ teaspoon salt
4 large eggs, divided - 1 + 3
1 unbaked 9- or 10-inch
  deep-dish pastry shell
1¼ cups pecans, chopped
1 cup corn syrup

- Preheat oven to 375°.
- Combine cream cheese, ¼ cup sugar,
  1 teaspoon vanilla, salt, and 1 egg.
- Pour into pastry shell, and sprinkle with pecans.
- Combine remaining ¼ cup sugar, 1 teaspoon
  vanilla, 3 eggs, and corn syrup.
- Pour carefully over pecans. Do not mix.
- Bake at 375° for 40 to 45 minutes or until
  center is set.

Serves 8.

Bourbon Pie
Pecan   *Supper Club*
10-30-99

6

2c

1c

½c

1 t.

½c

2

1¼-1½c
pecans

3 large eggs
1 cup firmly packed light
  brown sugar
½ cup light corn syrup
¼ cup butter, melted
½ teaspoon salt
¼ cup bourbon
1 unbaked 9-inch pastry
  shell

- Preheat oven to 375°.
- Beat first 6 ingredients at medium speed with an
  electric mixer until smooth.
- Pour into pastry shell.— *Pillsbury in box*
- Bake at 375° for 45 minutes.

1¼ - 1½ C. chopped pecans

Serves 8.

Filled 9" + 10" glass pie plates

Wicked Peanut Butter Pie

1 cup graham cracker crumbs

¼ cup firmly packed brown sugar

¼ cup butter, melted

2 cups creamy peanut butter

2 cups sugar

2 (8-ounce) packages cream cheese, softened

2 tablespoons butter, melted

2 teaspoons vanilla extract

1½ cups whipping cream

4 ounces semisweet chocolate morsels

3 tablespoons plus 2 teaspoons hot coffee

Miniature peanut butter cups, cut into fourths

- Combine first 3 ingredients, and press into the bottom of a 9-inch springform pan.

- Beat peanut butter and next 4 ingredients at medium speed with an electric mixer until smooth.

- Beat whipping cream in a separate bowl at high speed with a handheld mixer until soft peaks form. Fold into peanut butter mixture.

- Pour into prepared crust, and chill 6 hours.

- Combine chocolate morsels and coffee in the top of a double boiler; bring water to a boil. Cook, stirring constantly, until chocolate is melted.

- Pour over pie, and chill until hardened.

- Top each serving with a peanut butter cup fourth.

Serves 12.

S'mores

A great camp treat consists of graham crackers, marshmallows and a Hershey's chocolate candy bar. Roast the marshmallow over an open camp fire until it gets real mushy (don't let it catch on fire!), then squish it between two graham crackers and the chocolate bar. You'll want s'more. Guaranteed.

try con press

Creme de Menthe, Kahlua, etc

no bake

Chocolate-Amaretto Cream Pie

2- 1 (3-ounce) package cream
cheese, softened

1c ½ cup sugar

2+½ ½ teaspoon vanilla extract,
divided

⅔c ⅓ cup amaretto, divided

⅔c ⅓ cup cocoa, divided

8 ounces cream, whipped

½ cup warm fudge sauce

2 1 (6-ounce) chocolate
cookie pie crust

Whipped cream

- Beat cream cheese and sugar at medium speed with an electric mixer until smooth; add half each of vanilla, amaretto, and cocoa, beating well and scraping down sides. Add remaining half each of vanilla, amaretto, and cocoa, beating well.

- Gently fold in 8 ounces whipped cream using a wooden spoon.

- Spread half of chocolate mixture over piecrust; drizzle evenly with fudge sauce, and top with remaining chocolate mixture, smoothing top.

- Cover with plastic wrap, and chill at least 1 hour.

- Top each serving with additional whipped cream.

Serves 8.

It is easy to make two pies at a time and freeze one for later use. This pie will keep well for several days in the refrigerator but only if you keep it hidden! The variation possibilities on this pie are unlimited. You can make it with or without cocoa, substitute different liqueurs (orange, Kahlúa, crème de menthe, raspberry, cherry) for amaretto, substitute fruit toppings for fudge sauce, or substitute grated citrus rind for cocoa.

Chocolate Silk Chess Pie

July 01
CIK, E, LA
Can Freeze

4 (1-ounce) unsweetened chocolate squares

2 sticks butter

½ cup milk, warmed

2½ cups sugar

1 teaspoon vanilla extract

4 large eggs, lightly beaten

2 unbaked 9-inch pastry shells

chopped pecans, opt.

Makes 2 pies

- Preheat oven to 350°.

- Cook chocolate and butter in a large saucepan over low heat until melted; stir in milk and next 3 ingredients.

- Pour mixture into pastry shells.

- Bake at 350° for 40 minutes.

- Turn off oven, and leave pie in 8 more minutes.

Serves 16.

These pies freeze well. You may also use 16 (4-inch) tart shells. Fill with chocolate mixture. Bake at 350° for 25 minutes. Turn off oven, and leave in 45 minutes.

Do not overcook

Award-Winning North Carolina Pecan Shortbread

1 cup all-purpose flour

½ cup pecans

Salt

1 stick butter (no substitutions)

¼ cup firmly packed dark brown sugar

½ teaspoon almond extract

¼ teaspoon ground cinnamon

- Preheat oven to 300°.

- Process first 3 ingredients in a food processor until finely chopped.

- Beat butter and sugar by hand or at medium speed with an electric mixer until creamy; add almond extract and cinnamon, beating well. Beat in flour mixture.

- Shape dough into a ball, and chill overnight.

- Roll dough out on a lightly floured surface to ¼-inch thickness.

- Cut using a cookie cutter.

- Bake on baking sheets at 300° for 25 minutes.

Serves 24.

Vanilla extract can be substituted for almond extract.

Old-fashioned Gingersnaps

1½ cups solid shortening

2 cups sugar

½ cup molasses

2 large eggs

4 cups all-purpose flour

4 teaspoons baking soda

1 teaspoon salt

4 teaspoons ground cinnamon

2 teaspoons ground cloves

1 teaspoon ground ginger

- Preheat oven to 375°.

- Beat shortening and sugar at medium speed with an electric mixer until creamy; add molasses and eggs, beating well.

- Sift together flour and next 5 ingredients. Add to shortening mixture, beating well. Chill 1 hour.

- Roll dough into walnut-size balls, and place 2 inches apart on greased baking sheets.

- Bake at 375° for 7 to 10 minutes.

8 dozen.

Old-fashioned Oatmeal-Raisin Cookies

½ pound butter, softened

½ cup sugar

1½ cups firmly packed brown sugar

2 large eggs

1½ teaspoons vanilla extract

2 cups all-purpose flour

1 teaspoon baking soda

1 teaspoon baking powder

½ teaspoon salt

1½ teaspoons ground cinnamon

2½ cups uncooked regular oats

1 cup raisins

- Preheat oven to 375°.

- Beat first 3 ingredients at medium speed with an electric mixer until creamy; add eggs, and beat just until blended. Beat in vanilla.

- Combine flour and next 4 ingredients in a separate bowl.

- Gradually add flour mixture to butter mixture, beating well at low speed after each addition.

- Add oatmeal, and beat at low speed until blended. Stir in raisins.

- Drop dough by rounded tablespoonfuls onto ungreased baking sheets.

- Bake at 375° for 10 to 12 minutes or until lightly browned around edges. Remove from oven, and let cool on pans 2 to 3 minutes.

- Remove cookies to wire racks, and let cool completely.

2 dozen.

Too Good To Be a Box Cookie! - *Pinkerman Markus Bars?*

1 package yellow or
    chocolate cake mix

1 stick butter, melted

4 large eggs, lightly beaten

1 package powdered sugar

1 (8-ounce) package cream
    cheese, softened

- Preheat oven to 325°.

- Combine cake mix, butter, and 1 egg; press into the bottom of a 13- x 9-inch pan.

- Beat remaining 3 eggs, sugar, and cream cheese at medium speed with an electric mixer until smooth.

- Spread over bottom layer.

- Bake at 325° for 55 minutes to 1 hour. Remove from oven, and let cool completely.

- Cut into squares.

2½ dozen.

Cowboy Cookies - *Flo's*

1 cup butter, softened

1 cup granulated sugar

1 cup firmly packed brown
    sugar

2 large eggs

2 cups all-purpose flour

1 teaspoon baking soda

½ teaspoon baking powder

½ teaspoon salt

2 teaspoons vanilla extract

2 cups uncooked regular
    oats

2 cups pecans, chopped

3 cups (18 ounces)
    semisweet chocolate
    morsels

- Preheat oven to 350°.

- Beat first 4 ingredients at medium speed with an electric mixer until smooth. Add flour and next 3 ingredients, beating well.

- Beat in vanilla. Add oats, pecans, and chocolate morsels, stirring until well blended.

- Roll dough, ¼ cup at a time, into balls, and place on ungreased baking sheets, 8 per sheet.

- Bake at 350° for 13 to 15 minutes. Remove from oven, and let cool on wire racks.

- Store in airtight containers.

3 dozen.

These can also be made into bar cookies. Bake in a 13- x 9-inch pan at 350° for 25 to 27 minutes. These cookies are so good they ought to be outlawed!

You'll Never Have a Better Brownie!

2 (19.8-ounce) packages
fudge brownie mix

5 ounces vegetable oil

1 cup whipping cream

3 large eggs

1½ cups pecans, chopped
(optional)

8 (1.45-ounce) milk
chocolate bars

- Preheat oven to 350°.

- Combine first 4 ingredients, stirring well
  (50 strokes). Stir in pecans, if desired.

- Spread half of batter into a greased 13 x 9-inch
  pan; top with chocolate bars.

- Spoon remaining half of batter over chocolate.

- Bake at 350° for 40 minutes (do not overbake).
  Remove from oven, and let cool completely.

- Cut into squares.

Serves 8.

Pecan Bars - *clubs* ?

1 package yellow cake mix

⅓ cup vegetable oil +1 -88

4 5 large eggs, divided (4 + 1)

1 cup dark corn syrup

1 cup sugar

¼ cup butter, melted

2 cups chopped pecans

- Preheat oven to 350°.

- Combine cake mix, oil, and 1 egg, stirring until
  crumbly.

- Press mixture into the bottom of a greased
  13- x 9-inch pan.

- Bake at 350° for 20 minutes.

- Beat remaining 4 eggs, corn syrup, sugar, and
  butter at medium speed with an electric mixer
  until smooth. Stir in pecans, and pour over
  bottom layer.

- Bake at 350° for 45 minutes or until filling is
  set. Remove from oven, and let cool completely
  before cutting.

2 dozen cookie bars.

**Add a scoop of vanilla ice cream on top for a
fancy dessert.**

Cookie Wisdom

*Each time I start making
cookies, I remember the
loving lady who taught
me her secret recipe. As a
child, I found nothing
better than licking the
bowl and waiting for her
hot cookies to come out of
the oven. They were the
best! I learned several
things from her which I
still use with regularity. I
always soften my butter
naturally. I use a wooden
spoon, and I always use
the best ingredients.*

Strawberries and Sabayon in Cookie Shells

1 large egg

¾ cup powdered sugar

2 tablespoons brown sugar

½ teaspoon vanilla extract

⅛ teaspoon salt

⅓ cup all-purpose flour

2 tablespoons butter,
   melted

4 cups fresh strawberries

Sabayon

½ cup chopped pecans

- Preheat oven to 350°.

- Beat first 3 ingredients at high speed with an electric mixer until fluffy; stir in vanilla and salt. Fold in flour and butter.

- Spoon 2 tablespoonfuls batter into a 5- to 6-inch circle, spreading evenly, on a greased and floured baking sheet.

- Repeat procedure once.

- Bake, 2 at a time, at 350° for 4 to 5 minutes or until brown. Remove from pan while hot using a spatula, and mold each over the back of a small bowl. Let cool completely, and remove from bowl.

- Repeat procedure with remaining batter.

- Divide strawberries evenly among cookie shells; spoon Sabayon evenly over berries, and sprinkle with nuts.

Sabayon

6 egg yolks

¼ cup sugar

⅓ cup Grand Marnier

½ cup heavy cream,
   whipped

- Whisk together yolks and sugar in the top of a double boiler; bring water to a simmer, and cook, whisking constantly, until fluffy.

- Gradually whisk in Grand Marnier, whisking until slightly thickened.

- Chill mixture 1 hour; fold in whipped cream.

Serves 6.

Spirited Fruits

2 cups fresh strawberries
1 orange, sectioned
2 to 3 tablespoons
powdered sugar
2 tablespoons fresh orange
juice
2 tablespoons Grand
Marnier
1 tablespoon kirsch
1 tablespoon cognac
1 tablespoon framboise

- Combine strawberries and orange in a large bowl; sprinkle with powdered sugar. Chill at least 1 hour.
- Combine orange juice and next 4 ingredients in a small bowl.
- Pour over fruit when ready to serve, stirring gently.

Serves 6.

Other liqueurs can be substituted. Just be sure to use 5 tablespoons of liqueurs.

The Best Strawberry Sorbet

4 cups pureed strawberries
2 cups sugar
2 cups nonfat buttermilk

- Combine all ingredients.
- Pour into a 13- x 9-inch baking dish, and freeze 1 hour and 30 minutes.
- Beat at medium speed with an electric mixer until slushy.
- Return to baking dish, and freeze until hardened.

Serves 8.

Mock Cream Caramel on Strawberries

Sour cream
Brown sugar
Fresh strawberries

- Spread sour cream in the bottom of an oven-proof glass baking dish.
- Cover with brown sugar, and broil until sugar melts.
- Spoon over strawberries.

Lemon Roll and Chocolate-Coffee Cream

6 large eggs

1 cup sugar

Grated rind from ½ a lemon

½ teaspoon vanilla extract

1 cup unbleached all-
   purpose flour

1 teaspoon baking powder

½ cup powdered sugar

Lemon Filling

Garnish: powdered sugar,
   fresh mint leaves

Chocolate-Coffee Cream

- Preheat oven to 350°.

- Butter a 13- x 9-inch pan, and line with buttered parchment or wax paper.

- Beat first 4 ingredients at high speed with an electric mixer until light and tripled in volume.

- Combine flour and baking powder, and gently fold into egg mixture using a rubber spatula and being careful not to deflate egg mixture.

- Pour batter into a prepared pan.

- Bake at 350° for 18 to 20 minutes or until very lightly browned. Remove from oven, and let cool 8 to 10 minutes.

- Invert onto a damp kitchen towel, and sprinkle with powdered sugar.

- Peel off parchment paper, and roll up, jellyroll fashion, lengthwise in towel. Let cool.

- Unroll cake, and cover with Lemon Filling.

- Roll up, jellyroll fashion, without towel. Transfer to a serving platter.

- Garnish, if desired. Chill at least 1 hour.

- Serve with Chocolate-Coffee Cream, reserving remaining cream for another use.

Lemon Filling

2 large eggs

2 egg yolks

1 cup sugar

Grated rind from 2 lemons

½ cup butter

- Whisk together first 4 ingredients in a heavy saucepan; add butter, and cook over low heat, whisking constantly, until thickened.

- Remove from heat, and let cool.

Lemon Roll and Chocolate-Coffee Cream (continued)

Chocolate-Coffee Cream

12 ounces imported
  semisweet chocolate

½ cup sugar

5 cups strong-brewed coffee

1 teaspoon ground
  cinnamon

½ teaspoon vanilla extract

• Cook first 4 ingredients in a heavy saucepan over low heat, stirring constantly, until chocolate is melted.

• Remove from heat, and stir in vanilla. Let cool slightly.

Serves 10.

Freezer Lemon Sorbet

1¼ cups sugar

Grated rind of 1 lemon

½ cup fresh lemon juice

2 cups milk

Garnishes: lemon slices,
  fresh mint sprigs

• Combine first 4 ingredients in a freezer-safe bowl, stirring until sugar is dissolved. Freeze until slightly firm.

• Beat mixture at medium speed with an electric mixer until slushy. Freeze until firm.

• Garnish each serving, if desired.

Serves 4.

Sinfully Rich Chocolate Bombe

½ angel food cake, cut into
½-inch slices

½ cup Grand Marnier

4 (12-ounce) packages
semisweet chocolate
morsels, divided

2 cups unsalted butter,
softened

4 cups sifted powdered
sugar

16 egg yolks

1½ tablespoons vanilla
extract

2 tablespoons unsalted
butter

Garnish: orange slices

• Brush cake slices with Grand Marnier.

• Line a plastic wrap-lined 2-quart bowl with cake slices, reserving extra slices.

• Place 3 packages chocolate morsels in the top of a double boiler; bring water to a simmer. Cook, stirring constantly, until melted.

• Beat 2 cups butter, sugar, and egg yolks at high speed with an electric mixer until fluffy. Gradually add melted chocolate and vanilla, beating at low speed.

• Pour mixture over angel food cake in bowl. Top with reserved angel food cake slices. Chill overnight or until set.

• Invert the bombe onto a serving platter, removing plastic wrap.

• Cook remaining 1 package chocolate morsels and 2 tablespoons butter in a small saucepan over low heat, stirring constantly, until melted.

• Spread glaze over bombe. Chill slightly.

• Cut into thin wedges, and garnish, if desired.

Serves 24.

My favorite dinner table is encircled with family and friends, laden with good food and enhanced with the promising aroma of a glorious dessert still baking, to be served hot when we are ready.

Decadent Chocolate Soufflé

8 ounces German chocolate

2 teaspoons instant coffee granules

1 cup sugar

½ cup boiling water

2 sticks butter, softened and each cut into 6 pieces

4 large eggs

1 tablespoon cognac

1 cup whipping cream

2 tablespoons sugar

2 teaspoons cognac

Garnish: candied violets, if desired

Butterscotch Rum Sauce

1 cup firmly packed light brown sugar

¼ cup light corn syrup

½ stick butter

Salt

½ cup cream

1½ teaspoons vanilla extract

¼ teaspoon lemon juice

1½ tablespoons dark rum

½ cup pecans, chopped and toasted (optional)

- *Cook first 4 ingredients in a heavy saucepan over medium heat, stirring with a wooden spoon and washing down sides.*
- *Bring to a boil. Reduce heat to very low, and cook without stirring 12 minutes.*
- *Remove from heat, and stir in cream, next 3 ingredients, and, if desired, pecans.*
- *Serve warm or at room temperature.*

2 cups sauce.

- Preheat oven to 350°.

- Line a 5-cup soufflé dish or mold with aluminum foil.

- Cut a piece of foil long enough to fit around soufflé dish, allowing a 1-inch overlap. Fold foil lengthwise into thirds. Lightly grease 1 side of strip, and wrap around outside of soufflé dish, oiled side against dish, allowing foil to extend 3 inches above rim to form a collar. Secure with freezer tape.

- Pulse first 3 ingredients in a food processor 4 times; process until well blended. With machine running; add ½ cup boiling water through food chute, and process until chocolate is melted. Add butter, and pulse 3 times; process until well blended. Add eggs and 1 tablespoon cognac, and process 10 seconds.

- Spoon into prepared soufflé dish, and bake at 350° for 40 minutes or until a crust has formed. Remove from oven, and let cool.

- Wrap airtight, and chill up to 2 weeks, or freeze, if desired.

- To serve, peel off foil. (Mixture will look sticky and irregular.)

- Beat whipping cream at high speed with an electric mixer until stiff peaks form; gradually beat in sugar. Add 2 teaspoons cognac, beating well.

- Spoon mixture into a pastry bag fitted with a medium star tip; pipe rosettes over entire mold, and garnish, if desired.

- Chill until ready to serve.

Serves 6 to 8.

Luscious Lemon Mousse

1 tablespoon unflavored
    gelatin
2 tablespoons water
¼ cup sweet white wine
½ cup sugar
Juice and grated rind of
    2 lemons
4 large eggs, separated

- Soak gelatin in 2 tablespoons water.

- Combine wine, sugar, lemon rind, and juice in the top of a double boiler; bring water to a simmer. Add gelatin mixture, and cook, stirring constantly, until gelatin is dissolved.

- Beat egg yolks at high speed with an electric mixer until thick and pale; stir into lemon mixture.

- Beat egg whites at high speed with an electric mixer until stiff peaks form. Fold into lemon mixture. Remove from heat.

- Pour into a glass serving bowl, and chill until firm but still light and foamy.

Serves 4.

Raspberry Mousse Parfaits

1 (10-ounce) package frozen
    red raspberries in syrup,
    thawed
½ cup heavy cream
½ cup powdered sugar
Salt
2 tablespoons kirsch
Fresh raspberries

- Crush frozen raspberries in syrup to make a thin puree; force through a wire-mesh strainer into a bowl. Discard seeds.

- In another freezer-safe bowl, beat cream at high speed with an electric mixer until thick; beat in sugar and salt. Add raspberry puree, beating at low speed.

- Freeze 30 minutes or until just slightly firm.

- Stir in kirsch. Spoon into parfait glasses and freeze until firm. Let stand at room temperature briefly before serving.

- Top with fresh raspberries.

Serves 4.

Brandy Alexander Mousse

1 cup (6 ounces) semisweet
  chocolate morsels
1 cup heavy cream
1/2 cup sugar
1/8 teaspoon salt
4 egg yolks
5 or more tablespoons
  brandy

- Cook first 4 ingredients in a heavy saucepan over low heat, stirring constantly, until chocolate is melted. Whisk mixture until smooth.

- Process yolks in a food processor until blended.

- With machine running, add chocolate mixture in a slow steady stream through food chute. Stir in brandy.

- Pour into cordial glasses or demitasse cups. Chill.

Serves 8.

Crème Brûlée

5 egg yolks
2 cups heavy cream
2/3 cup half-and-half
1/3 cup plus 1 tablespoon
  granulated sugar
1/2 teaspoon vanilla extract
Brown sugar

- Preheat oven to 325°.

- Lightly whisk egg yolks in a large bowl; add cream and next 3 ingredients, and beat at medium speed with a handheld mixer until smooth.

- Pour mixture through a wire-mesh strainer, and distribute evenly among 6 ramekins.

- Bake in a 2-inch-deep water bath at 325° for 30 to 40 minutes or until set. Remove from oven, and let stand in hot water 20 minutes.

- Remove from water bath, and chill 2 hours or overnight.

- Sprinkle each serving with 1 to 2 tablespoons brown sugar.

- To caramelize sugar, use a propane torch or run under broiler, watching carefully.

Serves 6.

The sugar is caramelized when a dark golden hard-crack surface is formed.

Sugar secrets

Brown sugar gone rock hard in the package? Add a slice of soft bread, close the bag tightly, and in a few hours the sugar will be soft again. If you need it in a hurry, grate the amount called for with a hand grater.

Tarheel Tiramisu

4 egg yolks

1 cup sugar

1 cup crème fraîche

1 cup whole-milk ricotta cheese

1 cup heavy cream, chilled

3 tablespoons cognac or other brandy

48 ladyfingers, divided

1 cup strong-brewed coffee

1½ teaspoons cocoa

- Beat yolks at medium speed with an electric mixer; gradually add sugar, beating until thick and pale.

- Beat crème fraîche and ricotta in a separate bowl at high speed with a handheld mixer until soft peaks form.

- Beat cream in a separate chilled bowl at high speed with a handheld mixer until soft peaks form.

- Fold crème fraîche mixture and whipped cream into yolk mixture. Fold in cognac.

- Determine the number of ladyfingers needed to line the bottom of a 9- x 5-inch loaf pan or serving dish of similar width.

- Dip ladyfingers into coffee, and arrange in the bottom of loafpan. Top with 1 layer of cream mixture.

- Repeat layers using remaining ladyfingers and cream mixture, ending with cream mixture.

- Chill overnight or longer.

- Top with sifted cocoa before serving.

Serves 8.

This recipe tastes best when made a day or two ahead.

Crème Fraîche

1 cup heavy cream

1 cup sour cream

- Whisk together in a bowl. Cover and let stand in a warm place overnight. Stir well, cover and refrigerate for at least 4 hours. Crème Fraîche will keep for up to 2 weeks. Use as a topping on fresh berries.

English Trifle

Pound cake slices or
  ladyfingers, divided

½ cup sherry, divided

2 cups fresh fruit (peaches,
  strawberries, etc.),
  divided

Vanilla Custard, divided

Whipped cream

Toasted sliced almonds

- Place 1 layer of pound cake slices in the bottom of an 8-inch crystal bowl. Sprinkle with ¼ cup sherry.

- Top with 1 cup fruit; spread half of Vanilla Custard over fruit.

- Repeat layers once. Chill several hours or overnight.

- When ready to serve top with whipped cream, and sprinkle with almonds.

Vanilla Custard

1½ cups sugar

½ cup all-purpose flour

Salt

4 egg yolks, lightly beaten

3 cups milk

1 teaspoon vanilla extract

- Combine first 3 ingredients in the top of a double boiler. Combine yolks and milk; gradually add to sugar mixture, stirring well.

- Bring water to a boil; cook mixture over medium heat, stirring constantly, until thickened.

- Remove from heat, and stir in vanilla.

- Let cool. Strain or beat in blender if lumps develop.

Serves 12.

Low fat

Does anything low fat <u>really</u> taste good? The answer is no. But if you lose weight and don't clog up your arteries, you're going to live longer. According to a recent article, eating right can add up to seven months to your life. Question is, is it worth it?

Thanksgiving Pudding

¼ cup butter, melted

2 cups sugar

5 large eggs

½ cup all-purpose flour

½ cup evaporated milk

2 cups mashed cooked
  pumpkin

1 teaspoon ground
  cinnamon

½ teaspoon ground nutmeg

½ teaspoon ground ginger

½ teaspoon ground mace

½ teaspoon ground cloves

2 teaspoons vanilla extract

Pecan halves

- Preheat oven to 350°.

- Beat butter and sugar at medium speed with an electric mixer until smooth; add eggs, beating well. Beat in flour and milk.

- Add pumpkin and next 6 ingredients, beating until smooth.

- Pour batter into a well-greased 2-quart baking dish.

- Bake at 350° for 55 minutes or until firm.

- Top with pecan halves.

Serves 10.

Mocha Madness Sauce

½ cup butter

1 cup sugar

⅛ teaspoon salt

1 teaspoon instant coffee
  granules

1 tablespoon rum

⅓ cup cocoa

1 cup heavy cream

1 teaspoon vanilla extract

- Melt butter in a saucepan over low heat, stirring often. Add sugar and next 4 ingredients, stirring well.

- Stir in cream, and simmer, stirring often, 5 minutes.

- Remove from heat, and stir in vanilla.

Makes about 2 cups.

Serve this decadent sauce over ice cream, fruit, or pound cake.

Try for supper club

Sinful Bread Pudding

1 (16-ounce) stale French bread loaf, torn into pieces

1 quart milk

2 cups heavy cream

4 large eggs, divided

1½ cups granulated sugar

3 tablespoons vanilla extract

sauce

8 tablespoons unsalted butter, at room temperature

1 cup powdered sugar

4 to 5 tablespoons bourbon whiskey

Grated rind of 1 lemon

• Preheat oven to 325°.

• Combine first 3 ingredients in a large bowl, mixing with your hands. Let stand at room temperature 30 minutes to 1 hour.

• Beat 3 eggs, granulated sugar, and vanilla at medium speed with an electric mixer until smooth; add to bread mixture, stirring well.

• Pour into a well-buttered 13- x 9-inch baking dish.

• Bake at 325° for 1 hour and 10 minutes or until browned and set. Remove from oven, and let cool to room temperature.

• For sauce, combine butter and powdered sugar in the top of a double boiler; bring water to a simmer.

• Cook, stirring often, until sugar is dissolved. Remove from heat; lightly whisk remaining egg, and whisk into butter mixture.

• Whisk mixture until cooled to room temperature. Stir in bourbon.

• To serve, cut pudding into squares, and place on individual ovenproof plates.

• Top with sauce, and broil until bubbly.

Serves 8.

This is good cold from the refrigerator.

Queen of Puddings

4 ounces fresh white
   breadcrumbs

5 tablespoons sugar,
   divided

1½ cups milk

2 tablespoons butter

3 large eggs, separated

Vanilla extract

Grated lemon rind

3 tablespoons raspberry or
   other jam

- Preheat oven to 375°.

- Combine breadcrumbs and 2 tablespoons sugar in a large bowl.

- Bring milk and butter to a boil in a saucepan; cook, stirring constantly, until butter is melted. Pour butter mixture over breadcrumb mixture.

- Add egg yolks, vanilla, and lemon rind, and beat at medium speed with a handheld mixer until well blended. Pour mixture into a buttered 4-cup baking dish; level off.

- Bake at 375° for 30 to 35 minutes or until set. Remove from oven, and let cool slightly.

- Reduce oven temperature to 325°.

- Beat egg whites at high speed with a handheld mixer until soft peaks form; gradually whisk in remaining 3 tablespoons sugar. Beat mixture at high speed until stiff peaks form.

- Spread jam evenly over pudding, and top with meringue, using a rubber spatula to form swirls and peaks.

- Bake 10 to 12 minutes or until lightly browned.

- Serve immediately.

Serves 4.

From age 2 in the high chair to age 11 at the dining room table, the child's father had monitored her table manners by saying "Are you going to eat like that when you eat with the Queen?" If elbows were on the table or no napkin in her lap, it was always, "What will the Queen say?" After years of not living up to such rigorously royal expectations, the little girl finally responded "Daddy, it doesn't matter... I intend to BE the Queen."

BACK TO THE TABLE
Menus

Janie Wood

Pathway to success

Like great composers, accomplished cooks understand the timeless principles of harmony and rhythm. They know, almost instinctively, that any meal — whether it's an old-fashioned church picnic or a state dinner — must be born of the creative, deliberate blending of tastes and textures and colors and smells.

These gifted chefs, whether they hold forth in five-star restaurants or humble country kitchens, have learned to subtly manipulate the palate, the eye and the nose just as a composer weaves the intricacies of sound and an artist blends the effects of light, color and value.

In the end, it is a wholly creative process. One which touches the edges of sensitivity and captures the fullness of the experience of eating.

The menu, like a musical score or the table of contents of a literary work, is a roadmap to the approaching culinary experience. But it is more than a list of "what's to eat." It is a plan, a blueprint, a pathway, a carefully studied and exquisitely crafted chart which helps diners "navigate" the meal, course by course. From aperitif to dessert it is a preview, a program and, ultimately, a keepsake.

The menu is the arrangement. It is the orchestration. It is, in fact, the composition itself.

The following section of our cookbook addresses the menu as a work of art. This is as it should be, of course, since the creation of truly memorable meals for family and friends demands careful thought, planning and sheer imagination.

And, done right, menus are not only a reflection of the cook, but truly a compliment to the guests they are intended to please, to delight, and sometimes to astound.

Movin' On

There are times in life when the children move on. They are baptized as babies and confirmed as teenagers. They graduate from high school and head off to college. They graduate from college and dash out into the world. They get engaged and married and start families of their own in Albuquerque. At each of these milestones, there is a celebration or a bittersweet farewell meal. It's almost as though, if we eat enough, time will stand still and life will get back to normal again. Well, it won't. But a helping of Elegant Beef Tenderloin and Queen of Puddings can help.

Baptismal or Confirmation Brunch Buffet

Eye Opening Bloody Marys
Governor's Mansion Punch
Easy Cheese Straws
Breakfast for a King (or Queen)
Asparagus Milan
Sausage and Spinach Bread
Raspberry Cream Cheese Coffee Cake
Orange Currant Scones
Seasonal Fresh Fruit
Bishop's Cake

Graduation Dinner

Mandarin Orange Salad
Elegant Beef Tenderloin
Vidalia Onion Pie
Dillicious Green Beans
Heavenly Rolls
Chocolate Silk Chess Pie

Bridesmaids' Luncheon

Glencoe Champagne Punch
Gazpacho
Bride's Chicken Salad
Haricots Verts
Heavenly Rolls
Raspberry Mousse Parfaits

Feast Easy

If there's one thing this book won't advocate, it's fast food. But there are times when an easy but good meal is called for. Like when two of Ralph's golfing buddies decide to follow him home for supper, or you get tapped for the bridge group's dinner party two nights beforehand. Or perhaps you're just in need of a meal your family will love and will request over and over again. So, if you want to (or have to) fix a hurry-up meal folks will rave about, these recipes are for you.

Southern Simplicity

Carolina Crab Cakes with Basil Tartar Sauce
Brown Rice with Pecans
Mixed Greens with Dijon Vinaigrette
Uptown Cornbread
Blender Lemon Pie

Cook It Again, Mom

Sassy Meat Loaf
Creamy Mashed Potatoes
Cherry Tomatoes and Green Beans
Quick Butter Biscuits
Cowboy Cookies

A Portable Feast

Remember the folks who just moved in from "somewhere in the Midwest?" Well, here's an idea for a real nice way of saying "welcome to the neighborhood" Southern style. Once they've sampled "Christ Church Chicken Pie," well, heck, you've made a friend for life!

Dinner for the New Neighbors

Christ Church Chicken Pie
Roquefort Waldorf Salad
Pecan Bars

And while we're talking portable feast…Remember those special family picnics, or the picnic your mother fixed for the long trip (pre-fast foods) to Aunt Susie's? It was everyone's job to look out the window for just the right picnic table and shady tree along the road to stop and eat. And don't forget those fall football tailgating picnics, when there's a cool breeze in the air and pride and bragging rights are on the line for the entire next year. Now, why not just gather the kids and go to the local park for an old-fashioned family picnic—they'll love the novelty of this idea and "You'll Never Have a Better Brownie" will become a family favorite forever.

Perfect Picnic Basket

Picnic Sandwiches
Pimiento Cheese Sandwiches
Layered Potato Salad
Cherry Tomatoes for a Tailgate
You'll Never Have a Better Brownie
Old Fashioned Oatmeal Raisin Cookies
Summertime Iced Tea
(Football, kite, blow-bubbles, and a good book also recommended)

Dining with God's Creatures

In the days before air conditioning—that's when we all used to talk to one another across the back fence, remember?—A lot of folks would have dinner outside. Out on the terrace, or these days the deck. There's something magic about eating outside. There's an openness. Freedom. The sound of birds and the breeze rustling through the tops of the pine trees. If you're really lucky a rabbit will hop across the yard, which means your wish will come true. Here are wonderful menus which will make your little table in the backyard something really special.

Dinner on the Terrace

Grilled Pork Tenderloin
Applesauce with Pears and Grand Marnier
Green Corn Pudding
Tomato and Mozzarella Salad
Herb Foccacia
Strawberries and Sabayon in Cookie Shells

Great Grills Afire

Country Style Barbeque Ribs (pork or beef)
Drunk Roasting Ears
Grilled Vegetables with Basil Mayonnaise
Southern Spoonbread
The Best Strawberry Sorbet

Puttin' On the Dog

The dog's in the crate. Children are in the upstairs playroom armed with "Bambi" and the "Little Mermaid." The guest china is out along with your best silver and grandmother's linen tablecloth. Crystal. Napkin rings. Fresh cut flowers and candlelight. There are simply occasions—for two or for twenty, going out or coming in—when only the best will do. Here are some menus guaranteed to evoke memories.

Candles and Conversation

Crab Crostini
Heart Ball Salad
Roasted Fish Fillets (Red Snapper) on a Bed of Spinach
Lemon Rice with Almonds
Tomato Herb Bread
Brandy Alexander Mousse

Saturday Night Supper Club

Cream of Brie Soup
Filet Mignons with Green Peppercorn Sauce
A Colorful Salad
Potatoes and Tomatoes
Lemon Chess Pie

Or

Roasted Red Pepper Soup
Poached Salmon with Dilled Sour Cream
Asparagus Vinaigrette
Dilly Casserole Bread
Raspberry Mousse Parfaits

Holiday Feast

Gourmet Upside Down Turkey
Holiday Hot Panned Oysters
Elegant Beef Tenderloin
Bourbon Sweet Potatoes
Green Beans with Mustard Vinaigrette
Broccoli in Orange Shallot Butter
Holiday Cranberry Salad
Herbed Wild Rice
Angel Biscuits
English Trifle

Social Graces

Episcopalians don't need a reason to gather, but the springtime is one of the best reasons we know. Springtime in the South is special. It is the time to enjoy the beautiful color of azaleas and tulips, the warm Carolina sun, the beauty of green-laden golf courses, the excitement of the NCAA final four, the bounty of the vegetable garden, and the first visits to the beach. The perfect time to gather people together. And when folks around here gather just to have a good time, good things are bound to happen. Good fellowship. Tall tales. Exaggerated golf scores. Amazing children's feats. But most of all there's wonderful food. And if you've never sampled a "Melvin Biscuit" or "Celebration Chocolate Cake," why, you are about to find out why so many Episcopalians walk around smiling.

Springtime Cocktail Party

Grilled Pork Tenderloin with Melvin Biscuits and Horseradish Sauce

or

Grilled Butterflied Leg of Lamb with Melvin Biscuits, Chutney and Mint Jelly
Brie with Cranberry Marmalade or Blue Cheese Mousse
Chinese Asparagus
Mushroom Pâté
Prosciutto Palmiers
Tomato and Herb Bruschetta
Shrimp for a Crowd or Crabmeat Crescents
Lemon Curd Tartlets
Perfect Pound Cake with Mocha Madness Sauce

March Madness Half-Time Supper

Capital City Chicken
Greens and Grapefruit Salad
Parmesan and Garlic Potatoes
Herb Cheese Biscuits
Celebration Chocolate Cake

Christening The Beach Season Supper

Frogmore Stew or Louisiana Baked Shrimp
Zippy Cole Slaw
Blue Corn Bread
Freezer Lemon Sorbet

Kiki Farish

A prayer for those who clean up

Well, Lord, here we are at the sink again. Just you and me and the dog. Please steady my hands so I don't chip another plate or drop a spoon down the disposal. As I look at the remains of this wonderful dinner, Lord, I am again reminded of your great bounty. We are thankful for the fruits of your good earth, especially for the meat loaf tonight. We know that when our family gathers at the table your spirit moves amongst us. We are reminded that mealtime is family time. A time for children. A time for love. A time for giggling. A time when we know that life is good, and families really count, and that mealtime is a celebration of being together. It will not always be like this. The children will grow up too fast, and we will grow old too soon. And when they have their own families and homes, I pray, for them, the joy and love we have come to know at our humble table. Most of all, Lord, I pray that mankind will invent a pair of dishwashing gloves that look good on a guy. In the name of the Father, Son and Holy Spirit, I pray here, again, at the sink. Amen.

Back To The Table
Contributors

Chairmen
Sandy Anthony
Tricia Arnett
Judy Charles
Katie Medlin

Art and Graphics
Ginger Jernigan
Lane Nash

Computer
Trina Blanton
Mary Tucker

Editing and Proofing
Ann Berry
Jenny Herbert

Marketing
Diana Harris
Cissy Elmer

Public Relations
Margaret Bratton
Susie Small

Recipe Testing
Jean Maupin
Libbie Ward

Treasurers
Gale Nichols
Mary Tucker

Advisor
Rachel Smith

Martha Abernethy
Ann-Louise Aguiar
Mickie Alexander
Nancy Allison
Dot Andrews
Sandy Anthony
Sara Ellen Archie
Maxine Arnett
Patsy Arnett
Tricia Arnett
Trip Auray
Blanche Bacon
Beverley Bahin
Marcia Barham
Jane Barnes
Margaret Barringer-Willis
Doris Bason
Ann Berry
Beth Betts
Trina Blanton
Louise Blosser
Harriett Bobbitt
Bill Bost
Cathy Bouggy
Meb Bowers
Jane Brady
Katherine Bratton
Margaret Bratton
Paige Bratton
Lillian Bremer
Beau Brewer
Stannie Brewer
Virginia Brewer
Margaret Brickell
Sloan Bridger
Sue Tucker Briggs
Carol Brinkley
Ginny Broughton
Mary Ann Broughton
Robert Brown
Mary Jane Bryant
Sarah Tayloe Bulla
Kim Bunn
Emily Burgess
Christy Byers
Ruth Bynum
Copie Cain

Lynn Calder
Cameron Callaway
Betty Cannon
Susan Carter
Alta Chalmers
Collins Chalmers
Anne McCann Chaney
Judy Charles
Julia Charles
Winston Charles
Mabon Childs
Carson Clark
Peggy Coe
Eloise Cofer
Louise Coggins
Lee Colhoun
Catherine Cox
Valerie Cozart
Jill Cramer
Frances Crawford
Randi Crawford
Randy Croft
Ed Curtis
Ann Daniel
Ann Daniel-Croft
Edna Davis
Elma Davis
Maryann Davis
Gail Dembicks
Pam Dickson
Elizabeth Dixon
Helen Dixon
Miriam Dixon
Chip Dodd
Ami Dombalis
Georgia Donaldson
Terri Dowdee
Nancy Duckett
Mary Jarvis Duerson
Mary Eberhardt
Ellen Edmunds
Alison Eisenstadt
Cissy Elmer
Sarah Emrich
Bob Estill
Peggy Fain
Harriet Fairfield

The creation of *Back to the Table* represents a three year labor of love which involved many Christ Church family members. The Committee thanks all who shared in the common vision, making this book a reality.

Robin Falls
Kiki Farish
Deborah Fernandez
Peg Fisher
Terry Fisher
Terry Flanagan-Knott
Ann Nicholson Flint
Jan Floyd
Daphne Forbes
Jane Forde
Cynthia Franken
Geri Fricke
Carla Frost
Julie Funkhouser
Elizabeth Gant
Mary Garner
Mahala Garrett
Barbara Geiger
Patty Gibson
Trudy Gilbert
Alice Gillespie
Caroline Gilly
John Glover
Sallie Glover
Tina Glover
Alan Godfrey
Kim Gottshall
Lisa Grable
Martha Gray
Linda Green
Hennie Gregory
Katherine Gregory
Linda Grew
Anita Griffin
Brenda Griffin
Sandra Griffin
Pickett Guthrie
Sally Habermeyer
Ann Hale
Bill Hale
Deneece Ham
Janice Ham
Olivia Ham
Brent Hamilton
Betty Harper
Diana Harris
Mary Ellen Harris
Liz Hartzell
Alice Haywood
Jinny Haywood
Margie Haywood

Beth Headley
Annette Heath
Cindy Henderson
Annette Henry
Jenny Herbert
Millie Herget
Carolyn Hicks
Elizabeth High
Margaret Hill
Leslie Hilliard
Anna Ball Hodge
Elizabeth Hodge
Kathie Hoffman
Elizabeth Hogan
Anne Hogewood
Doug Holbrook
Cindy Holmes
Brooke Holt
Lynn Holtzclaw
Mary Anne Howard
Mike Hoyt
Nancy Hugus
Jane Hunter
Linda Hunter
Polly Ingram
Ellen Jackson
Eric Jackson
Mary Jackson
Mary Lewis James
Ann Janvier
Jane Jarvis
Ginger Jernigan
Marian Jernigan
Lou Johanson
Carolyn Johnson
Karen Johnson
Luci Johnson
Margie Johnson
Virginia Johnson
Betsy Jones
Coles Jones
Neville Jones
Susie Burnett Jones
Beth Joyner
Marj Jurek
Ellen Kautz
Cathie Kelly
Ginny Kirkland
Helen Kirven
Meredith Kittrell
Alice Knowles

Debbie Krisulewicz
Tom Krisulewicz
Ann Kurtz
Ann Laird
Jenny Bunn Lamb
Marshall Lamb
Suzy Lamb
Trish Kirby Lancaster
Cynthia Landvater
Spencer Landvater
Martha Leak
Judith LeGrand
Barbara Lewis
Mack Little
Marriott Little
Susan Little
Belle Long
Linda Long
Tommy Long
Linda Loomis
Angela Lord
Edythe Lumsden
Elizabeth Lynch
Jensen Mabe
Walker Mabe
Jennifer Maddrey
Dabney Mann
Candace Martin
Molly Masich
Martha Mason
Parker Mason
Deborah Matthews
Jewell Matthews
Jean Maupin
Caroline McCall
Hargrave McElroy
Rick McElroy
Callaway McKay
Ginny McKay
Arthur McKimmon
Suzanne McLarnon
Joyce McLarty
Kari McMichael
Cornelia McMillan
Verna Medeiros
Katie Medlin
Emily Meymandi
Martha Michaels
Martha Michaux
Ethel Miller
Kelly Mitchell

Pat Moody
Julie Moore
Jennifer Moran
Lynn Mosier
Jill Moye
Georgia Carolyn Moyer
Melanie Mudge
Sis Mullen
Shirley Mullinax
Lillian Murray
Lane Nash
Gale Nichols
Jack Nichols
Bob O'Brien
Carolyn O'Brien
Ihrie O'Bryant
Barbara O'Herron
Grace O'Neill
Pat Odell-Kelly
Jan Page
Peggy Page
Barbara Parker
Betty Anne Parker
Lynette Parker
Jewell Parker
Betsy Parry
Elizabeth Parsons
Theo Parsons
Dell Paschal
Mishew Paynter
Susan Pennington
Diane Pergerson
Edna Pergerson
Gail Perry
Emily Vaill Pfaff
Margie Pfaff
Cheryl Phillips
Janet Pittard
Lisa Pittman
Pat Poe
Marilyn Poole
Ann Proctor
Nancy Pruden
Jane Pullen
Beth Purrington
Charlotte Purrington
Suzy Purrington
David Purser
Debbie Purser
Evan Purser
Wes Ragland

Dody Ragsdale
Grayson ReVille
Lynn Reyonolds
Lillian Richardson
Marjorie Riepma
John Robertson
Anna Robinson
Hunter Rogers
Jane Rogers
Laura Rogers
Marty Rumley
Caroline Russell
Molly Safrit
Stagg Sanders
Dan Sapp
Jackie Savage
Lynn Scarborough
Mary Schofield
Anne Scruggs
Helen Sewell
Edwina Shaw
JoAnn Shea
Nora Shepard
Kelly Shipley
Kim Shirley
Kathy Shonerd
Wendy Shull
Bill Sigmon
Carolyn Simons
Kathleen Sinnott
Sheila Sinnott
June Small
Susie Small
Stuart Small
Anna Smith
Clark Smith
Eve Smith
Landon Smith
Leigh Smith
Nan Smith
Rachel Smith
Roberta Smith
Sandra Smith
Addie Soldin
Renee Souza
Margie Springer
Carol Spruill
Eva Stancil
Hannah Stephens
Caroline Stone
Nell Styron

Toni Talton
Dora Taylor
Kate Taylor
Sophia Taylor
Nancy Teague
Adriane Thomasian
Marte Thompson
Lynn Titchener
Gay Todd
Marian Troxler
Caroline Truex
Don Tucker
Greyson Tucker
Mary Tucker
Mary Conyers Tucker
Elizabeth Tyler
Ainslie Uhl
Robert Uhl
Martha Underwood
Bob Upton
Ellen Vitek
Frances Waddill
JoAnn Wainright
Martie Walsh
Libbie Ward
Lee Weaver
Edie Webb
Zoe Webster
Kim Whitley
Anne Williams
Catherine Williams
Margaret Williams
Mary Clark Williams
Pam Williams
Ray Williams
Barbara Williford
Cheri Wilson
Gwyn Wilson
Kate Wisz
Elaine Wood
Janie Wood
Lee Worth
Alice Yates
Kakie Yelverton
Louise York
Tempe Younger
Aat Zevenhuizen
Cathryn Zevenhuizen
Robin Zevenhuizen
Barbara Ziko
Anne Bailey Zschau

Back To The Table
Episcopal Church Women
Christ Church
P.O. Box 25778
Raleigh, North Carolina 27611-5778
Voice Mail: (919) 834-4013 ext. 19

Please send _____ copies of *Back To The Table* .... @ $19.95 each _____

Add postage and handling.. @ $ 4.00 each _____

North Carolina residents add 6% sales tax .... @ $ 1.20 each _____

Total _____

☐ Check or money order enclosed. Make checks payable to *Back To The Table*.

☐ Please charge to: ☐ MasterCard ☐ VISA Card Number: _____

Expiration Date: _____ Signature of Cardholder:_____

Ship to: Name _____

Street Address _____

City _____ State _____ Zip _____

- -

Back To The Table
Episcopal Church Women
Christ Church
P.O. Box 25778
Raleigh, North Carolina 27611-5778
Voice Mail: (919) 834-4013 ext. 19

Please send _____ copies of *Back To The Table* .... @ $19.95 each _____

Add postage and handling.. @ $ 4.00 each _____

North Carolina residents add 6% sales tax .... @ $ 1.20 each _____

Total _____

☐ Check or money order enclosed. Make checks payable to *Back To The Table*.

☐ Please charge to: ☐ MasterCard ☐ VISA Card Number: _____

Expiration Date: _____ Signature of Cardholder:_____

Ship to: Name _____

Street Address _____

City _____ State _____ Zip _____

Tried

Bourbon Pecan Pie - 229 - Supper Club - '99
Elegant Beef Tenderloin - 158 ✳ very tender + goo
Ann Majors Coffee Cake - 37
Cowboy Cookies - 234 ~ Flor
Club's Pecan Bars ? 235
Neikman Marcus Bars ? 234
Texas Sheet Cake - 221

Try - Easy recipes
231 Choc. Amaretto Cream Pie (makes 2 - can freeze)
231 ✓ Choc Silk Chess Pie - +made '01
225 Blender Lemon Pie - Easy Try - use whole lemon
196 Vidalia Onion Pie
122 Chicken + Cr. Cheese (Mabianski)
104 Easy Cheese Sauce
104 Scrambled Egg Make ahead Casserole
32 Easy Pean Walnut Salad
77 Easy white Gaspacho - FP
64 Fat Free Black Bean Soup
60 Pimento cheese
38 Easy Orange Butter Syrup